WHITE PROTESTANT AMERICANS

ETHNIC GROUPS IN AMERICAN LIFE SERIES
Milton M. Gordon, *editor*

ANDERSON	WHITE PROTESTANT AMERICANS: From National Origins to Religious Group
GOLDSTEIN/GOLDSCHEIDER	JEWISH AMERICANS: Three Generations in a Jewish Community
KITANO	JAPANESE AMERICANS: The Evolution of a Subculture
MOORE	MEXICAN AMERICANS
PINKNEY	BLACK AMERICANS

WHITE

CHARLES H. ANDERSON
University of Umeå, Sweden

PROTESTANT AMERICANS

From

National Origins

to Religious

Group

PRENTICE-HALL, INC., ENGLEWOOD CLIFFS, NEW JERSEY

WHITE PROTESTANT AMERICANS

*From
National Origins
to Religious
Group*   ANDERSON

P: 13–957415–8   C: 13–957423–9

Library of Congress Catalog Card No.: 73–108810

Current printing (last digit):

10   9   8   7   6   5   4   3   2

Printed in the United States of America

PRENTICE-HALL INTERNATIONAL, INC., London
PRENTICE-HALL OF AUSTRALIA PTY. LTD., Sydney
PRENTICE-HALL OF CANADA LTD., Toronto
PRENTICE-HALL OF INDIA PRIVATE LTD., New Delhi
PRENTICE-HALL OF JAPAN, INC., Tokyo

To F. O. M. Westby

Foreword

The problem of how people of diverse racial, religious, and nationality backgrounds can live together peaceably and creatively within the same national society is one of the most crucial issues facing mankind, second in importance only to the overriding problem of international war itself. Indeed, these two problem areas, while not identical, are, from the viewpoint of recurring social processes of group interaction, interrelated at many points. The United States of America, as the classic example of a highly industrialized nation made up of people of diverse ethnic origins, constitutes, both in its history and its current situation, a huge living laboratory for the serious study of various underlying patterns of ethnic interaction—patterns which produced in this country both corroding failure (particularly with respect to the treatment of racial minorities) and certain modified successes which, however, have by no means been free of a residue of unfulfilled personal hopes, psychological scars, and unjustified hardships for those who were not born with the majority sociological characteristics of being white, Protestant, and of Anglo-Saxon cultural origins.

The explosion in the 1960's of the Negro's or black American's anger and growing revolt against centuries of white prejudice and discrimination have shocked the nation out of an attitude of mass complacency with regard to ethnic group relations. Now, not only social scientists, academic liberals, and well-meaning humanitarians, many of whom had waged valiant battles against racism before, but also millions of other Americans in all walks of life are becoming aware that to devalue another human being simply on the grounds of his race, religion, or national origins, and to act accordingly, is to strike at the very core of his personality and to create a living legacy of personal hatred and social disorganization. All the great religious and ethical traditions have spoken out prophetically against ethnic prejudice (however weak their followers have been in implementation). Now it has become increasingly clear that sheer self-interest and the desire to preserve a viable nation sternly countenance the conclusion that prejudice and discrimination are dubious luxuries which Americans can no longer afford.

We have spoken of the social scientific knowledge to be derived (and, hopefully, to be creatively used) from intensive study of American ethnic groups. There is another reason to commend such focused scientific attention. The history and the decisive contributions of the various racial, religious, and national origins groups to the warp and woof of American life is not a story that, to say the least, has been overly told in American publication or pedagogy. The important pioneer studies on the Negro of E. Franklin Frazier, John Hope Franklin, and Gunnar Myrdal, and on the white immigrant of Marcus Hansen, Oscar Handlin, and John Higham, all stem from either the present generation or the one immediately preceding it. In the main, American minority ethnic groups have been, by patronizing omission, long deprived of their past in America and of a rightful pride in the nature of their role in the making and shaping of the American nation. It is time for a systematic overview, group by group, of this long neglected portion of the American experience, one that on the one hand avoids filiopietistic banalities and, on the other, does justice to the real and complex nature of the American multiethnic experience.

A final and equally compelling reason for instituting a series of studies of America's ethnic groups at this time is that more adequate theoretical tools for carrying out the respective analyses are currently at hand. In my book, *Assimilation in American Life,* published in 1964, I presented a multidimensional approach to the conceptualization of that omnibus term "assimilation" and endeavored to factor it into its various component processes, at the same time offering certain hypotheses concerning the ways in which these processes were related to each other. Such an approach appears to facilitate dealing with the considerable complexity inherent in the functioning of a pluralistic society. Furthermore, studies of social stratification or social class which have burgeoned to become such an important part of American sociology in the past few decades have made it abundantly clear that the dynamics of ethnic group life, both internally and externally, constantly involve the interplay of class and ethnic considerations. And, lastly, the passage of time, producing a third generation of native-born children of native-born parents even among those ethnic groups who appeared in large numbers in the last great peak of emigration to America in the early part of the twentieth century, has emphasized the need for considering generational change and the sociological and social psychological processes peculiar to each successive generation of ethnic Americans.

For all these reasons, I am proud to function in the capacity of general editor of a series of books which will attempt to provide the American public with a descriptive and analytic overview of its ethnic heritage in the third quarter of the twentieth century from the viewpoint of relevant social science. Each book on a particular ethnic group (and we include the white Protestants as such a sociologically definable entity) is written by an expert in the field of intergroup relations and the social life of the group about which he writes, and in many cases the author derives ethnically himself from that group. It is my hope that the publication of this series will aid substantially in the process of enabling Americans to understand more fully what it means to live in a multi-ethnic society and, concomitantly, what we must do in the future to eliminate the corrosive and devastating phenomena of prejudice and discrimination and to ensure that a pluralistic society can at the same time fulfill its promised destiny of being truly "one nation indivisible."

MILTON M. GORDON

Preface

The status of the word "ethnic," it would seem, has finally come of age in America, though the status of many to which the concept applies has not. Journalists, newsmen, politicians, clergymen, educators, and businessmen, among others, speak often of America's ethnic groups, their conflicts, their needs, and their aspirations.

In the language of the historian, "ethnic group" has usually referred to national origin groups who emigrated to America from Europe. "Racial group" has been applied to Negroes, Orientals, Indians, Mexicans, and Caucasians. America's religious groups are Protestants, Catholics, and Jews. Scores of combinations of national origin, race, and religion have existed in American society. Nearly every American embodies, with various degrees of attachment to each, national origin, racial, and religious attributes. Every American, as we shall use the term, is a member or potential member of an ethnic group—racial, religious, or national origin.

If, in fact, a person is a member of an ethnic group, he will in some measure sustain meaningful social relationships with others of the same ethnicity, psychologically identify with "his people," and probably select a spouse from among them, and act out the group's beliefs and values. With the exception of the latter, American society has tended to tolerate though not always approve of ethnic pluralism. We are now seemingly in the process of more fully accepting the legitimacy and contributions of various ethnic groups in our nation.

Our concern in the present context, however, does not involve an ethnic group which for the most part has had to struggle for legitimacy or acclaim from other ethnic groups. Indeed, it has not always been aware of itself as an ethnic group. But white Protestants, like other Americans, are as much members of an ethnic group as anyone else, however privileged the majority of them might be. As non-white, non-Protestant persons climb the social ladder, the image of the ethnic group as being lower class fades. As Catholics, Jews, and blacks press in around them, and as internal differences decline, white Protestants increasingly per-

xiii

ceive that they, too, constitute a definable group with distinctive social and familial networks, and psychological and cultural moorings.

White Protestants are, of course, an amalgam of several national origin groups, vestiges of which are still present in our society. English, Welsh, Scottish, Scotch-Irish, Swedes, Norwegians, Danes, Finns, Germans, and Dutch form the national origin constituency of white Protestantism. The assimilation of these northern European ethnic groups into the core society, English in the colonial period and Old American thereafter, shall be the topic of discussion in the first part of the book.

Each of the national origin groups tended to be affiliated with a Protestant denomination, e.g., English with Episcopal (Anglican) and Congregational, Scottish with Presbyterian, Scandinavians, Germans, and Finns with Lutheran, and Dutch with Reformed. Methodists and Baptists drew heavily from all quarters. Denominational differences remain, next to social class, as the most important internal dividing influence among white Protestants. Both popular and theological ecumenism is in the air, however, and with the exception of important sectarian and conservative groups, white Protestants increasingly join the church most convenient to them.

The task before us, then, is a broad one, as we trace the process of assimilation of the various Protestant national origin groups, and then, in the second part of the book, evaluate from several aspects the current status of white Protestants.

Valuable editorial assistance has been given by Donald W. Hastings and Milton M. Gordon. My intellectual indebtedness to Professor Gordon is great indeed. I should also like to thank my mother for some "interviews" as she told me "how it was" with first- and second-generation Scandinavians in the Midwest.

CHARLES H. ANDERSON

Acknowledgments

I am grateful to the following publishers for permission to use their copyrighted material:

Harvard University Press, *British Immigrants in Industrial America* by Rowland T. Berthoff.

C. Wendell King, "Branford Center: A Community Study in Social Cleavage," a doctoral dissertation, Yale University.

J. B. Lippincott Company, *Americans From Norway* by Leola Nelson Bergmann, 1950.

The University of Minnesota Press, *A Pioneer in Northwest America: The Memoirs of Gustaf Unonius, Vol. I,* edited by Nils W. Olsson.

The University of North Carolina Press, *The Scotch-Irish: A Social History,* by James G. Leyburn.

Social Forces, Sociological Analysis, and *Review of Religious Research* for previously published tables.

Wayne Wheeler, "An Analysis of Social Change in a Swedish Immigrant Community," a doctoral dissertation, University of Missouri.

Contents

Part Two

**WHITE PROTESTANTISM:
ITS PAST AND PRESENT STATUS
IN AMERICAN LIFE, 95**

Once, while interviewing a Protestant economics professor for a sociological study, I asked him to what extent he felt that he belonged to the white Protestant community in America. The professor replied that he had "never heard of a white Protestant community, to say nothing of membership." Another study participant, a Protestant history professor, responded to the same query by saying that he had a "strong sense of Protestant group membership" and was "very self-consciously a Protestant." The ethnic sentiments of the history professor are shared by an increasing number of white Protestants; a declining number feel that *they* inhabit America while *others* live in groups.[1]

Native white Protestants have undisputably inhabited dominant American groups and institutions for nearly three hundred years. Indeed, white Protestants conceived and developed the social framework of America. The public interest and the institutions designed to achieve that interest were at once American and white Protestant. That the social life of the

Introduction

larger community was organized to serve the needs of a particular religious group was given but slight thought by participants. Why should such an awareness have existed when for the first two centuries white, mainly British, Protestants were the only viable ethnic group in America and for still another century the only one that was materially successful on the whole? For most of American history, only white Protestant needs and interests have been publicly recognized as legitimate. If a member of another ethnic group would not or could not become socially and culturally like white Protestants, then that person did not qualify for the material rewards and social acceptance available through the larger society. As a member of an illegitimate ethnic group, he remained a second-class American.

In the course of the twentieth century, first members of other religious groups, then members of other racial groups have challenged the premise that community interests and institutions belong solely to white Protestants. Catholics and Jews have demanded and generally received recognition as legitimate Americans with equal rights of participation in community-wide groups. For more than a generation now, white Protestants have been facing the difficult task of making room in domi

[1] See the general arguments on white Protestant community presented by Will Herberg, *Protestant-Catholic-Jew* (Garden City, N.Y.: Doubleday & Company, Inc., 1960); and Milton M. Gordon, *Assimilation in American Life* (New York: Oxford University Press, Inc., 1964).

nant community institutions for persons of other creeds. Further, all whites, Protestant or not, are being challenged by the demands of racial and ethnic minorities for first-class citizenship.

As many white Protestants begin to perceive that community institutions are no longer coextensive with those of their own group, they may respond in two ways, the first essentially negative, the second positive. First, they may defend Protestant hegemony by opposing social change. Second, they may enlarge the arena of self-defined white Protestant community through increasing participation and identification. The majority of white Protestants have variously engaged in both types of action.

WHITE PROTESTANTS IN AMERICA

Protestantism in America has its beginnings in America's beginning. Jamestown, Plymouth, and Massachusetts Bay were, of course, the first seventeenth century Protestant settlements in the New World. Anglican (Episcopalian) and Congregational churches enjoyed early state support. Among other large Protestant churches of today, the Baptist and Reformed also trace American congregations back to the seventeenth century. By the first decades of the eighteenth century, Presbyterians, Lutherans, and sectarians secured firm positions in American Protestantism.[2] Methodists outstripped all Protestant churches in size in the first half of the nineteenth century.

Despite low formal church membership, Protestantism was the chief and virtually sole religious influence in the colonial period (Catholics comprised less than 1 per cent of the white population). In the first half of the nineteenth century, revivals generally heightened Protestant religious identity and brought an increasing proportion of the population into organized churches. By the mid-nineteenth century, an estimated three-fourths of the population claimed denominational ties and a sixth church membership.[3] Protestants and Protestant churches in American society then exercised an unprecedented religious-based influence that was to be sustained well into the twentieth century. In Hudson's words, "Protestantism had been the dominant religious and cultural force in the United States from the beginning, but by the middle of the nineteenth century it had established undisputed sway over almost all aspects of the national life."[4]

---

[2] See Edwin S. Gaustad, *Historical Atlas of Religion in America* (New York: Harper & Row, Publishers, 1962).

[3] S. M. Lipset, *The First New Nation* (New York: Basic Books, Inc., 1963), p. 144.

[4] Winthrop S. Hudson, *American Protestantism* (Chicago: University of Chicago Press, 1961), p. 109.

The English, of course, were numerically and socially the dominant national origin group in colonial America. By the end of the eighteenth century, at least 60 per cent of the white population of more than 3 million were of English stock.[5] Scots, Scotch-Irish, and Germans comprised most of the remaining white population. Despite the much smaller numbers of Scots, they were keen rivals with the English in economic and political affairs. The Scotch-Irish and Germans predominated in many frontier areas, especially in Pennsylvania. The lopsided English numerical advantage was reduced in the heavy immigration of the nineteenth century, but English social privileges were sustained. As the descendants of European Protestant immigrants assimilated into the British-dominated core society, they shared the social privileges of the preferred ethnic group.

Much as an English majority was eliminated in the nineteenth century, so has a large white Protestant majority been curtailed in the twentieth. With 25 per cent of the population Catholic, 10 per cent black Protestant (over 90 per cent of blacks are Protestant) and 10 per cent Jewish, other, or without religious preference, self-identifying white Protestants now compose about 55 per cent of the population. Approximately three-fifths of these self-defined Protestants are on church rolls, the highest proportion in Protestant church history.[6] Less than half of those on Protestant church rolls are weekly attenders. Thus, whereas more than five in ten Americans are nominally white Protestants, only about three in ten Americans are white Protestant church *members,* and fewer than two in ten are active on a weekly basis. The latter group constitutes the social center of white Protestant community. Surprisingly enough, the number of white Protestants who attend church weekly (recently at an unprecedentedly high level) is smaller than the number of Catholics who attend church weekly.

The decline of the white Protestant majority and of white Protestant hegemony in twentieth century America has encouraged the growth of self-conscious Protestant community. This awareness of separate and identifiable group interests is not, however, entirely new to American Protestantism. Large numbers of Protestants have always experienced and continue to experience minority status as members of national origin groups or in fundamentalistic and sectarian churches. In certain geographical areas, white Protestants have had to operate as at least a local minority, usually, however, without incurring the handicaps of most

[5] *Annual Report of the American Historical Association,* 1931, Vol. I (Washington, D.C.: Government Printing Office, 1932), 124.

[6] *Yearbook of American Churches* (New York: National Council of the Church of Christ in the U.S.A., 1967).

minorities. The newly self-conscious white Protestant minority has at its nucleus the 15 to 20 per cent of Americans who have relatively active Protestant church ties. Many more, of course, are involved to lesser degrees in Protestant community activity.

Although Protestant America may be approaching obsolescence in the sense of nineteenth century hegemony, few persons would debate with Killian when he says that "the white, Anglo-Saxon Protestant remains the typical American, the model to which other Americans are expected and encouraged to conform." [7] And as we shall see in Chapter Eleven on social class, white Protestants are still the most powerful and privileged ethnic group in America.

The Agrarian Outlook

The outstanding hallmark of white Protestantism in America is its ruralism. As William Petersen has remarked, "The Protestant churches are rooted in rural America, linked to rural institutions, made up of rural-bred people." [8] In terms of the group's own distribution, two-thirds of all white Protestants live in localities of under 100,000 people. An even larger majority were *raised* in even smaller communities. The clergy is even more rural in family background than the laity. By contrast, two-thirds of all Catholics live in cities of *over* 100,000 people. One in two Catholics and black Protestants lives in a metropolitan area of 250,000 persons or more, as do nine in ten Jews. Only one in four white Protestants resides in a city of that size.[9]

The proportion of white Protestants in the population rises sharply in the rural areas. In metropolitan areas of over 250,000 persons, white Protestants number on the average less than two-fifths of the total. However, in smaller towns and cities with populations of over 2,500, the white Protestant proportion is two-thirds and in the most rural areas that increases to three-fourths.[10]

White Protestants, irrespective of rural or urban residence, cling tenaciously to an agrarian world view. An urban white Protestant will often be heard denouncing urbanism and eulogizing rural virtues. The farmer no more than the businessman anathematizes the city and apoth-

---

[7] Lewis M. Killian, *The Impossible Revolution* (New York: Random House, Inc., 1968), p. 18.

[8] William Petersen, "The Protestant Ethos and the Anti-Urban Animus," in *The Church and the Exploding Metropolis,* ed. Robert Lee (Richmond, Va.: John Knox Press, 1965), p. 63.

[9] U.S. Bureau of the Census, "Religion Reported by the Civilian Population of the U.S.: March, 1957," *Current Population Reports,* Series P-20, Number 79 (Washington, D.C.: U.S. Government Printing Office, February 2, 1958), Table 3, p. 7.

[10] *Ibid.*

eosizes the country. Trends in technology force reluctant rural-oriented white Protestants, both skilled and unskilled, to metropolis and megalopolis. To a majority of white Protestants, urbanism signifies congestion, big government, Democrats, minority groups, rebellious youth, corruption, and crime. The white Protestant is both impressed and repulsed by life in the large city. In the Protestant ethos (many non-Protestants share it), the large city is a "nice place to visit" but not to live in. The farm or small town, middle-sized city, and metropolitan fringe area, often in roughly that order of preference, are the comfortable milieus of white Protestants in America.

FROM NATIONAL ORIGINS
TO RELIGIOUS GROUP

Men share numerous common denominators upon which it is possible to build social relationships and group life. Common kin, neighborhoods, jobs, and leisure interests are important pivots of personal relationships. Ethnicity is a further such common denominator, one that has usually been closely related to family, residence, work, and leisure as each has separately and in combination contributed to the shape of group life and personal identity.

The word "ethnicity" stems from the Greek word *ethnos,* which means "people." [11] The sharing of a sense of peoplehood and commonality serves to bind men together into kinship networks, cliques, and organizations. The resulting system of social relationships constitutes the ethnic group. Myriad and overlapping smaller groups and social circles collectively form the larger ethnic group.

Settlers and immigrants from England, Germany, Sweden, and other European countries developed a sense of peoplehood with other newcomers from their homelands, creating the various national origin communities of American history. Interestingly enough, most European immigrants developed a sense of collective national origin identity *after* coming to America.[12] Group consciousness and activity often centered in the immigrants' churches, especially in the non-English-speaking communities.

As knowledge of and feeling for the Old World faded in the first American-born generations, religion rather than national origin became

[11] For an elaboration of the concept "ethnic group," see Gordon, *Assimilation in American Life,* pp. 23–30. Following Gordon, I shall apply the term "ethnic group" to race, religion, or national origin and any combination thereof.

[12] Oscar Handlin, *The Uprooted* (New York: Grosset & Dunlap, Inc., 1951), p. 186; and Joshua A. Fishman, et al., *Language Loyalty in the United States* (The Hague: Mouton & Company, 1966), p. 27.

the repository of ethnic feeling and the family church the main locus of ethnic group life. As churches gradually shed distinctive national origin identifications, still later generations of Protestants no longer found themselves members of very special and fixed congregations established by their own immediate ancestors. Rather, modern Protestants are more often participants in comfortable yet fluid churches belonging to denominations considered of a piece with the larger Protestant faith.

The shift in ethnic identity and social participation from national origin communities and their churches to the larger body of white Protestantism involved the process of assimilation. Ethnic community and assimilation stand at opposite ends of a continuum. In order to ascertain the degree of convergence between two ethnic groups, say Protestants and Catholics, or the extent of movement of a minority group into the host society, say Scandinavians into the British-dominated core society, we are in need of a measure of assimilation (or viewed from the opposite perspective, a measure of ethnic communalism).

The Process of Assimilation

Assimilation is not a single event or unitary process. It is a complex event that includes several subprocesses or steps. Milton Gordon has analyzed assimilation into its component parts.[13] The first step of assimilation is a cultural one: the acquisition of possibly a new language, patterns of consumption, customs, values, norms, and belief systems held by the dominant or host society, in this case, the white Protestant. Non-British Protestant national origin groups were largely acculturated to Anglo-America within two or three generations and most Britishers, of course, even sooner.

Cultural assimilation is a prerequisite, and not an automatic one as American Indians can attest, to full participation in the social groups of the host society. The distinction between cultural and group or structural assimilation is important: the former refers to the content of a person's speech and behavior and the latter to a person's network of social interaction. Speech and behavior must usually change in the direction of that found in the host society before a person is socially accepted. However, acculturation does not guarantee structural assimilation. A person may speak the same language, place value on the same goods and services, and share similar norms with his neighbors, but at the same time be denied or not prefer acceptance into their families, close friendship groups, clubs, and organizations. Similarly, members of two ethnic groups may commingle with one another in schools, work places, and community organizations (secondary-group assimilation) without ex-

---

[13] Gordon, *Assimilation in American Life,* pp. 60–83.

tending invitations to one another for an informal evening in the home or at the club (primary-group assimilation).

Large-scale intermarriage is a further important subprocess of assimilation. Although marrying outside the ethnic group does not necessarily mean that the intermarried person has been lost to the group (we may convert as well as be converted), the existence of strong taboos against intermarriage attests to the seriousness of the act. Intermarriage follows closely after members of one ethnic group begin to participate in the informal group life of another. The close connection between structural and marital assimilation is fully grasped by persons who endeavor to preserve ethnic solidarity by organizing ethnic-bound clubs and activities within which young people will hopefully confine their close personal relationships.

Identification with the host group is a further aspect of the assimilation process. The loss of traditional ethnic identity into that of the host society is a by-product of intermarriage. Furthermore, if identified with the host group, the offspring of mixed marriages cease to be targets of prejudice and discrimination from the dominant society. Finally, the reduction of value and power conflict, or civic assimilation, completes the process of assimilation. Socially dispersed, intermarried, and with attenuated group identity, descendants of an ethnic group scarcely could or would wish to stand together behind an old interest or value position that conflicted with interests and values of the dominant society.

The above scheme, then, shall serve us as a working guide in charting the course and speed of assimilation of the Protestant national origin groups with one another and into the core society. The same scheme shall serve as a touchstone in the analysis of white Protestant community in the second part of the book.

THE ASSIMILATION OF
THE PROTESTANT NATIONAL
ORIGIN GROUPS

Part One

In this part of the book, we take up from a sociological viewpoint a largely historical problem: the assimilation into American society of the Protestant peoples of northern Europe. The task of knitting the immigrant Anglo-Saxon, Scandinavian, or Teuton into the generalized garment of American culture and society was only occasionally regarded by native Americans as a difficult or dangerous one and almost never as an insurmountable one. Since the colonial period, Dutch, Scots, Germans, and Scandinavians at times seemed too steeped in their foreign adaptations to the New World to suit the more impatient Americans. However, they were not long considered by many as a serious threat to the integrity of Anglo-Saxon institutions.

As foreigners flooded the cities in the early years of this century, a distinction between northern Europeans and those from the southern and eastern regions assumed prominence in the alarmed minds of native

Americans. The developing immigration policy of the period drew a sharp distinction between northern European immigrants and those from the south and east. As Handlin has pointed out, "In the minds of those who framed the laws of 1917–1924 that distinction was more important than restriction itself." [1]

André Siegfried, a French observer of the time, articulated the popular wisdom regarding the assimilative potential of national origin groups:

> A century of experience has proved that Protestants of Nordic origin are readily assimilated, and Calvinists particularly so. There is almost no question of Americanizing an Englishman or a Scotchman, for they are hardly foreigners and feel quite at home for many reasons that go far deeper than the mere similarity of the language. The Dutch, the Germans, the Scandinavians, and the German Swiss all have low melting-points. . . . Assimilation only begins to be troublesome with the Catholics, even German and Anglo-Saxon Catholics. . . .[2]

Siegfried's observation contained considerable validity strictly from the standpoint of the social assimilation of non-Protestants. However, the implications of immigration restrictionist views usually extended beyond group life to the biological preferability of Protestants as opposed to non-Protestants. As a secretary of the Immigration Restriction League posed the problem, do we ". . . want this country to be peopled by British, German, Scandinavian stock, historically free, energetic, progressive, or by Slav, Latin, and Asiatic races, historically down-trodden, atavistic, and stagnant?" [3] A fledgling and naïve social science further buttressed the popular images regarding the inherent desirability and undesirability of the "old" and "new" immigrants, respectively, by reporting their social and mental differences as if immutable correlates of their national origin.

The Immigration Act of 1924 embodied in law the distinction between old and new immigrants. Protestants were thereby, in thinly concealed terms, considered superior to non-Protestants. The annual quota of small but Protestant Norway, for example, was set at a number similar to that of gigantic but non-Protestant Russia. Not until 1968 was the immigration law rewritten so as to be free of the religious bias.

Two demographic points concerning the so-called old immigration are of special preliminary interest to the study of the white Protestant. First, although the percentage of immigrants from northern Europe declined from over 90 per cent of the total before 1860 to a low of 17 per

1 Oscar Handlin, *Race and Nationality in American Life* (Garden City, N.Y.: Doubleday & Company, Inc., 1957), p. 75.

2 André Siegfried, *America Comes of Age* (New York: Harcourt, Brace & World, Inc., 1927), pp. 22–23.

3 Prescott F. Hall, "Immigration and the Educational Test," *North American Review*, LXV (October, 1897), 395.

cent for the years 1911–1920 (Table A–1, Appendix A), a greater percentage of the post-colonial total from northern Europe arrived after
1880 than before. If 1880 is taken as a cutoff point, we may note that
about 48 per cent of the old immigration entered the country before
that time and 52 per cent after (Table A–2, Appendix A). If British
Canadians are included as "old" immigrants, an even greater percentage
of the old immigration arrived after 1880. The post-colonial immigrant
flow from northern Europe is "old" only in comparative terms and not
when considered by itself in a time perspective. Thus, the numerical base
of ethnic community among the Protestant national origin groups was
not curtailed at some historical pivot point signaling the end of the
old immigration and beginning of the new. Rather, large reinforcing
contingents of British, Germans, and Scandinavians continued to arrive
through the 1920's.

A second preliminary observation concerning the old immigration
is that far from all northern European and Canadian immigrants were
Protestants. Less than two-thirds of the over 21 million immigrants from
northwest Europe and Canada were Protestant in religious background
(Table A–3, Appendix A). Only the Scandinavian immigration was in
both relative and absolute terms almost solidly Protestant. Often neglected are the some 750,000 Protestants who came from central and
eastern Europe.[4]

Much of the present white Protestant population has derived, of
course, from colonial stock, the truly "old immigrants" (called emigrants
at the time) and their descendants. In 1920, the colonial stock (defined as
those who arrived before 1790) was estimated at 41 million out of a white
population of 94 million.[5] If this figure is roughly correct, and in view of
the fact that nearly all of the white colonial population was Protestant
in origin, the respective colonial and immigrant contributions to the
existing total white Protestant population of well over 100 million persons
have been proportionately quite similar. Considerable intermarriage between colonial and immigrant stock and many religious conversions to
and from Protestantism within both stocks has obviously taken place. In

[4] Protestant immigrants to the United States from the countries of central and
eastern Europe, mainly Hungary and Austria, comprised less than 5 per cent of the total
from south and east Europe. Jews comprised 25 per cent and Eastern Orthodox persons
over 5 per cent. Interestingly, the Roman Catholic contribution was to the new
immigration (something less than two-thirds) what the Protestant contribution was to
the old immigration. These estimates are based on the same sources and methods as
those used in Table A-3 of Appendix A to arrive at the religious totals for the
northern countries.

[5] Warren S. Thompson and Pascal K. Whelpton, *Population Trends in the
United States* (New York: McGraw-Hill Book Company, 1933), p. 91.

very broad terms, however, American Protestants today are half colonial and half immigrant in origin. Yet, colonially derived white Protestants possess considerably more than half of all power and prestige held by white Protestants in America.

The phrase "White Anglo-Saxon Protestant" (WASP) has become commonplace in American parlance. Over 85 per cent of all United States Protestants are indeed various shades of white from pink to beige, but far fewer are of Anglo-Saxon stock. In point of fact, even the English were composed of more than Angle and Saxon. A glance at English history establishes a variegated tribal past. The original neolithic inhabitants of the Britain mainland were early subdued by Celts whose forebears had first appeared in central Europe (probably by way of Russia) and later moved into northern France, south Britain, and finally, Ireland. Raids from the north by Scots and Picts after the Roman withdrawal prompted the Britons to appeal to Germanic tribes for assistance.[1] Thus came belligerent bands of Angles and Saxons.

The Angles had originated in the district of Angle on the Danish peninsula. The Saxons inhabited the district between the Elbe and the Weser. The name "Saxon" was initially used to refer to an alliance of tribes that were users of the *seax* or *sahs,* a short one-handled sword. Once in Britain, the Angles and Saxons became so closely linked that they and their enemies alike referred to them interchangeably as Angles and Saxons. *Angelcynn,* or "English people," denoted Saxons as well as Angles, and the Saxons were content to call their language English.[2]

Angles, Saxons, and Others

The first contingents of Angles and Saxons left the Continent as war parties in the fifth century and were shortly followed by major tribal emigrations. By the middle of the seventh century, Germanic peoples occupied much of the British mainland. The indigenous Britons either withdrew to the west or were absorbed. In appearance, the English were purportedly tall, long-headed, and light in complexion compared to the shorter, broad-headed, and darker Briton.

Another large migratory stream, possibly as large as the Saxon, entered eastern and northern England from the Scandinavian peninsula,

---

[1] For a discussion of the expansion and the culture of the Germanic tribes, see Francis Owen, *The Germanic People* (New Haven: College and University Press, 1966).
[2] See R. H. Hodgkin, *A History of the Anglo-Saxons* (London: Oxford University Press, 1952).

mainly Norway, in the ninth and tenth centuries.[3] Unlike their bellicose Viking brothers, these Scandinavians were farmers and fishermen. Other Norse and Norse-Irish came to the west coast of Britain from Ireland during the same period. About the time these Vikings were settling in northern areas, the more aggressive Danes moved into southern England. After a century and a half of Danish-Saxon warfare, the Danes like the Norse eventully fused with the English. Normans—themselves of Danish ancestry—made a minor contribution to the Anglo-Saxon stock, especially the nobility. Later, thousands of Protestant refugees came to England from the Low Countries and France during the Reformation.

In short, the genetic composition of the "Anglo-Saxon" is hetero-geneous and embraces elements of Mediterranean, Alpine, and Nordic racial stocks through Celtic, Teutonic, and Scandinavian peoples. Yet, much as the Anglo-Saxon cultural mould has prevailed over successive waves of immigration in America, so did the Anglo-Saxon world of early England absorb Celts, Norse, Danes, and Frenchmen.

ENGLISH IMMIGRATION TO AMERICA

The English were not the first European emigrants to what is now the continental United States. They had been preceded in the Southwest by Spaniards. The English were, however, the first Europeans to colonize in force. Most important, the English gave an Anglo-Saxon stamp to American culture and gradually emerged as the host society.

Since English newcomers span the entirety of American history, we might for discussion purposes divide English migration into two major eras: the colonial period to the Revolutionary War, and the industrial period from about 1820. Few Englishmen or any Europeans arrived in the interim period, in large part owing to European wars. The division of periods was named linguistically as well: Marcus Hansen has pointed out that the first use of the word "immigrant" dates from about 1817. In the seventeenth and eighteenth centuries, the newcomer was known as an "emigrant." "He migrated *out* of something; by 1817 he was migrating *into* something." [4]

The colonial English have received much more scholarly attention than their industrial age counterparts. Numerous accounts are available

---

[3] For a brief discussion of the Scandinavian movement to England, see *ibid.*, pp. 481–90.

[4] Marcus Lee Hansen, *The Immigrant in American History* (New York: Harper & Row, Publishers, 1964), p. 11.

of English life in the colonies and on the early Appalachian frontier.[5] Indeed, a chronology of colonial life is nearly tantamount to that of English life, since nearly two-thirds of the population of more than 3 million in 1790 were English and even larger proportions in the key states of Massachusetts and Virginia.[6] By contrast, as Berthoff has pointed out in his seminal work on the industrial British immigrant, historians have hardly noticed nineteenth century English newcomers.[7] But then, neither did many of the English immigrant's contemporaries.

Although religious and ideological interests were germane to many colonizers, a complex of socioeconomic forces was behind most English immigration. Indentured servants, both voluntary as workers for passage and involuntary as convicts or vagrants, accounted for possibly more than half of all white people who came to colonial America.[8] A moderate but continuous flow of English laborers, artisans, merchants, and professionals arrived in the colonial period, most of them with the foremost goal of economic gain in a new life.

In the nineteenth century, increasing religious tolerance and political reform in England dulled these incentives to emigration, but the desire for material improvement continued to loom large. Abundant and cheap labor and a stagnating economy intermittently forced down incomes in the first part of the century, and sporadic employment and wages depressed English workers in the latter half.[9] Yet, the decision to emigrate was frequently made during prosperity in the English economic cycle, because this usually meant that wages in America were commensurately higher. In assessing the "push-pull" of structural factors on immigration, we may easily over-intellectualize the problem. Individual impulses to move are often not readily reduceable to neat categories; they may be spontaneous decisions for change, fresh experiences, or a "new sense of self."

Magnitude and Settlement

Englishmen have migrated to America on a very large scale, yet they have not always been the most numerous immigrants (even when one adds English Canadians to the total). Immigration statistics are not available

[5] For an interesting social account of early America, see Oscar Handlin, *The Americans* (Boston: Little, Brown and Company, 1963), pp. 3–192.

[6] *Annual Report of the American Historical Association,* Vol. I, 1931 (Washington, D.C.: Government Printing Office, 1932), p. 124.

[7] Rowland T. Berthoff, *British Immigrants in Industrial America* (Cambridge, Mass.: Harvard University Press, 1953).

[8] Maldwyn Allen Jones, *American Immigration* (Chicago: University of Chicago Press, 1960), p. 9.

[9] See Berthoff, *British Immigrants in Industrial America,* for a detailed discussion of the socioeconomic push and pull of British immigration.

before 1820, so about all one may safely say regarding the numerical role of the English in colonial immigration is that they were overwhelmingly predominant among the settlers of the seventeenth century, but later fell behind incoming Scotch-Irish and Germans in the eighteenth. England never again regained the top position in American immigration, trailing Ireland and Germany throughout the nineteenth century, and Italy, Austria-Hungary, and Russia in the twentieth.

Nevertheless, the English contribution to American immigration has been consistently great. From 1820 to 1929, well over 2.5 million Englishmen were counted by immigration officials. The English contribution to total immigration was greatest in the 1870's (16 per cent), but the 1880's were the numerical apogee (650,000).[10] The number of first and second generation Englishmen (English stock) totaled 2.8 million by 1910, or 9 per cent of all foreign stock.[11] As recently as 1950 over 2 million English immigrants and their children resided in this country.

Owing mainly to language and cultural similarities with the host society, the English population in the United States has always been more evenly distributed by state than any other major national origin group. This wide dispersion in settlement promoted the assimilation and inconspicuousness of the English. Even in the colonial period, only Massachusetts (82 per cent), Vermont (76 per cent), and Rhode Island (71 per cent) were more heavily English and Pennsylvania (35 per cent) less English than the average for the English population in the United States.[12]

In the eighteenth and early nineteenth centuries the English pushed west across the Appalachians into Kentucky and Tennessee and from New England into western New York and northern Ohio. The average Yankee, unlike the typical German, did not attempt to carve out a permanent farm home on the frontier. Rather, he possessed a gargantuan appetite for new and hopefully more productive land, perhaps anticipating enough gain to start a small business. Later English agriculturalists in the Old Northwest were less migrant, yet rarely huddled together in frontier or agricultural enclaves as did the Welsh, Germans, and Scandinavians.

As American industry advanced, English newcomers began turning in larger numbers to the cities. In certain New England industrial communities, English stock lived in particularly heavy concentrations. In

---

[10] *Annual Report of the Commissioner General of Immigration,* 1929 (Washington, D.C.: Government Printing Office, 1930).

[11] E. P. Hutchinson, *Immigrants and Their Children* (New York: John Wiley & Sons, Inc., 1956), p. 5.

[12] *Annual Report of the American Historical Association,* 1931, p. 124.

Fall River, Massachusetts a British dialect writer saw so many Englishmen in 1885 that he wrote, "I soon forgeet wheere I wur, and fancied I're i'England, an'wur th' only Yankee i' th' company. I towd 'em I wouldn't foret 'em when igeet back to Ameriky." [13] English and English Canadians and Irish crowded into the mill and factory towns of the East, viewing each other with suspicion and often open hostility. Inasmuch as the pattern of English settlement in this country has always been very similar to the population distribution as a whole, all of the major industrial states of the North and West became significant repositories of English stock. Regardless of where the English immigrant chose to settle, he would be sure of finding Anglo company; thus he went where he thought economic or personal opportunities were greatest.

In addition to sheer numbers and wide distribution, the English immigrants of the industrial period had several other demographic assets working in their advantage in the economic struggle and the assimilation process. First, nearly all were literate, a virtual prerequisite to social mobility in an industrial society. Secondly, English families tended to be smaller than those of other ethnic groups; small family size augments the material chances of its members, and material success facilitates social acceptance and assimilation. And thirdly, the English immigrant tended to be much better equipped with industrial skills than the majority of his foreign counterparts.

SKILLS, POWER, AND MOBILITY

The English have easily been the most successful national origin group in America, economically, politically, and socially. Together with the Scots, they largely dominated commercial activity in the colonial period. Many Yankees, of course, were poor farmers and laborers. The majority of English immigrants in the first half of the nineteenth century were indigent agricultural workers. Indeed, primarily New Englanders and English immigrants extended the agricultural frontier from western New York to the Great Plains.[14] As Marcus Hansen has put it, "The first white man to pioneer in any township was not a Schultz or a Meyer, a Johnson or an Olson. He was a Robinson, a McLeod, or a Boone." [15] These transient Yankees were in the vanguard of the northwest migration, clearing and breaking the land and then often yielding it to Germans or Scandinavians.

13 Berthoff, *British Immigrants in Industrial America,* p. 33.
14 W. S. Shepperson, *British Emigration to North America* (Minneapolis: University of Minnesota Press, 1957), pp. 5–31.
15 *The Immigrant in American History,* pp. 66–67.

The English played a pivotal role on the industrial frontier as well. By 1870 only one-fourth of the English-born labor force were in agriculture. English workers were rapidly accumulating in the burgeoning industrial centers of the North. Englishmen were instrumental to the development of practically every major industrial sector of the economy. The demand for supervisory skills and mechanical expertise in the mills and factories stimulated a regular flow of skilled workers from England to New England. Children of Yankee farmers often performed unskilled tasks in the mills under imported English direction. Irish, however, increasingly occupied the menial and lowest-paying jobs.

In the coal fields of Pennsylvania, the English and the Welsh held the top jobs both inside the mines and at the supervisory level. An Immigration Commission survey of 1907–1910 reported that 83 per cent of English coal miners had had previous experience in England.[16] In copper and iron and steel industries, the majority of English immigrants were also trained in their work, and thus they moved directly into the better jobs. Later research on Connecticut industry was summed up thus: "The analysis demonstrates quite definitely the superior position held by certain groups, notably the British-Americans . . . the latter clearly predominate in the most remunerative fields and positions." [17]

As demonstrated in the community studies of the 1930's and 1940's, British Americans were vastly overrepresented in professional and managerial occupations.[18] For example, two-thirds of all professional and managerial persons in New Haven were British American, yet they constituted but 12 per cent of the city's population.[19] Regardless of whether they were a majority or a small minority, British monopolized the upper levels of the occupational hierarchy.

The very top of the occupational ladder has also had a decidedly British, and especially English, composition. Keller's investigation of topmost executives of the largest American companies disclosed that 87 per cent were of British descent in 1870, 77 per cent in 1900, and 65 per cent in 1950.[20] Two-thirds of the British executives were English. Another

[16] Berthoff, *British Immigrants in Industrial America*, pp. 47–74.

[17] Samuel Koenig, "Ethnic Groups in Connecticut Industry," *Social Forces,* XX (October, 1941), 105.

[18] For example, Elin Anderson, *We Americans* (Cambridge, Mass.: Harvard University Press, 1938); Robert S. Lind and Helen Lind, *Middletown in Transition* (New York: Harcourt, Brace and World, Inc., 1937); W. Lloyd Warner and Paul S. Lunt, *The Social Life of a Modern Community* (New Haven: Yale University Press, 1941); and W. Lloyd Warner, *Democracy in Jonesville* (New York: Harper & Row, Publishers, 1949).

[19] John W. McConnell, "The Influence of Occupation Upon Social Stratification" (doctoral dissertation, Yale University, 1937).

[20] Suzanne I. Keller, "The Social Origins and Career Lines of Three Generations of American Business Leaders" (doctoral dissertation, Columbia University, 1953).

trend study by Newcomer revealed that a substantial majority of the executives in the largest industries, public utilities, and railroad corporations of 1900, 1925 and 1950 were British.[21]

Accordingly, American millionaries have been predominantly English. In a study published in 1925, Sorokin noted that at least half of both deceased and living millionaires were English and a majority were British.[22] The list of America's centimillionaires of 1968 was heavily scored with Anglo names.[23]

In political life, too, the English have surpassed all other groups in power and position. Approximately two-thirds of American presidents have been of largely English parentage, beginning with George Washington, the great-grandson of a Yorkshireman. Reporting on the judiciary, Schmidhauser noted that from 1789 to 1957, 78 per cent of all Supreme Court justices were British and more than half English or Welsh.[24] Even since the 1930's, the majority of justices have been of British descent. Finally, in the legislative branch of the federal government, lawmakers have been very disproportionately British.[25]

In brief, English have been extraordinarily successful in the occupational world. At the apex of economic and political institutions, they have extended their predominance far beyond mere representation. Moreover, Americans of English descent seem to be only very gradually losing their hold on the top industrial posts. Indeed, in certain of the most venerable areas of the economy, such as manufacturing, mining, transportation, and finance, they were as strongly represented in 1950 as they were in the nineteenth century. But of course, not all Americans of English ancestry have been high occupational achievers. There have been and continue to be indigent "swamp Yankees," impoverished dirt farmers, hill folk and miners from Maine to Georgia, destitute rural Southerners bypassed by twentieth-century progress, and generations of unskilled urban laborers of English descent. On the whole, however, English Americans have gained far more than their share of the occupations most highly valued in American society.

Why were the English so successful? We have already touched upon some of the reasons, such as literacy, small family size, geographical mobility, and transplanted skills. In addition, as the first and largest

21 Mabel Newcomer, *The Big Business Executive: The Factors That Made Him* (New York: Columbia University Press, 1955).

22 Pitirim Sorokin, "American Millionaires and Multi-Millionaires," *Social Forces,* III (May, 1925), 627–40.

23 Arthur M. Lewis, "America's Centimillionaires," *Fortune* (May, 1968), 152–57.

24 John R. Schmichauser, "The Justices of the Supreme Court: A Collective Portrait," *Midwest Journal of Political Science,* III (February, 1959), 1–57.

25 Donald W. Matthews, *The Social Background of Political Decision Makers* (New York: Random House, Inc., 1954), pp. 26–27.

group in colonial America, the English established themselves economically before anyone else did. With each successive wave of newcomers, English Americans were elevated to a higher level in the occupational structure. Occupational gains may be converted into permanent family possessions by transmitting privilege in life chances from generation to generation. That there has been considerable occupational inheritance, especially at the upper levels where British are found, has been amply demonstrated for specific sets of fathers and sons.[26] Furthermore, the English have always enjoyed the enviable advantage of being members of the preferred ethnic group. A person's employment has not always been in one-to-one correspondence with his ability and talent. Although the technological sophistication of the present makes ethnicity no longer germane to occupational selection, ethnic status has traditionally been a factor of perhaps equal importance to work history and credentials in the job market. And again, past advantages tend to be self-perpetuating.

The role of Protestantism in English success must also be considered. The larger question of the Protestant ethnic will be considered later in the book. Suffice it to say here, to the extent that Protestantism has been influential in economic success (over and above preferred ethnic group status), the English have benefited favorably.

CULTURAL COMPATIBILITY

Americans had developed a culture and identity of their own by 1750, but it was, in Rowland Berthoff's words, "a British acorn from which the young oak had sprouted." [27] The colonial English adapted Anglo-Saxon institutions to the environment of the New World and gradually emerged as the host society and core culture. Thus, later English immigrants did not confront the arduous task of learning new ways of life in the same manner as did the non-Anglo-Saxon. Moderate differences between English and American life styles existed, but congruence was maximal. The English immigrant often found tea-drinking ridiculed, ale illegal, and his favorite sport, cricket, an exclusive diversion of the rich—none of these difficulties being too serious. The failure of the English American press attested to the security of the English immigrant in American culture. The British American press, with its broader base of appeal, was moderately successful and printed weeklies with news from home under various publishers for over a century, beginning in 1822.

---

26 See, for example, Elton F. Jackson and Harry J. Crockett, Jr., "Occupational Mobility in the United States," *American Sociological Review*, XXIX (February, 1964), 5–15.

27 *British Immigrants in Industrial America*, p. 5.

Probably to no one's surprise, the image of the English as extraordinarily staid and proper in their behavior is more fiction than fact. Cleveland Amory has suggested that, despite a proliferation of books on etiquette, that the nineteenth century Boston upper class had "customs but no manners." [28] On the frontier, a Norwegian in Wisconsin wrote home to friends about an experience in a Yankee home where in the midst of a conversation the Yankee lady belched so loudly that the room resounded.[29] At Paterson, New Jersey, an American observer alleged in 1832 that the English millhands were usually drunken and unruly, and were the most beastly people he had ever seen.[30] This is not to single out the English; as we shall see, spontaneous and rowdy behavior has been characteristic of segments of nearly every Protestant immigrant group at some early point in their American experience.

In brief, English Americans were culturally assimilated with rather painless celerity; their hyphenated status was short-lived, if even recognized. They simply adopted the American version of the Anglo-Saxon life styles prevailing at their own particular social status level, be it professional, business, industrial, or agricultural. English forebears resided at the cultural core, and within a generation or two at the most, the newcomers joined them.

GROUP LIFE IN THE CORE SOCIETY

As the host society, the communal interests of the English and Anglo-American (read British American) easily may be overlooked. To be sure, structural assimilation has different implications for the Anglo-American than it does for non-Anglo (read non-British) groups. Owing to their early social and cultural establishment, Anglo-Americans were generally not themselves involved in the assimilation process, but were on the receiving end. The groups and institutions of the larger society were in fact their groups and institutions. Though largely acculturated to begin with, many first and second generation Britishers were involved in the process of structural assimilation as they moved out of cliques, families, and neighborhoods dominated by Old World people and into those of the "Old Americans." [31] The extent of communal solidarity

28 Cleveland Amory, *The Proper Bostonians* (New York: E. P. Dutton & Co., Inc., 1947).

29 Theodore Blegen, *Land of Their Choice* (Minneapolis: University of Minnesota Press, 1955), p. 318.

30 Berthoff, *British Immigrants in Industrial America*, p. 146.

31 To make it explicit, by "Old American" I mean a descendant of Britishers (though very successful first-generation persons, particularly English, may be included) and completely assimilated non-British Protestants.

within the core group is nevertheless of considerable importance, because it relates directly to the prospects of assimilation of other ethnic groups. Moreover, social merger or fusion of the British with the remainder of the population would also be an empirical possibility.[32]

Empirical evidence bearing on the communal tendencies of the British comes to us mainly from the earlier community studies. These studies rarely distinguished between American generations or among the separate British national origin groups, but rather treated them all together as Yankees, Old Americans, or Anglo-Americans. From this we should not infer that generation and particular British origin have never been relevant to the shaping of British American group life. These studies were carried out at a late date in the histories of the British national origin groups, and at an earlier point in time immigrant English, Scotch, Scotch-Irish, Welsh, and Old Americans formed separate social units. As Berthoff has pointed out, "Through most of the nineteenth century the Welsh, Scottish and English immigrants showed little sign that they would ever fuse into a truly British-American community." [33] The Welsh, Cornish, and Scotch-Irish often formed extremely close-knit groups. A Scottish American is reported to have said in 1865 that all that distinguished the so-called Anglo-Saxons of the South Province of Britain was tow-colored hair, dough faces, spindle shanks, and shovel-built feet, a not very ingratiating appraisal.

Old or Anglo-Americans also formed cohesive social groups at the primary level. In his study of Burlington, Vermont, Elin Anderson discovered that of all ethnic groups in the city Old Americans were the most socially exclusive: 87 per cent declared that all of their intimate friends were also Old Americans.[34] English Canadians were preferred as neighbors and friends second only to members of their own group because "they are like our own people." Anderson noted that within the Anglo-American group ". . . [T]here are the usual divisions of classes and cliques, of rich and poor; but the common elements of culture and tradition give an impression of a common unit in relation to other ethnic groups in the community." [35] Through the famous Yankee City studies, we learn that higher-status Yankees rarely associated with people of other ethnic stocks and other Yankees tried hard not to do so.[36]

Anglo-Americans residing in a Connecticut town studied by C. W.

[32] For a distinction between fusion and assimilation, see Walter P. Zenner, "Ethnic Assimilation and the Corporate Group," *The Sociological Quarterly,* VIII (Summer, 1967), 340–48.

[33] Berthoff, *British Immigrants in Industrial America,* p. 185.

[34] Anderson, *We Americans,* p. 126.

[35] *Ibid.,* pp. 23–24.

[36] Warner and Lunt, *The Social Life of an American Community,* p. 242.

King in the early 1940's remained socially aloof from other ethnic groups, with the occasional exception of Scandinavians.[37] As an indication of the extent of ethnic separation, fully three-fourths of the Anglo-Americans belonged to predominantly Anglo-American cliques. That the British made some room in their social life for culturally assimilated Scandinavians has also been noted by Vogt in his study of a Minnesota township. Yankees were organized into three levels of self-contained status groups, but each was relatively open to acculturated third generation Norwegians who wished to participate.[38] Studies such as these hint strongly at the notion of the multiple-melting-pot thesis, according to which acculturated non-Anglo Protestants are socially accepted by Anglo-Americans to the exclusion of other minorities.

Relations with the Irish were especially tenuous and sometimes violent. The growing presence of the Irish, in fact, provided the impetus to greater inter-British solidarity. Various "United British Societies" of English, Scots, and Welsh symbolized British solidarity around the turn of the century. In New England the British-Irish rivalry was most intense. Rancorous precedents and bitter memories were there first established between the two groups. The Irish had acquired a dubious reputation among Old Americans and other Protestant groups of being heavy drinkers, ferocious fighters, and loose in morals. To quote one early Anglo writer's image of the Irish:

> The pure Celt has, to those who know how to take him, the value and charm which belong to a rather primitive man of a high order. The rich fund of simple human nature; the keen uncalculating sympathy, with its attendant sportive wit; the immediate joy of living, at its best in the moment, with scant sense of the morrow; and an honesty that makes him the least furtive of men, are combined with a remnant of the old man-slaying brutality which greatly inclines him to violent deeds.[39]

In an even less favorable vein, we have from another New England writer:

> Given to excess in drink, quick to violence, they seemed barbarous to the staid Puritans. Even sea captains were shocked by their blasphemous language.... A simple business dispute that would cause two New Englanders to do no worse than call bad names and quote biblical texts at each other would drive an Irishman to blind rape and murder.[40]

[37] C. Wendell King, "Branford Center: A Community Study in Social Cleavage" (doctoral dissertation, Yale University, 1943).

[38] Evon Z. Vogt, "Social Stratification in the Rural Midwest: A Structural Analysis," *Rural Sociology*, XII (December, 1947), 364–75.

[39] Nathaniel S. Shaler, "The Scotch Element in the American People," *Atlantic Monthly*, LXXVII (April 1, 1896), 508–16.

[40] Clifford K. Shipton, "Immigration to New England, 1680–1740," *Journal of Political Economy*, XLIV (April, 1936), 225–39.

Reflecting on Anglo-Irish relations in Vermont, Anderson writes, "To be an Irishman—a Papist and a Democrat—is as a red flag to a bull to many a Puritan Yankee." [41]

British-Irish relations in the Pennsylvania coal fields were also turbulent. Violence stemming from English and Welsh monopolization of skilled jobs and Irish strike-breaking activity frequently erupted between the two groups. A policy of avoidance was adopted by both. Yet, as we shall see later, the most incendiary ethnic relations existed between the Irish and Scotch-Irish.

Although they relied mainly on the organizations of the larger society, the English also formed some of their own voluntary associations. The first specifically English voluntary associations were organized in the eighteenth century as charitable societies whose purpose was to help indigent newcomers make their way in the cities and guarantee English respect, which the paupers threatened. St. George charitable societies, named after England's patron saint, were located in a number of the nation's larger cities. In the nineteenth century, English immigrants organized recreational clubs, fraternal organizations, professional and businessmen's societies, and workingmen's associations. [42] Some British American associations, such as the Anglo-American Association of Boston, were anti-Irish and had mainly political aims. Most, however, were social and recreational. Many ostensibly non-ethnic service clubs, such as Rotary, frequently have been composed entirely of Anglo-Americans, pointing up one of the reasons why there were not as many ethnic institutions per se among the English and their descendants as there were in other ethnic groups: the organizations of the core society were perforce Anglo-American, and English immigrants soon viewed them as their own. Why should English Americans build up a network of schools, presses, clubs, and churches when those of the community would comfortably accommodate them?

Intermarriage and the Protestant Melting Pot

Intermarriage is a most crucial aspect of intergroup relations. It signifies the most intimate kind of social acceptance. Conversely, marriage within the group is a prerequisite to the maintenance of communal solidarity. In the colonial and early industrial period, in-marriage among the English was naturally quite high, because opportunities for out-marriage were relatively low. Even with the heavy influx of non-British groups, however, persons of English background continued to display a strong

41 Anderson, *We Americans*, p. 25.
42 Berthoff, *British Immigrants in Industrial America*, Chap. 11.

propensity for marriage with members of their own and other British groups.[43] A perusal of the data in Table 3–1 will reveal a remarkable uniformity in the difference between expected and actual rate of English or British in-marriage across time and space. The differences suggest that in the present century up to a half of the English and British population have gone out of their way (beyond random choice) to marry within their own group.

The English intermarried with increasing frequency in second and later generations, but out-choices were mainly limited to members of other Protestant national origin groups. An excellent example of this pattern may be found in Julius Drachsler's classic work on intermarriage in New York City: 46 per cent of first generation English persons took English spouses in America, compared to only 16 per cent of the second generation. However, two-thirds of *both* first and second generations married British, German, or Scandinavian spouses.[44] Ruby Jo Reeves Kennedy later reported a similar pattern in New Haven and was among the first observers of the assimilation process to note empirically the tendency for national origin groups to intermarry within religious categories.[45] Yet, as the data in Table 3–1 suggest, British intermarriage has not proceeded as far as some might think.

The in-marriage tendencies of the British, or any other ethnic group, reflect not only conscious preference but also social opportunities as found in residential propinquity, common church, school, and club affiliations and similar status-group memberships. As pointed out in the introduction, the consequences of primary-group solidarity is endogamy in marriage.

"OLD AMERICANS" ALL

The question of ethnic indentity as it pertains to the English, and to other British groups, may be couched in two closely related ways. First, to what extent have English Americans thought of themselves as English qua English? and second, to what degree have Americans of

[43] An excess of females or males (the latter was nearly always the case) predisposes an ethnic group to higher intermarriage rates. The English were rather well-balanced in sex ratio, and thus intermarriage rates were largely unaffected by it. In 1920, for example, there were 109 English-born males to every 100 females, compared to Denmark's 158 at one extreme and Northern Ireland's 83 at the other. See Hutchinson, *Immigrants and Their Children*, p. 19.

[44] Julius Drachsler, *Intermarriage in New York City* (New York: Columbia University Press, 1921), computed from Table VI, Appendix.

[45] Ruby Jo Reeves Kennedy, "Single or Triple Melting-Pot?" Intermarriage trends in New Haven 1870–1940," *American Journal of Sociology*, XLIX (January, 1944), 331–39.

TABLE 3–1

ENGLISH AND BRITISH IN-MARRIAGE RATES
IN THE UNITED STATES, SELECTED STUDIES

Location	Time	Percentage Expected In-Marriages [a]	Percentage Observed In-Marriages [b]	Percentage Difference
New York City [c]				
(English only)	1908–1912	2	34	32
Nebraska [d]	1909–1913	13	49	36
	1921–1925	12	37	25
Wisconsin [d]	1908–1912	10	64	54
	1921–1925	7	56	11
New York State [d]	1908–1912	45	56	11
	1921–1925	39	47	8
Woonsocket, R.I.[e]				
(English only)	1926	9	59	50
Derby, Conn.[f]	1940	5	53	48
Wright County, Minn.[g]	1942	3	59	56
New Haven, Conn.[h]	1900	20	72	52
	1930	12	59	47
	1950	10	54	43
Protestant City [i]	1967	12	54	42
Catholic City [i]	1967	7	55	48

[a] The expected in-marriage rates were computed and represent the per cent of English or British (females if given) in the sample or community population.

[b] The observed in-marriage rates represent the percentage of English or British males married to English or British females of all English or British males in a given sample except in Derby and Protestant and Catholic City, where the over-all male and female rate is given to maximize sample size. All marriages were contracted in the United States.

[c] Julius Drachsler, *Intermarriage in New York City* (New York: Columbia University Press, 1921), first and second generations only.

[d] Edmund deS. Brunner, *Immigrant Farmers and Their Children* (Garden City, N.Y.: Doubleday & Company, Inc., 1929), first and second generations only.

[e] Bessie Bloom Wessel, *An Ethnic Survey of Woonsocket, Rhode Island* (Chicago: University of Chicago Press, 1931).

[f] Milton Barron, *People Who Intermarry* (Syracuse: Syracuse University Press, 1946).

[g] Lowry Nelson, "Intermarriage Among Nationality Groups in a Rural Area of Minnesota," *American Journal of Sociology*, XLVIII (March, 1943), 585–92.

[h] Ruby Jo Reeves Kennedy, "Single or Triple Melting-Pot? Intermarriage in New Haven 1870–1950," *American Journal of Sociology*, LVIII (July, 1952), 56–59.

[i] See Appendix B for source. A marriage between a British American with a mixed British–non-British spouse was considered an in-marriage.

English descent identified themselves as "Old Americans"? The former involves the traditional type of ethnic identity lodged in Old World ties; the latter refers to a special British modification of ethnic identity, which takes British origin as a frame and embellishes it with pride in American traditions.

In answer to the first question, a rather strong sense of ethnic feeling existed among first generation Englishmen. As Berthoff has written, "Although as the years passed the immigrants' personal ties came to be in America rather than in Britain, their fondness for and pride in the old country waxed. British travelers found them everywhere, 'British in heart and memory . . . always with a touch of the exile eager to see an English face and to hear an English voice!' " [46] Few of the second generation, however, felt strong kinship with English traditions as such, even though they were fully appreciative of their Anglo-Saxon background.

Perhaps because Old American identity was so closely related to English identity and so easily accessible to English Americans, the transition from one to the other could be made with great alacrity in the second generation. Thus, in answer to the second question, Americans of English or British ancestry were quick to identify themselves individually and collectively as Old Americans. For Yankees with colonial roots, writes Barbara Miller Solomon, "The common tie of rural antecedents, religious affiliations, and Revolutionary experience cemented a strong feeling of kinship. . . ." [47] Nearly a century later, according to Elin Anderson, "The Old Americans, more than any group, emphasized their ethnic origin or expressed race-consciousness." [48] Regardless of how recent the American stock, persons of English descent could consider themselves *the* Americans. Children of English immigrants were able to chide their parents with *"We* beat *you* in 1776." Though the weakest in the usual sense of maintaining a hyphenated-American status, the English were the first to claim Old American identity.

Nor were those with longer American lineages inclined to reject the ethnic claims of more recent Englishmen. The English have always been preferred by native Americans above any other immigrant group as friends, associates, neighbors, and marriage partners.[49] Englishmen were scarcely considered "immigrants" in the usual condescending sense of the word. They had simply switched old for new and were considered little more foreign than a Philadelphian in Boston. The English were assigned

46 Berthoff, *British Immigrants in Industrial America,* p. 138.

47 Barbara Miller Solomon, *Ancestors and Immigrants* (New York: John Wiley & Sons, Inc., 1965), p. 3.

48 Anderson, *We Americans,* pp. 246–47.

49 See any one of a number of studies generated by and including Emory Bogardus, *Immigration and Race Attitudes* (Boston: D. C. Heath & Company, 1928).

no opprobrious corollary to "dagoe" or "mick." "John Bull," the American appellation for Englishmen, carried no invective but only affectionate jest. The English posed no civic threat, no alternative value system, no point of religious conflict. On the contrary, they were not only accepted, but considered a welcome addition to the strength and fortification of the core culture.

SOME NOTES ON THE WELSH

In many ways the Welsh experience in America has been very similar to that of the English, although the language difference set the first generation of Welsh further apart from the core society than their English counterparts. Partially as a result of their language, Welshmen relied more heavily on their own ethnic institutions in social life, particularly the church.

Welsh immigrants were attracted to industrial America by the prospect of high wages in American mines and mills, but to the crowded Welsh the promise of land held the greatest appeal. The Union Pacific Railroad described Nebraska to the Welsh as a land where "the gentle Spring and wonderful Summer pour down their blessings from overflowing coffers and only the playing of the red deer and the wonderful singing of the birds break the silence. Waggon roads which reveal the black earth, cross green and verdant slopes where the tall grass of the prairies waves in the breeze." [50] Images such as this may have seemed irresistible to the Welsh agriculturalist tilling his minuscule plot of land. To some, these expectations were fulfilled. In a letter home, an early Welsh farmer in Iowa wrote: "You urge me to come back to the Old Country but there is no likelihood of my doing that very soon as my adopted country is better than the land of my birth. . . ." [51] Others, perhaps more coal miners among them, were disillusioned. As one such miner wrote: "Many have emigrated this year to the coal districts and most of them are bitterly disappointed." [52]

Welshmen were among the first settlers in Jamestown and Plymouth and in the New England colonies generally. However, the first separate Welsh colony of any size was established near Philadelphia by religious dissenters on land negotiated from William Penn in 1682. Welsh farmers, most of them attracted by religious freedom, came to Pennsylvania in fairly large numbers over the next several decades. Almost two hundred

---

[50] Alan Conway, ed., *The Welsh in America: Letters from the Immigrants* (Minneapolis: University of Minnesota Press, 1961), p. 10.

[51] *Ibid.*, p. 111.

[52] *Ibid.*, p. 176.

years later the Welsh again became a recognizable minority in Pennsylvania, this time as miners rather than farmers.

The total Welsh immigration to industrial America was comparatively small, probably not much larger than 125,000 persons. Relative to the population of Wales and in terms of American industrial development, however, Welsh immigration was important. Because Welsh immigration was heaviest during the first decade of this century, Welsh stock reached a peak of 250,000 in 1920.

In contrast to the English, the Welsh clustered together in only a few states. At the turn of the century, four-fifths of all foreign-born Welsh resided in Pennsylvania, Ohio, New York, Illinois, and Wisconsin.[53] The majority of Welsh were farmers and miners, but Welsh populations could also be found in Pittsburgh and Scranton, Pennsylvania, and Columbus, Ohio. The immigrants tended to settle in Welsh-speaking enclaves, but later generations proceeded to disperse ecologically.

Aside from the language barrier and the related tendency to segregate residentially, the Welsh possessed most of the requisites for rapid assimilation. Most were literate. Virtually all were Protestant. Welsh families, though often quite large in the first generation, were on the whole smaller than those of other immigrant groups.[54] The large majority of urban dwellers were in white-collar jobs and the skilled trades. Very few were unskilled laborers. For example, 10 per cent of the Columbus, Ohio Welsh were professionals and most of the remainder were in white-collar or skilled positions.[55] In Columbus, the average Welsh home, according to an early observer, was ". . . comfortable and well equipped with good furniture, well located on respectable, improved streets, and its inhabitants enjoyed a wholesome and comfortable living." [56] Many Welsh farmers also enjoyed prosperity on the fertile land of Wisconsin, Iowa, and Nebraska.

Two-Generational Assimilation

For a time, however, the Welsh clung tenaciously to their cultural heritage. As Berthoff has remarked, ". . . Of all the British-Americans they were the most anxious to preserve the culture—particularly the language —of their fatherland." [57] A Welshman upon returning to Wales in 1912

53 U.S. Bureau of the Census, *U.S. Census of Population: 1900, Population,* Vol. I, Table 33 (Washington, D.C.: Government Printing Office, 1901), pp. 734–35.

54 Albert E. Jenks, "Ethnic Census in Minneapolis," *American Journal of Sociology,* XVII (May, 1912), 776–82.

55 Daniel J. Williams, *The Welsh of Columbus, Ohio* (Oshkosh, Wisconsin, 1913), pp. 92–93.

56 *Ibid.,* p. 91.

57 Berthoff, *British Immigrants in Industrial America,* p. 170.

reported that the emigrants were "ten times more Welsh than they were at home . . . and will travel hundreds of miles to hear anything Welsh." [58]

The Welsh language was widely maintained through three genera-tions in homogeneous Welsh communities, but often fell into disuse in the second or third generation in mixed areas. In Pittsburgh during the 1850's, a Welshman noted that Welsh was "the only tongue spoken in those quarters of the city where our ancestors resided. . . . Their children were likewise as 'Welshy' as their parents. . . ." [59] The Welsh church of Columbus was said to have lost many younger members because of the persistence of the language in religious services. Children were taught to read Welsh texts, because the immigrants made a strong effort to preserve the language into the second generation. The Welsh language press had the largest circulation per person of any British American newspaper and published until 1951. Nevertheless, Welsh language, literary, and singing societies, enthusiastically supported by the foreign-born, lagged in membership in American-born generations.

Most first generation Welsh were strongly religious and communally oriented. In Columbus, three-fourths held church membership, mainly Methodist. Amusements such as card-playing, theater-going, and dancing were not tolerated by the church. However, like many other immigrant parents, Welsh elders were more often than not disappointed by the younger generation's leisure activities. Most organized social activities were church-related and the religious commitment of the Welsh very much contributed to their reputation for clannishness. In his introduc-tion to a volume of Welsh letters, Conway has remarked, "A picture . . . emerges of the Welsh clinging more tenaciously together than most national groups." [60]

Welsh communal solidarity encouraged a rather high in-marriage rate for the size of the Welsh group. A number of empirical studies sug-gest that in-marriage rates for the first generation were around 50 per cent.[61] Owing to a moderate excess of Welsh males, in-marriage rates were higher for Welsh females. The second generation, and particularly the third, intermarried with much greater frequency; out-choices, how-ever, were mainly English.

The Welsh, no less than the English, were at loggerheads with the Irish. In the anthracite coal areas of Pennsylvania, conflict with the Irish promoted Welsh solidarity. In an 1844 letter home, a Welsh lady

58 *Ibid.*, p. 91.
59 *Ibid.*, p. 170.
60 *The Welsh in America*, p. 12.
61 For example, Jenks, "Ethnic Census in Minneapolis," p. 777; Drachsler, *Inter-marriage in New York City*, pp. 43–45; and Williams, *The Welsh of Columbus, Ohio*, pp. 84–85.

wrote, "There was fighting today between two of the men and a gang of Irish. The two Welshmen fought excellently and gave a pair of black eyes to the brother of D. O'Connell and beat them until they were hopping." [62] The Irish were despised by the Welsh as strike-breakers in the labor battles that swept the anthracite industry after the Civil War. Deploring the Irish as strike-breakers, a Welshman wrote home, "It is true that they got a number of old, spineless Irish to be blacklegs [strike-breakers] at one of the pits. . . . Had it not been for those old Irish we would have won a complete victory two months sooner had they been as united as the Welsh." [63]

Politically, the Welsh have traditionally been Republican, an affiliation initially encouraged by their strong anti-slavery feelings, and later through that party's links with Protestantism and the middle class. As a small and conservative British group, the Welsh have been popular foreigners, save for their labor organizing activities. Welshmen have posed few threats to fundamental American values. Rather, Welsh Americans offered support to the Anglo-Saxon Protestant mainstream, into which the second and third generations largely vanished.

ENGLISH CANADIANS

If immigrants from England attracted only slight attention from Americans, we might say that English Canadians have been ignored. Of course, not all immigrants to the United States from English Canada were English or even British. Many came from other European countries after a sojourn of a generation or more in Canada. Throughout most of the nineteenth century, Canada ranked among the top five immigrant-producing countries. In all, over 2.8 million persons immigrated to the United States from Canada during the period 1820–1929. [64] Although immigration figures do not distinguish English or French origin, probably about 2 million of these came from English Canada. Fully three-fourths of that number arrived during the first two decades of this century. As European immigration tapered off in the 1920's, 22 per cent of all immigrants were Canadians. In 1924 alone, over 200,000 Canadian entries were recorded.

The pattern of settlement of the English Canadians was similar to that of the English, the chief difference being that Canadians quite naturally were located in greater proportions along the border in New England, New York, Michigan, Minnesota, and Washington.

62 Conway, *The Welsh in America*, p. 24.
63 *Ibid.*, p. 191.
64 *Annual Report of the Commissioner General of Immigration*, 1931, p. 184.

English Canadians, if Protestant, have been accepted as virtual social equals by the white Protestant population in the United States. Inasmuch as most of the Canadian population has been concentrated near the United States border, most English Canadians who emigrated to this country had had previous exposure to American Anglo-Saxon culture. In this, and in other respects such as occupational skills, small family size, literacy, and geographical distribution, English Canadians have had a very low melting point, rapidly assimilating into the white Protestant core society. English Canadians have hardly recognized any basis or need for separate ethnic organizations; they became Old Americans almost as soon as they crossed the border.

SUMMARY

The English were the first large-scale national origin group in American life. They established the cultural moulds that were destined to prevail in American society. The supply of English immigrants to America has been longer and more consistent than that from any other country. In the tradition of national origin groups in America, the English immigrants maintained various amounts of social distance between themselves and other ethnic groups, though cultural differences with the Anglo-American core society were minor. Their small group of immigrant Welsh cousins, also similar in culture, were much more active within ethnic communities. Both English and Welsh participated in the development of a larger British American community, and the second generation assimilated into the Anglo-American core society. The English were geographically distributed throughout the country, whereas the immigrant Welsh congregated in a few states. As literate, often skilled, and culturally amenable groups, the English and Welsh enjoyed high occupational placement in the American economy; and most have sustained privileged social, political, and economic positions. Similar in culture, different in language, the Welsh have realized greater assimilative and economic success in America than any other foreign-language-speaking group.

Scots have been junior partners to the English in building Anglo-Saxon America. Scots have resided nearer the social center and dominant cultural tendencies in American society than any other non-English group. As a sizeable colonial British group, they were partially instrumental in shaping the American cultural mould. Yet, they were never at the English-dominated center when they arrived and nearly all were involved to some degree in the several processes of assimilation. The more isolated Scottish Highlanders and Scotch-Irish moved culturally and socially toward the emerging host society of the colonial period at a slower rate than the Lowlanders, though most colonial Scots had been assimilated by the turn of the nineteenth century. The majority of Scots who immigrated in the industrial period were quicker than colonial ones to complete the process of becoming members of the core society; but then, the core society of the nineteenth and twentieth centuries was better defined and the advantages of membership in the core society were more explicit than in the colonial period.

The Scots: Lowlanders, Highlanders, and Ulstermen

Scots who emigrated to America were very similar to the English in racial and cultural origin. The original ingredient of the Scottish amalgam stemmed from Gaelic-speaking Celtic tribes known as "Scoti," who were natives of Ireland but later resided in North Britain.[1] Scoti and Celtic Picts were dispelled from South Britain by Angles and Saxons who themselves subsequently inhabited the Lowlands. Rather sizeable contingents of Norse settled the same area at a later date. Vikings also mingled with Celtic tribes in the Highlands. The Scotch-Irish were originally inhabitants of the Lowlands, but emigrated to Ulster in northern Ireland in the seventeenth century, where they developed distinctive cultural patterns of their own.

IMMIGRATION AND SETTLEMENT

Scots were to play a conspicuous role in colonial development. Poverty had been proverbial among Highlanders, the English discrimi-

[1] See Peter H. Blair, *An Introduction to Anglo-Saxon England* (Cambridge: Cambridge University Press, 1956); or R. H. Hodgekin, *A History of the Anglo-Saxons* (London: Oxford University Press, 1952).

nated against the wool industry of the Lowlanders, and famines and exorbitant rents plagued the Scotch-Irish.[2] Then, too, Scottish Presbyterians were subjected to systematic religious discrimination by the English. These were among the precipitating influences that encouraged several hundred thousand Scotlanders and Scotch-Irish to set out for colonial America. Many additional Scots were sent to colonial America by the English as political and military prisoners. And after having fought for the British in the American Revolution, Scottish soldiers often remained behind when their regiments were disbanded. In the nineteenth century, social and economic dislocations similar to those experienced by the English induced further large-scale emigration.

There were some 200,000 Scotch-Irish and 250,000 Scotlanders in America at the end of the colonial period. Together they comprised nearly 15 per cent of the colonial population.[3] Then from 1820 to 1929, well over 750,000 persons came from Scotland and almost as many from Ulster. Interestingly enough, the decade of heaviest immigration from Scotland was the 1920's. However, both Scotlanders and Scotch-Irish conformed to the old immigration pattern of consistently heavy influx in the nineteenth century. Scotch stock in industrial America was at its greatest in 1930 when the census counted over 1.5 million first and second generation Scotlanders and Scotch-Irish.[4]

Along with the other British groups, Scots possessed demographic characteristics very favorable to rapid assimilation and mobility.[5] Scotch families, for example, tended to be smaller than those of other industrial immigrants; one large urban sample of Scots had an average of only slightly more than two children per family in 1910.[6] And they were second only to the English and Welsh in the percentage of skilled workers.

The pattern of Scottish settlement in industrial America was also favorable to assimilation; however, the colonial Scots often bunched closely together in homogeneous and even kinship communities. Whereas the Lowlanders often though not always arrived as families or individuals and dispersed themselves in the coastal cities, the Scotch-Irish and High-

    [2] Ian Charles Graham, *Colonists From Scotland: Emigration to North America 1707–1783* (Ithaca, N.Y.: Cornell University Press, 1956).

    [3] *Annual Report of the American Historical Association,* 1931, Vol. I (Washington, D.C.: Government Printing Office, 1932), p. 124.

    [4] E. P. Hutchinson, *Immigrants and Their Children* (New York: John Wiley & Sons, Inc., 1956), p. 5.

    [5] For a demographic description of American ethnic groups, see Stanley Lieberson, *Ethnic Patterns in American Cities* (New York: The Free Press, 1963).

    [6] Albert E. Jenks, "Ethnic Census of Minneapolis," *American Journal of Sociology,* XVII (May, 1912), 776–82.

landers frequently emigrated by entire congregations or in organized groups and settled in tightly knit rural enclaves. The Scotch-Irish initially streamed toward New England, but after 1725 they turned toward Pennsylvania and into the back country of Virginia and the Carolinas where they moved down into the valleys "like a stream inundating a plain." [7] The Scotch-Irish were to become legendary for their intrepid pioneering and Indian fighting along the Appalachian frontier. Many Highlanders farmed the river valleys of upper New York State.

By 1790, Virginia and North Carolina contained the most Scotlanders, but in no state did they constitute more than 15 per cent of the population. The Scotch-Irish were largely concentrated in Pennsylvania, constituting fully a third of that state's population. The Scotch-Irish spilled out from Pennsylvania into Virginia, the Carolinas, Kentucky, and Tennessee. Over a century later, Scots were found in greatest numbers in New York, Pennsylvania, Massachusetts, and elsewhere in the North and West, where their industrial skills were most applicable. In general, the colonial Scotch resided in the middle and southern colonies whereas the industrial Scotch focused on the Northeast.

Material Success

Next to the English and Welsh, the Scots were the highest-ranking occupation group in both colonial and industrial America. In the colonial period, Scottish merchants were rivals of the English.[8] Scotlanders also contributed more than their share of artisans, clerks, elected officials, and military officers. However, the vast majority of colonial Scots, especially Scotch-Irish and Highlanders, were frontiersmen and farmers.

The Scots contributed much to the early industrialization of the country. The first New England textile operators, for example, imported Scottish weavers. The granite, paper, pottery, coal, iron, and building industries all benefited from Scottish experience and skill.[9] A student of New England social life noted that "The Scotch or 'North Britons' were the most easily assimilated . . . for they were more frequently skilled and industrial workmen." [10] Yet, as in any immigrant group, the largest percentage of nineteenth century Scots worked as common laborers, servants, and farmers.

[7] See James G. Leyburn, *The Scotch-Irish: A Social History* (Chapel Hill, N.C.: University of North Carolina Press, 1962).

[8] Graham, *Colonists from Scotland*, p. 111.

[9] For a discussion of Scotch industrial activity in the nineteenth century, see Rowland T. Berthoff, *British Immigrants in Industrial America* (Cambridge, Mass.: Harvard University Press, 1953).

[10] Clifford K. Shipton, "Immigration to New England, 1680–1740," *Journal of Political Economy*, XLIV (April, 1936), 225–39.

Americans of Scottish descent have been solidly represented in the upper echelons of the business world and government. In studies of the business elite, men of Scottish ancestry consistently composed between 15 and 20 per cent of that top occupational group from 1870 to 1950.[11] Likewise, Sorokin's calculations indicated that Americans of Scottish derivation were second only to the English in total number of millionaires in the nineteenth century and ranked third or fourth in the twentieth.[12] In the history of the Supreme Court, Schmidhauser found that 25 per cent of all justices up to 1957 were primarily of Scottish origins.[13] By comparison, Scots have never constituted more than 10 per cent of the population in industrial America and less than that at mid-point in the twentieth century.

In short, early settlement, high literacy, smaller families, industrial experience, and whatever advantages have accrued to Protestants combined to promote a relatively high degree of material success among the Scottish. The Scottish strain in the American population—outside of Appalachia, where Scottish descendants have suffered economically with the rest of the region—is largely middle to upper-middle class.

SCOTTISH ANGLO-SAXONS

The three major Scottish groups of colonial America more or less differed culturally among themselves and to various degrees from the developing English core. Nevertheless, they all shared many cultural similarities. The foreign-speaking Highlanders and Scotch-Irish diverged the most culturally. Many early Highlanders in the Carolinas continued to wear their distinctive clan costumes. In Pennsylvania, the aggressive Scotch-Irish posed a sharp contrast to their more pious and ascetic German neighbors. Leyburn, in his study of the Scotch-Irish, has written, "It was usual to expect Germans to be orderly, industrious, carefully frugal.... Scotch-Irish by contrast, were regarded as quick-tempered, impetuous, inclined to work by fits and starts, reckless, too much given to drinking." [14]

Some of the isolated hollows and valleys of the Alleghenies allegedly

11 For example, William Miller, "The Recruitment of the American Business Elite," *Quarterly Journal of Economics*, LXIV (1950); and Suzanne I. Keller, "The Social Origins and Career Lines of Three Generations of American Business Leaders" (doctoral dissertation, Columbia University, 1953).

12 Pitirim Sorokin, "American Millionaires and Multi-Millionaires," *Social Forces*, III (May, 1925), 627–40.

13 John R. Schmidhauser, "The Justices of the Supreme Court: A Collective Portrait," *Midwest Journal of Political Science*, III (February, 1959), 1–57.

14 Leyburn, *The Scotch-Irish*, pp. 190–91.

preserved a slight Scottish tinge into the twentieth century, though one would probably have had to rely heavily on imagination. For example, one commentator on the Scots wrote some time ago that ". . . the original Scottish features remain, Scottish reserve, Scottish fervor, Scottish sentiment, Scottish practicality. I met last summer an old Scotch-Irish lady, in one of the lovely small valleys of southern Pennsylvania, who spoke with a distinctly Scotch accent, though she and her ancestors had lived in that spot since the middle of the eighteenth century." [15] Apparently at some point in history Scottish impetuosity and recklessness were transformed into practicality and reserve. Another early writer declared that "Among the descendants of the Scotch . . . a knowledge of the Bible is the surest and broadest basis for human intercourse," [16] indeed a long way from the Scotch-Irish reputation for inordinate drinking and ferocious brawling. After having tamed the frontier and the Indians, Scots were themselves apparently domesticated by missionaries and the sedentary life.

The amenability of the industrial Scots to American acculturation was never in doubt, nor was their enthusiasm for it. Whether in the cities or on the farms, from Scotland or Ulster, Scots were well on their way to cultural invisibility by the second generation. In religion, family life, education, leisure, or economic and political activity, Scots tended to harmonize with the ideals of Anglo-Saxon America.

The Scottish American press met with only mild success. The most successful publication, the *Scottish-American Journal,* survived from 1857 to 1919 but circulation was never very large.[17] Many more Scots, of course, read British American weeklies. Cultural ties with the homeland were nominally preserved through a number of societies. However, such groups more directly satisfied primary social needs of the Scots in America than Old World nostalgia.

COMMUNAL ACTIVITIES

Whereas cultural differences between Scots and the host society were comparatively minor, many Scots maintained separate social groups. Various Scottish American organizations and clubs existed for over two hundered years, beginning with the charitable societies in the seventeenth century. Scottish charitable and literary societies, usually called

15 George M. Harper, "The Scotch-Irish in America," *The Nation,* CIV (January 11, 1917), 45–46.
16 Nathaniel S. Schaler, "The Scotch Element in the American People," *Atlantic Monthly,* LXXVII (April 1, 1896), 512–13.
17 Berthoff, *British Immigrants in Industrial America,* p. 163.

St. Andrew's clubs, were founded in Boston in 1657 and eventually took root in many of the large cities.[18] St. Andrew's clubs were later often composed exclusively of well-to-do Scottish persons. Whatever the status level of a St. Andrew's society, writes Graham, "Scotsmen were sure to meet only with brother Scots." [19] St. Andrew's societies and similar societies of industrial Scots held banquets, sponsored lectures, provided entertainment, and made available reading materials and conversation rooms to community oriented Scottish-Americans.

In a more active and athletic vein, Caledonian clubs offered a variety of sports events, balls, and musical competition to interested Scotsmen. Scottish workingmen made up the main body of Caledonian clubs; Caledonians, however, came from all social backgrounds. The track and field games were often open to the public and attracted interest among Scots and non-Scots alike. The popularity of these games grew, until by 1918 they were held in over 125 places. Bagpipers and clansmen in costume often added Scottish color and feeling. A witness at a major event in 1896 remarked that he had seen "more wearers of the Highland costume . . . at the annual games of the New York Caledonian Club than at most similar gatherings in the Land o'Cakes." [20] In addition to St. Andrew's and Caledonian clubs, fraternal orders such as the Sons of St. George and the Order of Scottish Clans counted hundreds of lodges. These organizations also had their female counterparts in the women's auxiliaries. Scots also dominated many early Masonic lodges in this country.

The Presbyterian church in America was first organized by Scots in 1684 in Maryland and has remained an important locus of Scottish communal life. In education, Scots were instrumental in the establishment of William and Mary College in 1685, Princeton University in 1746, and the University of North Carolina in 1795. Scots and Scotch-Irish also established numerous smaller colleges. Before the Civil War, Presbyterians had organized 49 permanent colleges. Their prime function, however, was to train urgently needed clergymen.[21]

In primary-group life, colonial Scots tended to preserve social boundaries between themselves and other groups, especially in rural areas. Although the Scotch-Irish mingled freely with Scotlanders on the farming frontier,[22] Leyburn notes, "It is hardly too much to say that neither Germans nor Scotch-Irish liked each other, wanted the other as

---

[18] Graham, *Colonists from Scotland*, pp. 131–32.
[19] *Ibid.*
[20] Berthoff, *British Immigrants in Industrial America*, pp. 166–67.
[21] Leyburn, *The Scotch-Irish*.
[22] Graham, *Colonists from Scotland*, p. 110.

near neighbors, or engaged more than was necessary in social intercourse with the other." [23] The majority of the Scotch-Irish even remained separate from the English. Lowlanders who took up residence in the coastal communities mingled with the English to a greater degree than did rural Scots, but they, too, often recognized and observed ethnic differences in social life.[24] Nearly all Scottish peoples with colonial roots, however, had become participants in the core culture and society of the nineteenth century.

Though many Scots who came to this country in the nineteenth century continued to participate in Scottish group life, they became a part of a larger British American social world sooner than did their colonial counterparts. Commenting on the industrial Scots, one early writer declared, "There is a curious difficulty in tracing the distribution of the Scotch . . . which arises from the readiness with which they distribute themselves over the land . . . and the celerity with which they mingle in the social and business life of the places where in they cast their lot." [25] The various community studies carried out during the second quarter of this century strongly imply that Americans of Scottish descent, including those of more recent immigrant parents, formed an indistinguishable part of the larger Anglo-American community.

Empirical data on Scottish marriage patterns in the United States confirm the impression of considerable in-group solidarity in the first generation. Approximately two-fifths of first-generation marriages involving a Scot were endogamous.[26] A slight excess of males among Scotlanders and a moderate excess of females among Scotch-Irish roughly balanced each other out in the early decades of the century. Another two-fifths of immigrant Scotch marriages involved other British, Germans, or Scandinavians. Later generations of Scots followed the same intermarriage pattern but with greater frequency, suggesting Scottish conformity to the Protestant melting pot.

Ethnic Identity, Conflict, and Consensus

A sense of Scottish feeling and identification was keen among the foreign-born. As in subsequent generations of other British groups, the shift in self-image from Scottish to Old American was desired, entailed practically

---

23 Leyburn, *The Scotch-Irish,* p. 191.
24 Graham, *Colonists from Scotland,* p. 110.
25 Schaler, *"The Scotch Element in the American People,"* p. 514.
26 Bessie Bloom Wessel, *An Ethnic Survey of Woonsocket, Rhode Island* (Chicago: University of Chicago Press, 1931); Julius Drachsler, *Intermarriage in New York City* (New York: Columbia University Press, 1921); and Jenks, "Ethnic Census of Minneapolis."

no personal conflict, and was nearly everywhere accepted as legitimate. The immigrants, however, retained a sense of kindred with other Scots and the Old Country. A Scottish visitor to Pittsburgh in 1904 declared that he was impressed "to see glitter over songs that have the 'sough o' hame' in them and to find that after half a century, perhaps, Scotland is still the land of dollars." [27] Another Scot in America is said to have remarked, "When I am at home, I feel a man from Glasgow to be something of a rival, a man from Bara to be more than half a foreigner. Yet let us meet in some far country, and, whether we hail from the braes of Manor or the braes of Mar, some readymade affections join us on the instant." [28]

Writing on the colonial Scotch, Graham has noted that the Lowlanders tended to retain their sense of Scottish nationality and the Scotch-Irish held a "sense of distinctness from all other peoples, even including the Scots themselves." [29] Later generations that pushed west, however, placed the identificational emphasis less on European origin than on the place of family origin in America. The frontiersman was foremost a Virginian or a Pennsylvanian rather than a Scot.

Native Americans directed only slight prejudice toward Scots in industrial America; the colonial Scots, however, were sometimes less fortunate. At one point in the late seventeenth century, the elevation of Scottish persons to public office in the English colonies was prohibited. The Scotch-Irish, together with the Germans, were the principal objects of English enmity in the colonial period. "The Ulsterites were so looked down upon," wrote Shipton, "that the proper citizens of Boston refused to serve in the militia with them." [30] At Worcester a Yankee mob once pulled down a newly built Scotch-Irish Presbyterian church. Their poverty, Presbyterianism, drinking habits, blasphemous language, and propensity toward violence, suggests Jones, earned the Scotch-Irish the dislike of the English.[31] By contrast, the Lowlander's economic and political success incensed the English and native Americans. In Graham's words, "The conservatism of the great majority of the Scots in the colonies, coupled with the envy inspired by their commercial success and political power, exposed them to mounting unpopularity and abuse from Americans." [32] Although there were Scotlanders present at the Boston Tea Party and Bunker Hill, their frequent loyalty to the crown had

[27] Berthoff, *British Immigrants in Industrial America,* p. 138.
[28] *Ibid.,* p. 166.
[29] Graham, *Colonists from Scotland,* p. 142.
[30] Shipton, "Immigration to New England, 1680–1740," p. 237.
[31] Maldwyn Allen Jones, *American Immigration* (Chicago: University of Chicago Press, 1960), p. 45.
[32] Graham, *Colonists from Scotland,* p. 148.

garnered them an opprobrious name in America. The Scotch-Irish, in comparison, were nearly unanimously in support of the Revolution.

Social acceptance of Scots in industrial America was nearly universal though some natives were categorically anti-foreign. The remark by an early Scottish historian that "no new citizens are more cordially welcomed to the great republic than those who hail from the Land o' Cakes" was probably no hyperbole.[33] The Bogardus study of social distance in the 1920's corroborated that impression; the Scottish ranked next to the English in the degree of social acceptance by native Americans.[34]

Conversely, Scotlanders and especially Scotch-Irish played major parts in the virulent anti-Irish-Catholic activities that erupted sporadically in nineteenth century America. Pitched battles were waged between the Ulster Orangemen and the Irish Green. Death and bodily injury were often the consequence. Anti-Irish organizations such as the Loyal Orange Institution and the American Protestant Association enrolled thousands of Scotch-Irish in their cause. Though in the colonial period the Scots and English were often political enemies, both became part of a united British political front engaged to stand off the Celtic threat.

Despite occasional difficulties with native Americans and early frontier political opposition to the establishment, Scots for most of American history have belonged to the mainstream of the American value system. Who would doubt the allegiance of a group that claims John Paul Jones, Washington Irving, Andrew Jackson, Andrew Carnegie, and Alexander Graham Bell?

SUMMARY

Scotlanders and Scotch-Irish followed rather closely on the heels of the English colonizers, and in parts of the eighteenth century they came to America in larger numbers than the English. The Lowlanders were culturally most similar to English-established precedents, while the Gaelic-speaking Highlanders and Scotch-Irish had further to travel on the road to acculturation. Although the Lowlanders had their own social differences with the native population, they were more assimilable than the rural Highlanders and the Scotch-Irish. First generation industrial Scots formed separate social units despite fundamental cultural similarities with the host society. All Scottish groups eventually melted into the larger Anglo-Saxon Protestant core society.

[33] Peter Ross, *The Scot In America* (New York: The Raeburn Book Company, 1896), p. 2.

[34] Emory Bogardus, *Immigration and Race Attitudes* (Boston: D. C. Heath & Company, 1928).

Industrial Scottish immigration was smaller than the English influx; it continued, however, at a relatively high and consistent pace until the end of the immigration period in 1929. Scottish settlement patterns in industrial America were very similar to those of the English, Scots being rather well distributed throughout the North and West. Scottish material success in America has rivaled that of the English. Scots have always stood near or at the top of American political, social, and economic institutions. Most Americans of Scottish descent now participate fully in the nation's material abundance.

Though not Anglo-Saxon in culture, Scandinavians had early tribal links with the British. The early ancestors of the Scandinavians migrated from Europe to Scandinavia as hunting societies in pursuit of reindeer and game animals retreating northwards in the wake of glacial ice. Some of these same peoples later returned to the Continent as predecessors of certain Germanic tribes, including the Angles and Saxons. Whatever the actual sequence and direction of early migration, the inhabitants of Scandinavia were closely related to those of Northern Germany; both of these groups eventually made major contributions to the population of the British Isles.

Scandinavians, though now considered WASPs, thus do not belong historically to Anglo-Saxon culture and society. They have been granted WASP status on the basis of their successful adaptation to Anglo-Saxon America. In a sense, even today Scandinavians are second-class WASP's; nevertheless, Scandinavians know that it is better to be a second-class WASP than a non-WASP in American society.

American Vikings: The Swedes

The Swedes who left Europe were nearly all Lutherans. As Americans, Swedes and many more of their descendants became affiliated with Baptist, Methodist, and other Protestant churches. Regardless of which Protestant church they patronized, their anti-Catholic animus was unsurpassed save for the special nationalistic feud between the Protestant Scotch-Irish and the Irish. Though Swedes are much like Norwegians in culture and appearance, for a long time these two Scandinavian groups eyed one another warily from across city streets and country roads. But just as the British groups first came to terms with one another before they did with other Protestants, so did most Scandinavians first become friendly among themselves before moving out into the larger Protestant world.

NEW ENGLAND, NEW SWEDEN

The scale of Swedish immigration to America was unimpressive until the 1870's. Heavy Swedish immigration then was stimulated by rising population pressures and a scarcity of farmland in an economy that was only in the incipient stages of industrialization. As Martindale has pointed out, "The Swedish immigration ... was one of poor agricultural workers from a backward country with a shortage of land, lured on by the news of rich land in the American Middle West at a dollar or two an acre and even free under the Homestead Act of 1862." [1] Mechanization on Swedish farms created additional pressures on the rural population, encouraging many agriculturalists to leave their homeland for American prairies. Steamship, railroad, and emigrant companies conveyed in glowing terms the economic opportunities in America. American letters extolling life in the Midwest were passed on from family to family and reprinted in Swedish newspapers. Other Swedes left home mainly to escape the religious formalism of the state church, to evade military service, or to avoid the class legacy of feudalism and political privilege. Transportation was cheap in the decades after the Civil War: one could obtain American passage in steerage for as little as $12.50.

The first Swedes in America were not, however, the products of nineteenth century agricultural dislocations. The original Swedish settlement in America, New Sweden, was founded on the Delaware River in 1638. Before his death in the Thirty Years War, the indomitable Swedish king Gustavus Adolphus had developed rather far-reaching plans for colonial expansion in America. Following the advice of a Hollander, Gustavus founded the Swedish South Company in 1626. "Dutchman" Peter Minuit (Minuit was actually German-born) was contracted to lead the first expedition. Some five hundred Swedes, together with a few Finns, arrived in Delaware Bay in April of 1638. During its first few years, New Sweden proved to be a successful trading establishment. The Dutch took control in 1655 and New Sweden became a part of New Netherlands. Later, of course, New Netherlands itself fell under the domination of the English.

The Swedish language predominated in the Delaware area until William Penn opened Pennsylvania for settlement in 1682. By that time there were several Swedish settlements, with their churches, schools, and courts scattered throughout the region. The ethnic loyalty of colonial Swedes was nevertheless slight. In the words of an early Swedish pastor on the Delaware, "These descendants of the Swedes . . . have no more affection for anything from Sweden than if it were from Turkey." [2] Yet, the Swedes remained in the general geographical area they originally settled; 21,000 American Swedes comprised 9 per cent of Delaware's population in 1790 but less than 1 per cent of the nation's population.[3]

[1] Don Martindale, *American Social Structure* (New York: Appleton-Century-Crofts, 1960), p. 116.

[2] Quoted in Carl Wittke, *We Who Built America* (Englewood Cliffs, N.J.: Prentice-Hall, Inc., 1939), p. 37.

[3] *Annual Report of the American Historical Association,* 1931, Vol. I (Washington, D.C.: Government Printing Office, 1932), pp. 124–25.

Over two hundred years after New Sweden, another Swedish colony was founded at Bishop Hill, Illinois by peasants belonging to the Jansonist religious movement. Eric Janson, the charismatic-type leader of this communistically organized colony, was murdered by another member. At mid-nineteenth century, Bishop Hill numbered over one thousand souls—despite the fact that their ranks had been decimated by cholera and religious schisms. Bishop Hill prospered until 1861, when mismanagement culminated in the individualizing of property and the defection of most of the inhabitants to the Methodist church.

Other early Swedish settlements were those at New Upsala in Wisconsin and Scandia in Minnesota. However, before the Civil War, annual Swedish immigration never amounted to much more than several hundred persons. Swedish influx in the 1870's came to over 100,000 persons and approached 400,000 in the 1880's. In these decades, Sweden was the fifth ranking immigrant nation. Nor did Swedes stop coming then. About 250,000 arrived in the first decade of this century, and even as late as the 1920's another 100,000 Swedes disembarked in America. In all, from 1850 to 1929 approximately 1,250,000 Swedes entered the country; 250,000 fewer than the over-all Scottish total, but far more than came from either Scotland or Northern Ireland, respectively.[4]

At its height, in 1910, the foreign-born Swedish population totaled 660,000, or about 5 per cent of all the foreign-born.[5] At three census years —1880, 1890, and 1900—only Germany, Ireland, and England among all European nations counted more first-generation Americans than Sweden. A combined total of over 1,500,000 first and second generation Swedish Americans were enumerated in 1930. As of 1960, Swedish stock (immigrants and their native-born children) still numbered over a million.[6]

Swedes occupied a position intermediate to British and Eastern European groups on most demographic variables, literacy being an exception. The Swedes had the highest rates of literacy of any immigrant group.[7] Although rural families of eight or ten were not uncommon, Swedish fertility tended to be slightly higher than that of the British groups but lower than that of most others. For instance, among all immigrant women who bore children in 1929, those from Scandinavia (all Scandinavian countries displayed similar fertility rates) averaged 3.1 chil-

---

[4] *Annual Report of the Commissioner General of Immigration,* 1929 (Washington, D.C.: Government Printing Office, 1930), p. 186.

[5] E. P. Hutchinson, *Immigrants and Their Children* (New York: John Wiley & Sons, Inc., 1956), p. 5.

[6] *U.S. Bureau of the Census, U.S. Census of Population: 1960. Subject Reports. Nativity and Parentage* (Washington, D.C.: Government Printing Office, 1965).

[7] Stanley Lieberson, *Ethnic Patterns in American Cities* (New York: The Free Press, 1963).

dren, those from Britain 2.7, and those from Poland 4.9.[8] Urban families were smaller; Minneapolis Swedes of all generations reported an average of 2.5 children in 1910, more than the Scots and Welsh but fewer than the Irish.[9]

FARMERS, WORKERS, AND CLERKS

Inasmuch as they were foreign-speaking people in search of land, we should not be surprised that nineteenth-century Swedish immigrants first clustered in homogeneous rural settlements in the upper Midwest, especially Illinois and Minnesota. At the turn of the century, fully three-fourths of all Swedish Americans lived in a few Midwestern states. One of a handful of Swedes already in Minnesota in 1850 wrote home: "What a glorious new Scandinavia might not Minnesota become. . . . The climate, the situation, the character of the scenery, agrees with our people better than that of any other of the American states." [10] Others seemed to agree, for by the end of immigration in 1929, over 250,000 first and second generation Swedes resided in Minnesota alone. Illinois counted almost as many, and large contingents resided in Iowa and Nebraska as well.

With advancing industrialization, an increasing portion of the Swedish immigrant stream turned toward the cities of the Atlantic and Pacific Coasts. By 1930 over 40 per cent of persons of Swedish stock resided outside the Midwest. New York (122,000), California (104,000), Massachusetts (81,000) and Washington (77,000) were the major coastal strongholds of Swedish Americans. Obviously, in these areas Swedes were hardly a very noticeable minority.

By contrast, Swedes were one of the most conspicuous groups in the Midwest. A nineteenth-century writer remarked, "Travellers by train sometimes see apparently none but Swedes at certain stations in Minnesota and both of the Dakotas. . . ." [11] E. A. Ross conjectured in 1914 that 40 per cent of the Minnesota population was of Scandinavian descent.[12] In certain rural Minnesota counties, Swedes comprised virtually the entire population. The Swedes shared other counties with the Norwegians. Goodhue County's 1900 foreign-born population of 8,000 in-

[8] Warren S. Thompson and Pascal K. Whelpton, *Population Trends in the United States* (New York: McGraw-Hill Book Company, 1933), p. 92.

[9] Albert E. Jenks, "Ethnic Census of Minneapolis," *American Journal of Sociology*, XVII (May, 1912), 280–81.

[10] Charles Kendric Babcock, "The Scandinavian Contingent," *Atlantic Monthly*, LXXVII (May, 1896), 661.

[11] Julian Ralph, "Our Swedish Fellow-Citizens," *Harper's Weekly*, XL (April 25, 1896), 419.

[12] Edward A. Ross, "The Scandinavians in America," *The Century*, LXXXVIII (June, 1914), 291.

cluded 3,000 Swedes and 3,000 Norwegians, all of whom probably lived on opposite sides of the county. Philblad, in his early empirical study of Kansas Swedes, reported that the immigrants not only clustered together in certain counties and communities, but tended to settle in areas corresponding to the place of origin in Sweden.[13]

The large majority of nineteenth century Swedes were farmers or farm laborers. Next to Norwegians and Germans, Swedes had a larger proportion of agricultural workers than any other European group. Many started as "hired hands" on Yankee forms, working to save up enough money to purchase a farm of their own. Many others were homesteaders. Single Swedish females often worked as household servants to native Americans. However, as Swedish and American industrialization advanced, the proportion of Swedish American agriculturalists declined from three-fourths in 1870 to one-third in 1930.[14] The immigrants that settled in the Northeast and on the West Coast had among them a relatively large percentage of skilled workers, including carpenters, painters, masons, machinists, and iron and steel workers. Indeed, Swedes were second to the British in proportion of skilled and high-wage workers.[15]

Studies of the business elite have indicated that although Americans of Scandinavian descent were rarely found among the nineteenth and early twentieth century groups, by 1950 they had made noticeable inroads into this traditionally exclusive British circle.[16] Scandinavians were better represented in 1950 than were the much more numerous and longer resident Irish.

In brief, Swedes in America began mostly as farmers and laborers and by the turn of the century counted more than their share of skilled workers and clerks. Some of these middle-class and working-class persons came directly from Sweden; others were taking the step-by-step route up the occupational ladder filling the expanding white-collar sector of the occupational structure. A rapidly growing number are moving up into the upper middle class. A few are members of the economic elite. The main body of Swedish-descended persons are, however, middle to lower middle class, especially in the younger generation where the number of blue-collar workers has sharply declined.

[13] C. Terrence Philblad, "The Kansas Swedes," *Southwestern Social Science Quarterly*, XIII (June, 1932), 36.

[14] See Adolph B. Benson and Naboth Hedin, eds., *Swedes in America: 1638–1938* (New Haven: Yale University Press, 1938).

[15] Samuel Koenig, "Ethnic Groups in Connecticut Industry," *Social Forces*, XX (October, 1941), 105.

[16] Suzanne I. Keller, "The Social Origins and Career Lines of Three Generations of American Business Leaders" (doctoral dissertation, Columbia University, 1953); and Mabel Newcomer, *The Big Business Executive: The Factors That Made Him* (New York: Columbia University Press, 1955).

AMERICAN SMORGASBORD

Complete acculturation of the Swedes required a generation more than that of most Britishers. This difference in time was due more to the language barrier and geographical location of Swedes than to marked cultural differences with the Anglo-Saxon core. After all, Scandinavians and British shared the most important unifying factors of all: race and religion. That they first differed in speech, dress, diet, and values of lesser import did deter a basic understanding between the two groups. The majority of Swedes and nearly all of their children were anxious to become like Anglo-Saxon Protestants as quickly as possible. After having been in this country but a few years, most Swedish Americans at least externally resembled native Americans in similar economic circumstances. In the words of an early sociologist, "[N]o immigrants of foreign speech assimilate so quickly as the Scandinavians." [17]

A distinctive Swedish American subculture was rarely recognizable beyond the second generation. Even in areas where Swedes were in the overwhelming majority, they emulated American models and shed most Swedish customs with relative ease. Philblad observed about Kansas Swedes he studied in the 1930's, "The cultural heritage of Sweden among these people is rapidly disappearing" and "The present generation knows little of Swedish history and culture, and . . . has little interest in it." [18]

Indeed, the Scandinavians seemed to already possess the virtues extolled as genuinely American. Accolades to Scandinavian thrift and industry scored the pages of popular periodicals published in the immigration period:

> . . . as a class they are sober, earnest, industrious, and frugal. [19]

> Wherever Swedes are numerous all the other people speak of them as very good citizens. They have the reputation of being sober, law-abiding, industrious, thrifty, religious, and ambitious. [20]

> They will be sturdy, independent, and Protestant; they will be intelligent, persistent, patient, and thrifty. We shall not, therefore, expect the current of their life to run counter to that of the nation. [21]

Other descriptive words and phrases such as "steadying influence," "will not rock the boat," "conservatism," "Puritan," and "American" abound in the early popular literature on the Swedes and Scandinavians in

17 Ross, "The Scandinavians in America," p. 294.
18 Philblad, "The Kansas Swedes," p. 47.
19 Kendric C. Babcock, "The Scandinavians in the Northwest," *The Forum,* XIV (September, 1892), 102–9.
20 Ralph, "Our Swedish Fellow-Citizens," p. 422.
21 Babcock, "The Scandinavian Contingent," p. 663.

America. By implication, of course, non-Protestants display the reprehensible opposite traits.

Although the Swedish language was used in homes, churches, and even many Lutheran college classrooms for several decades, the Swedes rapidly became bilingual. Out of 67 homes in a Midwestern Swedish community studied in 1920, 44 were using both Swedish and English, 17 English only, and 3 Swedish only.[22] The initial stage of the linguistic transition was, as was typical among foreign-language groups, a mixture of the native language and English. For example, corn crib became "carn crebb," acre "aker," and fence "fans." Not much better was the remark of a disgruntled Norwegian who had for some time been mistaken for a Swede: "Ay ben dis coontry fourteen yahr and all er tame ay ben call'd gol durn son gun Swede and all er time ay been Nor-way-jun."[23] This Swedish-American dialect has often been the object of humorous anecdotes such as the one told about two Swedes who ran to catch a departing ferryboat. The first Swede leaped safely from the wharf to the boat, but the other jumped short and splashed into the water. "Good man, Ole," said the first, "ay dank you make it in two yumps." The Swedish accent seemed to complement the friendly epithet "dumb Swede," applied most often by equally "inept" Norwegians.

The Scandinavian press, both Swedish and Norwegian, has been among the most successful ethnic presses in America, in terms of both foreign-language and English-language publications. In 1910, the circulation of foreign-language publications, including 27 monthlies, 94 weeklies, and 2 dailies, was nearly one million.[24] As recently as 1960, there were still 120,000 subscribers to the four Scandinavian-language monthlies and fourteen weeklies. English-language publications aimed at Scandinavian readers had a circulation of 500,000 in 1960, second only to that of German and Jewish English-language publications.

A strong Lutheran asceticism typified Swedish communities in the Midwest. The churches deplored smoking, drinking, cards, gambling, dancing, most movies, and Sunday entertainment of all sorts. As we might expect, these stern proscriptions were often violated. In his study of "Swedeholm," Wheeler observed that there was a considerable amount of clandestine drinking and that several prominent families participated in a ritual known as the "bottle dumping," in which empty liquor bottles were thrown into the river after dark or on the way to church.[25] A quote

[22] Philblad, "The Kansas Swedes," p. 38.

[23] Ralph, "Our Swedish Fellow-Citizens," p. 419.

[24] See Joshua A. Fishman, *et al.*, *Language Loyalty in the United States* (The Hague: Mouton & Company, 1966), pp. 52–66.

[25] Wayne Wheeler, "An Analsyis of Social Change in a Swedish-Immigrant Community" (doctoral dissertation, University of Missouri, 1959), p. 149.

from an annual meeting of an early Kansas congregation expresses the concerns of the devout: "Some of our young people neglect both the Lord's word and the Holy Sacrament, and even many of the older members are seen only too seldom in church." [26]

As in most hyphenated-American communities, differences and discord sometimes separated the older and younger generations of Swedes. Members of the younger generation in large measure appropriated the American forms of leisure time activities, which often ran counter to the austere moral dictums of their parents and the church.[27] According to Wheeler, "The [Swedeholm] population was divided into two sharply separate factions—on one side the Swedish church people and the believing, moralistic element mostly older persons with old-fashioned ideas, on the other side Americans together with a portion of younger Swedes, less formal and grave...." [28] That intergenerational differences often separated the old and young may also be discerned in the following lines by White on ethnic celebrations among North Dakota Swedes:

> It is a gala time for everyone but the young people. They must listen to foreign languages as though they understood. Old folk songs with unfamiliar music are supposed to inspire them. They cannot dance with the gusto of the older people. They do not know the old games. They are out of color in their collegiate American clothes. Grandmother and her circle are a bit ashamed of their ignorance.[29]

The younger generation was occasionally placed in a position where cross-currents of American and Scandinavian life pulled them in opposite directions. Although some were faced with the choice of remaining with their families in the Swedish-American community or launching out on their own into the larger society, the majority of Swedish families were eager for their children to be socially mobile and often supported them psychologically and materially in their moves upward. Cultural assimilation was usually recognized and accepted as a prerequisite to that end.

Many Swedes, in fact, did preserve several cultural remnants of the Old World. For the more liberal Swedish Americans, the European Sunday, which included picnics, folk music and dancing, games, beer, and the art of conversation, revived feelings of ethnic community. A generation ago Scandinavian sponsored songfests, picnics, church suppers, and political rallies were commonplace throughout the Midwest. "On such days," observed White, "the air is filled with an old-world jargon and a

[26] Philblad, "The Kansas Swedes," p. 41.

[27] Carl M. Rosenquist, "The Swedes of Texas" (doctoral dissertation, University of Chicago, 1930).

[28] Wheeler, "Social Change in a Swedish-Immigrant Community," p. 157.

[29] George L. White, Jr., "Dakota Made," *Atlantic Monthly*, CLXIII (May, 1939), 697.

new-world dream." [30] In homogeneous communities, American holidays were given a Swedish flavor. Independence Day, for example, was celebrated by the usual fireworks and patriotic parades juxtaposed with folk dances and chorus concerts.

The Swedish customs of coffee break and coffee party have been taken up by the general populace as has the smorgasbord. Still largely a Scandinavian practice is the lavish Christmas Eve dinner featuring *lutefisk* (codfish steeped in a lye of potash), *lefse* (soft pan-fried flat bread made of mashed potatoes), lingon berries, *geitost* (goat's cheese), pickled herring, and *fattigmann* (a crisp pastry with powdered sugar). Although around Christmas lutefisk and lefse may be purchased at most grocery stores in the Midwest, a person may search in vain for it at other times.

SWEDES IN THE MELTING POT

Acculturated descendants of Swedish Americans gradually entered into the group life of the host society. Nevertheless, the majority of the second and even third generations remained within the social boundaries of the Swedish or Scandinavian community. Their strong commitment to the Lutheran church held many within the social life of the national origin group. Further, their early concentration in working-class and agricultural occupations placed them on the average a notch below the status of the host society. Nor were Swedes any different from other ethnic groups: many frankly preferred the security and comfort of being among persons of Scandinavian descent. Not until after World War II did most descendants of Swedes begin large-scale social participation in Anglo-Saxon cliques and clubs. Even today, considerable Scandinavian communalism remains in the older generations.

The first and second generation of nineteenth-century Swedes confined their primary relationships almost entirely to other Swedes. Even Norwegians were not considered good company. An early pioneer on the Wisconsin frontier recalled a visit by three Swedes and one native American: "Here I am afraid we were rather discourteous in leaving their American companion perhaps too much to himself, to hold his own meditations upon the language and manners of Swedes." [31] Yankees and Swedes, however, were not completely averse to social contact. The same pioneer related instances of mutually cooperative ventures between the two groups, such as a house-raising. But preference for fellow Swedes was foremost. As the same pioneer went on to say:

30 *Ibid.*
31 Nils W. Olsson, ed., *A Pioneer in Northwest America: Memoirs of Gustaf Unonius,* Vol. I (Minneapolis: University of Minnesota Press), p. 283.

The [Swedish] latecomers naturally find the best land taken by others; yet rather than go a few miles farther away, where a thousand times better land is available and where there are better opportunities of a livelihood, they elect, for the sake of being close to their countrymen, to dig in among the hills, hollow, and rocks. In this there is of course something creditable; that the Swede has not forgotten the old country and that he loves it are proved by his love for his countrymen.[32]

Another early observer of Swedish life contended that the Swedes "are very clannish, but they seem to band together for no worse purpose than to help one another along and to contribute both generally and generously to the support of their churches, schools, and colleges." [33]

Empirical investigations into Swedish communalism confirm the view that structural assimilation was far from complete 25 years ago and is not complete even today. King's analysis of ethnic relations in a Connecticut town in the early 1940's disclosed that half of all clique memberships held by Scandinavians (mostly Swedes) were in predominantly Scandinavian cliques.[34] However, the same investigator also discerned a considerable amount of inter-ethnic contact among Scandinavians and British: "The evidence points to a lack of cleavage between Scandinavians and Anglo-Americans; the groups which are consistently least separated from each other are the Scandinavians and Anglo-Americans." In "Swedeholm," Swedish solidarity was high as recently as the 1950's, when outsiders found it difficult to be accepted.[35] In another recent survey of a Midwestern county, Swedish Lutherans were found to be slightly more likely to choose members of their own church as close friends than were members of other denominations.[36] The Swedish Augustana Lutherans reported that 41 per cent of their closest friends belonged to their own congregation and the Swedish Mission Covenant group declared that 60 per cent did.

If the Scandinavians and British (German Protestants even more so than British in the Midwest) have displayed compatibility in primary relations, the opposite has been the case for Scandinavians and Irish. Again to quote King, "The two nationality groups between which social cleavage most consistently runs are the Irish and Scandinavians." [37] The traditional contempt between the two groups has been graphically portrayed in the memoirs of a Swedish pioneer on his way to Wisconsin

[32] *Ibid.*, p. 310.

[33] Ralph, "Our Swedish Fellow-Citizens," p. 422.

[34] C. Wendell King, "Branford Center: A Community Study in Social Cleavage" (doctoral dissertation, Yale University, 1943), p. 161.

[35] Wheeler, "Social Change in a Swedish-Immigrant Community."

[36] W. W. Schroeder and Victor Obenhaus, *Religion in American Culture* (New York: The Free Press, 1964), pp. 87–88.

[37] King, "Branford Center," p. 282.

via the customary route to the Midwest on the Erie Canal and Great Lakes:

> On this last leg of the trip we are unfortunate enough to add to our company a few Irish people. These are unpleasant enough as neighbors ashore, but having them on board made us wish they might depart for Blakulla [Hell], a more suitable destination for them and one I suspect most of them will eventually, willy-nilly reach. A genuine Paddy had seated himself at the table with us. In his entire person he reflected something of that rag-bag bully which generally characterizes the Irishman. . . . One can readily see by looking at him that he feels his citizenship entitles him to any public office just as his membership in the "only true Church" entitles him to a place in heaven by the side of St. Patrick and St. Columcille. With a clay pipe in his vest pocket and a whiskey bottle in his coat, he is fully prepared for a fist fight with anybody who dares dispute his right in either of these respects." [38]

As in primary group life, Americans of Swedish ancestry have also demonstrated their communal interests through participation in ethnic organizations. Fraternal orders such as the Vasa, Svithiod, Scandinavian Fraternity, and the Vikings counted over 100,000 members in the pre-World War II years. Americans of Swedish descent have supported a myriad of welfare organizations, hospitals, and schools through the Augustana Lutheran Synod. Among Swedish Lutheran colleges are Gustavus Adolphus (St. Peter, Minnesota), Augustana (Rock Island, Illinois), Bethany (Lindsborg, Kansas), Luther (Wahoo, Nebraska), Upsala (East Orange, N.J.), and Pacific Lutheran (Parkland, Washington). Swedes have tended to belong to the Augustana Lutheran Synod (now the largest body constituting the Lutheran Church in America) founded in 1860. Increasing numbers are now members of other Protestant churches more convenient for them. The Lutheran Church in America benefits from a similar kind of reverse flow of Anglo and German Protestants from outside the LCA.

As a consequence of solidarity in social group life, rates of Swedish in-marriage have in the past been quite high. A 25 per cent excess of immigrant males over females produced a higher intermarriage rate among Swedish males than among females. Easily the most frequent out-choice has been the Norwegians. Germans, Danes, and British have accounted for most of the remainder.

The information in Table 4–1 summarizes various studies that have included Swedes or Scandinavians in an analysis of intermarriage. The rate of Swedish in-marriage was in the vicinity of 70 to 80 per cent during the first few decades of this century, then manifested an over-all

[38] Olsson, *A Pioneer in Northwest America*, pp. 79–80.

TABLE 4–1

SWEDISH AND SCANDINAVIAN IN-MARRIAGE RATES
IN THE UNITED STATES, SELECTED STUDIES

Location	Time	Percentage Expected In-Marriages [a]	Percentage Observed In-Marriages [b]	Percentage Difference
New York City [c]				
(Swedes only)	1908–1912	2	73	71
Minneapolis [d]				
(Swedes only)	1912	15	82	67
Nebraska [e]	1909–1913	21	77	56
	1921–1925	21	62	41
Wisconsin [e]	1908–1912	24	84	60
	1921–1925	24	64	40
New York State [e]	1908–1912	3	61	58
	1921–1925	4	44	40
Woonsocket, R.I. [f]				
(Swedes only)	1926	1	82	81
New York State [g]	1939	6	40	34
Wright County, Minn. [h]				
(Swedes only)	1942	20	62	42
Northeastern Minnesota [h]				
(Swedes only)	1956	17	30	13
New Haven, Conn. [i]	1900	2	83	81
	1930	2	33	31
	1950	2	22	20
Protestant City [j]	1967	21	61	40
Catholic City [j]	1967	23	53	30

[a] The expected in-marriage rates were computed and represent the percentage of Swedish or Scandinavians (females if given) in the sample or community population.

[b] The observed in-marriage rates represent the percentage of Swedish or Scandinavian males married to Swedish or Scandinavian females of all Swedish or Scandinavian males in a given sample except in Minneapolis, Woonsocket, and Protestant City and Catholic City, where the over-all male and female rate is given to maximize sample size.

[c] Julius Drachsler, *Intermarriage in New York City* (New York: Columbia University Press, 1921), first and second generations only.

[d] Albert E. Jenks, "Ethnic Census of Minneapolis," *American Journal of Sociology*, XVII (May, 1912), 280–81.

[e] Edmund deS. Brunner, *Immigrant Farmers and Their Children* (Garden City, N.Y.: Doubleday and Co., Inc., 1929), first and second generations only.

[f] Bessie Bloom Wessel, *An Ethnic Survey of Woonsocket, Rhode Island* (Chicago: University of Chicago Press, 1931).

[g] Lowry Nelson, "Intermarriage Among Nationality Groups in a Rural Area of Minnesota," XLVIII (March, 1943), 585–92, first and second generations only.

[h] Lowry Nelson, *The Minnesota Community* (Minneapolis: University of Minnesota Press, 1960).

[i] Ruby Jo Reeves Kennedy, "Single or Triple Melting-Pot? Intermarriage in New Haven 1870–1950," *American Journal of Sociology*, LVIII (July, 1952), 56–59.

[j] See Appendix B for source. A Scandinavian with a mixed Scandinavian-non-Scandinavian spouse was considered an in-marriage.

decline. The diminishing tendency to marry within the Swedish group is apparent both in terms of longitudinal data and by comparison of different studies through time. Studies of Swedish communities also agree that Swedish Americans were at first very much opposed to intermarriage, but that by the third generation attitudes had moderated and mixed marriages occurred with considerable frequency.[39] The rate of in-marriage among Swedes, as is customary, tends to increase with their representation in the population.

Following the precedent set in primary-group life, Swedes conformed to the multiple-melting-pot thesis, as Julius Drachsler's New York City marriage data dramatically confirm: although the Swedish rate of in-marriage for males dropped sharply from the first (80 per cent) to the second generation (16 per cent), in-marriage within the limits of the several Protestant national origin groups declined only from a very high 93 per cent to 82 per cent.[40]

Almost Equals

In contrast to many other non-English-speaking immigrants, the Swedes were never the object of intense prejudice or systematic discrimination. To assert, as one early essayist did, that the Swede's "desirability is absolutely unquestioned"[41] was perhaps too sanguine in 1906. Still, the first generation rarely encountered debilitating rejection and subsequent generations have at worst been the butt of jokes. Though first generation Swedes would only occasionally be found in native American status groups, social distance studies indicate that Swedes were approved of as friends and neighbors by a majority of native Americans.

One of the reasons for the native American acceptance of Swedes is that few have been vocally opposed to any aspect of American culture. Unlike the Norwegian, Swedish American society produced few radicals of any stripe. From issues ranging from slavery to Prohibition, Swedes have been dependable allies of the Anglo-American. Swedes contributed to the ranks of the various anti-Catholic societies that flourished in the late nineteenth century and in the 1920's. They have typically been Republican since Lincoln except for a brief interlude with the Populists. Most backed the temperance movement. They have from the beginning been nearly unanimous in their support of the public school system. They have vigorously opposed federal aid to parochial schools.

[39] Philblad, "The Kansas Swedes"; Wheeler, "Social Change in a Swedish-Immigrant Community"; Rosenquist, "The Swedes of Texas."

[40] Julius Drachsler, *Intermarriage in New York City* (New York: Columbia University Press, 1921), p. 129.

[41] Hrolf Wisby, "The Scandinavian-American: His Status," *North American Review*, CLXXXIV (August, 1906), 213.

In contrast to the Norwegians, Swedish Americans displayed little interest in ethnic politics or political life (recently, however, Minnesota has had a run of governors of Swedish descent). Nor have Swedish Americans made a particularly strong impression in the arts, though poet Carl Sandburg, composer Howard Hanson, actor Warner Oland (Charlie Chan), and actress Greta Garbo, among others, might be mentioned. In athletics, the football prowess of Swedish farm boys at the University of Minnesota in the 1930's and 1940's is legendary. Perhaps one of the most famous Americans of Swedish parentage was Charles Lindbergh, Sr., the first man to fly nonstop across the Atlantic. Swedes in America have been too methodical, unemotional, and withdrawn ever to have incubated many noted politicians, artists, inventors, intellectuals, and adventurers.

FROM NATIONAL ORIGIN
TO RELIGIOUS GROUP:
A CASE STUDY

Typical of many Swedes who came to America was John Olson. Olson was born in Westergötland, Sweden in 1838. In 1855, at the age of seventeen, Olson left his farm home in Sweden for a sod house, 40 acres, and two oxen in Carver County, Minnesota. He soon became bilingual. Four years later he married a cousin, Christiana, who also had come to Minnesota from Sweden. Four of their 15 children survived into youth. Not surprisingly, Christiana succumbed at an early age, and Olson took another wife, a Swedish housekeeper by the name of Mary Johnson, who added another five children to the Olson family. By this time, the sod house was a log one, the oxen replaced by horses, and the acreage expanded. Olson had earlier enlisted in the First Minnesota Volunteer Regiment and fought in several engagements in the Civil War before being taken prisoner by the Confederate Army.

In 1882, Olson sold his farm and moved his family further west to Sioux Falls in the Dakota Territory, where he entered the grocery business. When Olson took up residence in Sioux Falls, it had a population of slightly over 2,000 and had barely emerged from frontier conditions. By the time of his death in 1928, Sioux Falls had become a city of nearly 40,000 people. In the interim, Olson with the help of a son Victor had become one of the community's most successful grocers.

Olson read widely and built up a large home library. He had been a member of the first class of Gustavus Academy, later to become Gustavus Adolphus College. Swedish American newspapers were part of Olson's reading agenda; he had a strong sense of Swedish identity. He was, however, an American first, and had been since the Civil War.

Olson was a charter member of the Augustana Lutheran Church in Sioux Falls, served as a deacon most of his life, and occasionally preached the Sunday morning sermon—in Swedish. At other points in his long career, Olson acted as city treasurer, participated fully in the G.A.R. veterans organization, acted as local agent for the Scandinavian-American Steamship Line, and voted the Republican ticket from Lincoln to Hoover. His Sioux Falls house stood until 1956, when it was torn down to make way for commercial development.

The ethnic status of the second generation of the Olson family can be illustrated by John's son and grocery partner Victor. Victor spoke fluent Swedish and read Swedish literature and newspapers regularly. Like his father, Victor was largely self-educated, but he had attended a two-year commercial course at Gustavus Adolphus. Most of his close associates were Swedish Lutherans. He was elected the first president of a Swedish fraternal organization called the Swedish Alliance. He was a deacon in the Swedish church and an authority on Lutheran church history, a subject upon which he delivered public lectures. As it was to his father, the Democratic party was anathema to Victor.

In 1898 Victor had married Amanda Hegstrom, a second generation Swedish farm girl from a family of 10 children whose father had settled on a farm near St. Peter, Minnesota after working as a blacksmith for several years in Galesburg, Illinois. In contrast to the large first generation family, the second generation family was limited to four children. Swedish identity, although still present, had waned; identification with the Lutheran church was far stronger than identification with national origin.

By the third generation, the Olson family had ceased to be Swedish American in the genuine sense. The third generation understood Swedish quite well, but had great difficulty in reading and speaking it. Frequently, their second generation parents addressed them in Swedish and they responded in English. There were no Swedish newspapers or literary monthlies in their own homes, and Swedish was not spoken in their own families. The only traces of any interest in Swedish culture and history were the ubiquitous coffee parties, the smörgasbords, the Christmas dinners, and the stories of how Sweden's hero-king Gustavus Adolphus saved Protestantism from the Catholics in the Thirty Years War. Friendships were still built mainly around the Swedish Lutheran church, but socializing with persons of Norwegian, British, and German origin became common. For the first time, marriage outside the Swedish line occurred, albeit with Norwegians and Germans. Identification had become transferred almost completely from the national origin group to religion. Most Catholics and all Democrats continued to be suspect and considered to be in league with one another against Protestantism and the virtues of rural life.

The fourth generation neither read nor understood Swedish, and knew nothing of Swedish culture and history. Yet, their friends were mostly Protestants, all were married to Protestants, and they had a strong sense of Protestant identity. In brief, the role of national origin was minor in the third generation and negligible in the fourth, whereas religion became the focal point of ethnic life.

SUMMARY

As white Protestants, Swedes and Americans of Swedish descent have occupied an enviable position among non-Anglo, foreign-speaking ethnic groups. Swedes arrived in strength several decades after large-scale British immigration to industrial America was underway. Swedes came with fewer industrial skills than the British, but as a highly literate group, their socioeconomic ascent has been, comparatively speaking, rapid. First heavily rural, later increasingly urban, the Swedes concentrated in the Midwest and a few coastal cities. Cultural assimilation of Swedes into American life was rather easily accomplished within a couple of generations, although Swedish American communal life has traditionally been strong, with remnants still in existence. Swedes merged first with other Scandinavians, then with Germans and Yankees. Considerable social distance has been maintained between Swedes and the remainder of European peoples.

Norwegians have displayed all of the classic traits of the national origin group in America. Accordingly, Norwegians have received more scholarly attention than any other Protestant national origin contingent.

Stimulants to Norse emigration were very similar to those that stirred the Swedes: in Norway religious and political restraints, military conscription, a formal class system, and rural poverty; and in America, the promise of new freedoms, an open class system, and especially, cheap land. Although the Norwegian church and government strongly opposed emigration, Norway lost a larger proportion of its population than either of its Scandinavian neighbors and nearly every other country in Europe.

American letters provided Norwegians with clues as to what life in America would be like. Some letters were discouraging in tone, especially in the earlier period. For example, a Wisconsin immigrant wrote back in 1844:

American Vikings: The Norwegians

I do not advise any of my relatives to come to America. If you could see the conditions of the Norwegians in America at present, you would certainly be frightened; illness and misery are so prevalent that many have died. One cannot imagine anything more misleading than the tempting and deceptive letters that reach Norway. . . .[1]

More typical, however, was the following message:

Every poor person who will work diligently and faithfully, can become a well-to-do man here in a short time, and the rich man, on the other hand, has even better prospects, for he can work out his career with less drudgery and fewer burdens and thus have a much more peaceful life here than in Norway.[2]

A verse from Norwegian folk literature candidly states what was perhaps the most compelling motive for the majority of poor farmers to venture to America: "Farewell, Norway, and God bless thee. Stern and severe wert thou always, but as a mother I honor thee, even though thou skimped my bread."[3]

[1] Theodore Blegen, ed., *Land of Their Choice: The Immigrants Write Home* (Minneapolis: University of Minnesota Press, 1955), pp. 185–86.
[2] *Ibid.*, p. 180.
[3] Leola Nelson Bergmann, *Americans from Norway* (Philadelphia: J. B. Lippincott Co., 1950), p. 53.

FROM MOUNTAINS TO PRAIRIES

After the Vikings' now well-publicized eleventh-century visits to American shores, the first Norse to come to America were a small group of seventeenth-century settlers who colonized a site at Bergen, New Jersey. Little is known about the disposition of this group, but it is assumed that they were assimilated into Dutch society. Between 1630 and 1674 some two hundred additional Scandinavians, mostly Norwegians, took up residence among the Dutch on the Hudson. These Norwegians adopted the Dutch language and Dutch names. Intermarriage with the Dutch was common. Many of the famous old Hudson River families, such as the Vanderbilts, can trace their origins to a Dutch-Norwegian beginning.

The first post-colonial settlement of Norwegians was located near Rochester, New York. In 1825, a party consisting of about fifty religious dissenters (Haugeans and Quakers) made the Atlantic crossing on a 40-ton vessel called the *Restauration,* the Norwegian version of the Mayflower. The "Sloopers," as the group was known, did not at all behave like sectarians once in America, but were split by factionalism and remained unchurched.[4] Upon the advice of the Norwegian adventurer Cleng Peerson, some of this first group of settlers moved on to the Fox River area of Illinois. Peerson, incidentally, thoroughly enjoyed his path-finding activities, since they took him away from a rich but aging widow whom he had married for material support in his adventures and idleness. The Fox River settlement, which Peerson had located, served as a point of entry and departure in the Midwest for numerous future Norwegian immigrants.

Immigration from Norway followed the Swedish pattern. However, the most productive decade for this "old" immigrant country was the first of this century, when nearly 200,000 Norwegians came to American shores. The 1880's were also bonanza years for Norwegian immigration with over 175,000 recorded entries. The 1820–1929 immigration total was approximately 800,000. The Norwegian foreign-born population reached its zenith of 400,000 in 1910. By 1930, the number of Norwegian-born and their children was placed at 2 million persons.

The first stream of Norwegian immigration flowed mainly toward southern Wisconsin. At the time of the Civil War, fully two-thirds of the Norwegian population resided in that state. Gradually, the Norse pushed west from their base in Wisconsin and northern Illinois into Minnesota, Iowa, and the Dakotas. Norwegians continued to favor these five or six

---

[4] See Phillip E. Hammond, "The Migrating Sect: An Illustration from Early Norwegian Immigration," *Social Forces,* XLI (March, 1963), 275–83.

states right to the end of the immigration period. New York City and Puget Sound area of Washington State also attracted a large number of Norwegians. Indeed, by 1940, New York (read New York City) was second only to Minnesota in Norwegian foreign-born population. Brooklyn counted twice as many foreign-born Norwegians as did the Norwegian "capitol" of Minneapolis. Nevertheless, three-fourths of all Norwegian Americans continued to reside in six North Central states.

With the possible exception of the Finns, the Norwegians evinced a more marked tendency toward ecological segregation than any of the other northern European groups.[5] Norwegian enclaves have been characteristic in the cities as well as in rural areas. A number of counties in Wisconsin, Minnesota, and North Dakota have literally been Norwegian counties, as have certain wards in Brooklyn, Chicago, and Minneapolis. Norwegians had a larger proportion of farmers in their group than any other national origin group in America. As late as 1940, half of all Midwestern Norse persons lived on farms or villages of fewer than 2,500 people.

To be sure, the early waves of settlers consisted almost entirely of farmers and farm laborers. Up to 1865, seven out of eight were agricultural workers. Even at the end of open immigration about one in five Norwegians still entered farming. Farming in the Midwest was very different from farming in Norway. The immigrant Norwegian had to learn from the start the rudiments of raising wheat, corn, hogs, and cattle on a large scale. Many of these same farmers worked seasonally in logging camps, on canal construction, and with railroad gangs, often leaving their families alone on the farm. Immigrant Norwegians, and thousands of other immigrants like them, performed a role in western American industrialization similar to that of conscript labor in Soviet industrialization.

Norwegians were also sailors, fishermen, boat builders, and dock workers—all skills of the variety transferred from Norway. An early census reported that about 90 per cent of San Francisco's foreign-born Norwegians were seamen.[6] Norwegians once owned the balance of Puget Sound salmon trawlers and played a major role in the West Coast halibut, herring, tuna, and sardine industries. Norwegians were once promi-

[5] For discussions of the Norwegian immigration and settlement patterns see Carlton C. Qualey, *Norwegian Settlement in the United States* (Northfield, Minn.: Norwegian-American Historical Association, 1938); and Einar Haugen, "Norwegian Migration to America," *Norwegian-American Studies and Records*, XVIII (Minneapolis: Lund Press, 1954).

[6] See Kenneth O. Bjork, *West of the Great Divide* (Northfield, Minn.: Norwegian-American Historical Association, 1958), for a discussion of the Norwegians in the Far West.

nent around the Manhattan and Brooklyn waterfronts.[7] They captained schooners during the height of the Great Lakes schooner trade; during the 1870's, half the seamen on the Great Lakes were Norwegian.

After the turn of the century, rising numbers of Norwegians with industrial skills entered the country, along with moderate numbers of professionals and white-collar workers. A 1941 survey of Brooklyn Norwegians by the Norwegian newspaper *Nordisk Tidende* revealed that 62 per cent were in skilled or semi-skilled jobs (mostly harbor and construction), 8 per cent were professionals, and 5 per cent were in business or sales.[8]

In short, the Norwegians experienced and reflected America's transition from the agrarian to the industrial way of life. Once nearly entirely an agricultural community, persons of Norwegian parentage are now well situated in the middle and upper working classes of a few large cities and hundreds of smaller villages and towns scattered throughout the upper midwest. They are also conspicuously present among the country's most prosperous remaining small farmers in northern Iowa, southeastern Wisconsin, southern Minnesota, and the eastern Dakotas—sitting, as it were, on man's richest soils.

GIANTS OF THE EARTH

Like their Swedish friends, the Norwegians had a longer course to travel en route to acculturation than did immigrants from the British Isles, but a shorter one than did many non-Protestant European peoples. The Norwegian language proved to be particularly hardy. The mother tongue persisted in the home, church, and ethnic organizations decidedly longer than did the Swedish. A 1905 tabulation of Norwegian Lutheran churches revealed that only 6 of 1,300 congregations held services in English only.[9] In Norwegian wards in Brooklyn, Chicago, and Minneapolis, and certain counties in Wisconsin and Minnesota, Norwegian was the language of trade until World War I, when a foreign tongue was considered unpatriotic. The conduct of programs of the Bygdelag societies (discussed below) shifted to English only at mid-century. As another indication of language interest, the Norwegian press was unusually successful, beginning in 1847 with Wisconsin's *Nordlyset*. Norwegians more than Swedes have contributed to the notable successes of the Scandinavian press that were pointed out in the previous chapter.

---

[7] See Christen T. Jonassen, "Cultural Variables in the Ecology of an Ethnic Group," *American Sociological Review*, XIV (February, 1949), 32–41.

[8] Reported in Bergmann, *Americans in Norway*, pp. 208–9.

[9] Kendric C. Babcock, "The Scandinavian Element in the United States," *University of Illinois Studies in the Social Sciences*, III (Urbana, Ill.: 1914), 122.

Though the language was rather well maintained, an observation by a Wisconsin Yankee suggests that Norwegians soon adopted at least the more superficial native cultural modes:

> Never have I known people become civilized so rapidly as your [Norwegian] countrymen; they come here in motley crowds, dressed up with all kinds of dingle-dangle just like Indians. But just look at them a year later; they speak English perfectly, and, as far as dress, manners, and ability are concerned, they are quite above reproach.[10]

The Norwegian-born author Ole Rolvaag was appalled at the paucity of Old World culture in the second generation. When Rolvaag came to America at the end of the nineteenth century, he was much chagrined by the fact that the immigrants' children had scant knowledge of Norwegian history, literature, or folkways.

The most virulent denunciations of Americanization emanated from the clergy, particularly if they happened to be trained in Europe.[11] The clergy championed European traditions and parochial schools. On the other hand, the most ardent advocates of assimilation, and often sharp critics of the church and clergy, were the majority of Norwegian intellectuals.[12]

The first clergymen on the scene from Norway were nearly overwhelmed by their ex-parishioners' conduct. An early missionary to a Norwegian area of Wisconsin declared: "Such gross immorality I never witnessed before—it was offensive to come within the sphere poisoned by their breath." [13] Another wrote:

> I am sorry to say that as is the old, bad Norwegian custom, the deplorable desire for drinking and rioting has held sway in the congregation, especially during Christmas but also at other times.[14]

A Norwegian saloonkeeper was once excommunicated from the church because he refused to sell a pastor his entire stock so that the pastor could dispose of it.[15] In another case, one Halvor Pedersen was summarily dismissed from church membership on the charges that he was "a drunkard and a hellion." [16] Not dismayed, Pedersen entered the church a following Sunday and sat in a front pew. Asked to leave, he refused and was removed with bodily force from the sanctuary. Apparently a man of some determination, Pedersen promptly charged his pastor with

---

[10] Blegen, *Land of Their Choice,* p. 209.

[11] For an analysis of the role of the Norwegian clergy in assimilation, see Nicholas Tavuchis, *Pastors and Immigrants* (The Hague: Martinus Nijhoff, 1963).

[12] For short biographies of several Norwegian-American intellectuals, see Bergmann, *Americans in Norway.*

[13] Marcus Hansen, *The Immigrant in American History* (Harper & Row, Publishers, 1964), p. 114.

[14] Blegen, *Land of Their Choice,* p. 148.

[15] Tavuchis, *Pastors and Immigrants.*

[16] *Ibid.*

assault and battery; the good reverend was found guilty by the court and fined. The dejected pastor was later subjectd to systematic harassment by a dissident group of Norwegians who had sympathized with Pedersen: "The tranquility of the parsonage was disturbed by constant swearing and filthy ballads composed about the pastor." [17]

The conservative element eventually prevailed and the Norwegians soon were to demonstrate a brand of asceticism that would be the envy of Puritans. As Warner has noted, the enforcement of a rigid moral code within the Norwegian community in "Jonesville" actually prevented them from gaining acceptance in community affairs.[18] Cocktail parties, country club dancing, poker and bridge, and Sunday recreation were systematically tabooed.

In a study of the youth of the same city, Hollingshead reported that the Norwegian Lutheran minister categorically denied the adolescents such things as dancing, cosmetics, permanents, motion pictures, alcohol, bowling, automobile rides, cards, pool, and high school parties.[19] Seeing the need for some sort of recreation, the minister approved roller skating parties, but only in a particular rink—one owned by a Norwegian. To be seen in the other local rink, owned by a Catholic, was from the viewpoint of the minister "an abomination in the sight of the Lord." Curiously, the Norwegian-owned rink had the reputation among non-Lutherans of being the location of a veritable blood bath on Saturday nights. The network of taboos complicated social acceptance for Norwegian adolescents, especially in the upper middle class, for which parties, dances, dinners, and movies on Saturday night or Sunday afternoon were social rituals. As a consequence, many families changed their church affiliation to a congregation more congenial with their social aspirations.

Among behavioral norms that set Norwegians apart even from other Protestants, at least in the degree of conformity, were (and in many cases continue to be) a steadfast belief in the ideology of the Norwegian Lutheran church and social participation within it, a deep-seated distrust of "city people," an evaluation of money as something to be produced rather than consumed, asceticism, and patriarchal authority.[20] There exist other less profound differences, such as snuff-chewing and clandestine drinking among men and nondescript dress and appearance among women. Norwegians, generally speaking, were slower to shed

17 *Ibid.*

18 W. Lloyd Warner, et al., *Democracy in Jonesville* (New York: Harper & Row, Publishers, 1964), p. 172.

19 August B. Hollingshead, *Elmstown's Youth* (New York: John Wiley & Sons, Inc., 1959), pp. 261–64.

20 Warner, et al., *Democracy in Jonesville*, pp. 254–55. If Warner was, as some contend, too eager to generalize on his findings regarding the Jonesville community, his generalizations are less subject to question regarding at least the Norwegians.

identifiable cultural traits than were Swedes. What remains of a unique Scandinavian cultural adaptation to America is much more Norwegian in origin than it is Swedish.

"SONS OF NORWAY"

The combination of common cultural interests and residential segregation helped produce an active group life among Norwegian Americans, more active than among Swedes. For over a century, many Norwegians confided only in their ethnic peers. The Norwegian Lutheran church has perennially been the focus of commonality.

The formation of Norwegian American communal life began early. An 1847 letter from America, for example, read: "There are, even now, so many of our people out here in the West that they already appear as a group and thereby are protected against influences foreign to themselves, because their relationship to one another is stronger than their relationship to other races." [21]

Until very recently, an impressive number of Americans of Norwegian ancestry remained securely within the closed social boundaries of their ethnic world. In a mid-century study of several Wisconsin communities, Peter Munch reported that over 90 per cent of Norwegian social visiting was confined to the national origin group.[22] At an earlier time, the same communities were ethnically stratified, with the Norwegians occupying a subordinate position to Yankees, but status distinctions were no longer based on ethnicity. Inter-ethnic contacts of Norwegians were largely with Yankees, and although there were ample Irish in the vicinity, there were virtually no mixed Norse-Irish groups. Similarly, in "Prairie Township" Vogt noted that the most recent generation of Norwegians were beginning to move out of the unified Norwegian social structure into the multi-layered Yankee status system. Yet, wrote Vogt, the majority of the Norwegian families "are participating members of the Norwegian Lutheran Church which functions as a closed interactive system within which individual Norwegians find satisfaction for most of their religious and social needs." [23]

According to Warner, Jonesville Norwegians constituted not only a religious but a social group "in which all of the interactions necessary to a life career may take place." [24] In the rural environs, nearly all

[21] Blegen, *Land of Their Choice*, p. 208.

[22] Peter A. Munch, "Segregation and Assimilation of Norwegian Settlements in Wisconsin," *Norwegian-American Studies and Records*, XVIII (Minneapolis: Lund Press, 1954), especially pp. 128–34.

[23] Evon Z. Vogt, Jr., "Social Stratification in the Rural Midwest: A Structural Analysis," *Rural Sociology*, XII (December, 1947), 364–75.

[24] Warner, et al., *Democracy in Jonesville*, p. 189.

families considered themselves as members of either the Yankee or the Norwegian group. But again, we find the familiar pattern of acculturated and mobile Norwegians reducing their social ties within the Norwegian community and increasing the number of native American contacts, and the equally familiar pattern of Norse-Irish avoidance.

In areas of the country where Norwegians constituted more of a minority, it is doubtful that the degree of solidarity found in the several Midwestern community studies noted above could have existed. A pastor to the San Francisco area, for example, wrote that "There is so little association among Scandinavians [mainly Norwegians] here that it is difficult to find them, especially since many seem to be ashamed of their homeland and prefer to be—Yankees." [25]

Norwegians have also supported a variety of ethnic organizations. The chief secular organization is the Sons of Norway. The Sons of Norway has had a membership averaging from 40,000 to 50,000 persons. *The Viking*, the news organ of Sons of Norway, is published monthly and carries notes, for example, on the various lodges, achievements of members, and short essays on Norwegian history in America. It is also heavily advertised by Norwegian and Scandinavian airlines, steamship lines, and travel agencies.

The other Norwegian-American organizations that maintained active membership at mid-century were the *Bygdelags,* societies made up of immigrants and their descendants from particular districts in Norway.[26] Some 50,000 Norwegians from fifty *lags* attended the 1929 annual conventions in the Midwest. A plethora of locally organized Norwegian clubs and societies could also be found performing the usual function of providing an arena for ethnic music, games, plays, lectures, conversations, and dinners.

Norwegians were often reluctant to participate in secular community organizations, and in some instances there were feelings among natives against admitting Norwegians. In general, however, the various professional, service, and fraternal clubs rarely excluded an American of Norwegian descent provided that the applicant held the appropriate social status credentials.

However, the church has been the foremost ethnic organization for Norwegians in America.[27] The first Norwegian Lutheran synod was

[25] Bjork, *West of the Great Divide*, p. 200.

[26] For a complete discussion of the *Bygdelags,* see Jacob Hodnefield, "Norwegian-American *Bygdelags* and Their Publications," *Norwegian-American Studies and Records*, XVIII (Minneapolis: Lund Press, 1954), 163–222.

[27] For a complete history of Norwegian Lutheranism in America, see E. Clifford Nelson and Eugene L. Fevold, *The Lutheran Church Among Norwegian-Americans* (Minneapolis: Augsburg Publishing House, 1960).

formed in 1853. Several Norwegian-based synods have since emerged and merged. The American Lutheran Church, based on a 1960 merger of largely Norwegian church bodies, has on its rolls most active Norwegian Americans. However, later immigrants to urban America were frequently very secular and only a minority held church membership of any kind.

The Norwegians, like the Swedes, have supported a variety of social welfare institutions and colleges through their churches. Although the clergy argued for a parochial school system, the Norwegian press and laity vetoed the clergy's position. However, several secondary schools or academies were founded and a few are still in operation. The German Lutheran success in the area of parochial schools had always been the envy of the Norwegian clergy, but the church school system was from the outset eschewed by the vast majority of Norwegian laymen. On the other hand, church colleges were actively supported, and several continue to prosper, among which are St. Olaf (Northfield, Minnesota), Luther (Decorah, Iowa), Augsburg (Minneapolis), and Augustana (Sioux Falls, South Dakota).

MARRIAGE PATTERNS

Endogamy has traditionally been a highly regarded norm in the Norwegian community. Minneapolis census data for 1910 indicated that of some 9,000 Norwegian family heads, 70 per cent were married to other Norwegians (10 per cent of the sample were Norwegians).[28] In two rural Minnesota areas, a survey disclosed that almost half of the persons in two Norwegian samples had married endogamously, an in-marriage rate roughly twice what one would expect by chance.[29] In the New York area, Drachsler's data revealed that of 330 Norwegian males, 65 per cent had Norwegian spouses.[30] The 1941 study of the Brooklyn Norwegians noted above indicated that 41 per cent of the second generation had married within the Norwegian group. In "Protestant City," 53 per cent of respondents of Norwegian extraction were married to Norwegians at the time of questioning in 1967 (15 per cent expected), a 20 percentage point decline, however, from the in-marriage rates reported for parents.

When Norwegians have moved out of their own circles in mate selection, they have displayed an unsurpassed tendency to choose from among other Protestant national origin groups. Census data indicate that

[28] Albert Jenks, "Ethnic Census in Minneapolis," *American Journal of Sociology,* XVII (May, 1912), 777.

[29] Lowry Nelson, *The Minnesota Community* (Minneapolis: University of Minnesota Press, 1960), pp. 45–46.

[30] Julius Drachsler, *Intermarriage in New York City* (New York: Columbia University Press, 1921), p. 124.

of some 30,000 Norwegian-born fathers who were intermarried in 1900, 56 per cent had Swedish spouses, 12 per cent Danish, 10 per cent German, and 10 per cent British, or nine in ten from Protestant national origin groups.[31] The 1941 survey of Brooklyn Norwegians found that the most frequent out-choices at this time and place were Anglo-Americans.

In his novel *Peder Victorious,* Rolvaag captured some of the emotions surrounding Norse-Irish relationships, specifically, the problem of intermarriage. Peder, a young Norwegian, had been courting Susan Doheny, an Irish lass. Peder's worried mother soon admonished him for his irresponsible behavior and issued him a warning: "What were you up to the night you were out with the Doheny girl? . . . Little did I dream that any of mine would take to fooling with the Irish—in that way! If the day should come that you get yourself mixed up with the Irish, then you have lost your mother—that I could not live through." [32] As one might expect, love prevailed over ethnic pressures and the mother managed to accept the inevitable. Nevertheless, church and family pressures have been successful in channeling most romances into more acceptable arrangements.

Norwegians and the Anglo-Saxon Consensus

Any group that has exhibited such pronounced tendencies toward communalism in group and family is almost certain to have developed a strong sense of ethnic identity. Empirical evidence confirms this expectation. The large majority of Wisconsin Norwegians interviewed by Munch were keenly aware of their ethnic identification, and expressed loyalty to their Norwegian background through pride in the achievements of Norwegians and in social preference. Despite the fact that Norwegians had been in the Jonesville area for over a century, people were highly aware of their Norwegian surnames and employed them as an index of ethnic group membership. However, mobile middle-class Norwegians attempted to play down their ethnic image, inasmuch as they considered it detrimental to business and professional success.

Considering the degree of in-group loyalty, it is somewhat surprising that Norwegians were rarely subject to serious nativist prejudice. They experienced no great difficulty in acquiring the educational and vocational skills required to compete successfully in American society, and once they possessed these prerequisites, they were allowed to use them to the fullest. Unacculturated Norwegians were often considered socially

---

[31] U.S. Bureau of the Census, *U.S. Census of Population,* 1900, Vol. I (Washington, D.C.: Government Printing Office, 1901), Table 56, pp. 850–65.

[32] Ole E. Rolvaag, *Peder Victorious* (New York: Harper & Row, Publishers, 1929), pp. 257–58.

inferior by Old Americans, but the acculturated descendants of the immigrants tended to be evaluated in universalistic terms.

As steadfast Protestants, reliable Republicans (except for a brief episode with the Populists), vociferous opponents of slavery, ardent supporters of the public school system, zealous Prohibitionists (early temperance legislation in several Midwestern states was passed with the help of nearly solid Norwegian support), and persons steeped in agrarian virtues, Norwegian Americans have never threatened the ideology of Anglo-Saxon America. On the contrary, Norwegians have been among its most strident advocates.

Not all Norwegian Americans, however, have supported the generally accepted system of values. Norwegian society in America has always had a palpable and often outspoken strain of recalcitrance within it. As a manifestation, one of the most trenchant critics of American society was a second generation Norwegian farm boy, Thorsten Veblen. Thorsten, the sixth of 12 Veblen children, grew up on his father's farm near Northfield, Minnesota. Veblen graduated from Carlton College in 1880 and later received his doctorate from Yale. Despite his academic qualifications, he was unable to obtain a suitable university position. Therefore, Veblen lived for several years on his father's farm and his wife's father's farm in Iowa. After further graduate study at Cornell, Veblen launched a career of erratic teaching but eminent writing that carried him to a number of universities. His alleged personal eccentricities contributed to his variegated teaching experiences. Among Veblen's best-known works are *The Theory of the Leisure Class* and *The Higher Learning in America,* both incisive critiques of the role of the business class in American institutions.

A COMMENT ON THE DANES

Little has been written about the Danes in America. More Danes have entered this country since 1820 than, for example, Dutch, yet we may learn much more concerning the Hollander's experience in America than the Dane's. If there is a relationship between the rapidity of a group's assimilation and the amount of literature concerning that group, the Danes have been one of the most assimilable peoples to come to this country.

Immigration from Denmark was, nevertheless, quite substantial. In all, some 330,000 Danes had emigrated to the United States by 1929, the largest group arriving with the old immigration in the 1880's. Danish stock passed the half million mark in 1920.

Danes first settled near other Scandinavians and Germans in Wisconsin as farmers and farm laborers. Danes became instrumental in developing Wisconsin into the nation's number one dairy state. Following the typical Scandinavian pattern of settlement, they concentrated in Wisconsin, Minnesota, Iowa, and Nebraska. A larger proportion of Danes than other Scandinavians went on to Utah as Mormon converts. In keeping with the trend, twentieth-century Danish immigrants often took up residence in New York, Chicago, and other large cities, working in increasing numbers as craftsmen and clerks. As a rule, the Danes did not congregate in either urban or rural enclaves, although there were a few districts in Iowa and Wisconsin where they comprised the largest single foreign-born element in the population.

A 50 per cent excess of Danish males contributed to a considerably higher rate of in-marriage among Danish females than among males. As an illustration of what effects an imbalance in the sex ratio can have on intermarriage, 61 per cent of first- and second-generation Danish women in New York City had married Danish men in America, whereas only 46 per cent of Danish males reported Danish wives.[33] Germans, Swedes, and Norwegians were about equally represented among outchoices and together accounted for most Danish intermarriages. For example, of the 34,416 Danish-born fathers who were married to non-Danish women in 1900, approximately 50 per cent had Swedish or Norwegian wives and 30 per cent German; another 10 per cent were married to Britishers.[34] Intermarriage increased very sharply in the second generation.

Danish assimilation moved with much greater rapidity than either Norwegian or Swedish assimilation. There were no Danish equivalents to the successful Norwegian press or national fraternal societies, and no intergenerational perpetuation of distinctly Danish subcommunities. In the words of an early observer of Scandinavian life in this country, "The Danish element in America has always lacked unity and solidarity."[35] The same writer had spent six weeks on a Danish farm in Minnesota in 1886 and perceived little difference between the Danes and their American neighbors in house furnishings, dress, food, and behavior.

Because the Danes often settled close to Swedes, Norwegians, and Germans, they merged first with these particular Protestant national origin groups. Danish intermarriage data clearly document this thesis. Danish customs and social ties were apparently short lived, and nowhere did Danes long persist as a self-conscious and identifiable national origin group. Given their linguistic and cultural similarity to their much more

---

[33] Drachsler, *Intermarriage in New York City,* pp. 108, 159.
[34] *U.S. Census of Population,* 1900, pp. 850–65.
[35] Babcock, "The Scandinavian Element in the United States," p. 64.

numerous Scandinavian and German neighbors, and their preference for assimilation, little basis was left for Danish community.

SUMMARY

The Norwegians sustained the ethnic community longer into the twentieth century than did any other Protestant national origin group. Other groups such as the Welsh and, as we shall next note, the Finns were equals to the Norwegians in ethnic solidarity in foreign-born circles, but failed to perpetuate ethnic community into subsequent generations as well as did the Norse. At the opposite end of the assimilation continuum were the Danes, though they entered the core society largely after assimilation into other Scandinavian and German groups. Because they developed a slightly atypical adaptation to the core culture, remained within the confines of the religiously based Norwegian clique, promoted ethnic organizations, maintained marital homogeneity, and emphasized ethnic identification and mutual recognition, one might argue that Norwegians have been more like various Catholic national origin groups than like other Protestant ones. However, these are merely formal similarities. Though they have maintained a few coastal communities, the Norse have been heavily concentrated in the rural north central United States. First as farmers and fishermen, Norwegians have participated fully in the means of mobility into the upper working and middle classes.

Finlanders occupy a paradoxical position in American immigration. Inasmuch as they were Protestants, northern Europeans, mostly literate, and primarily rural in American settlement, the Finns shared common ground with the old immigration. However, the large majority arrived with the new immigration as unskilled laborers, were considered racially different and inferior (despite their European origin), and shared the general stigma attached to the southern and eastern European peoples. Another similarity Finns shared with new immigrants, one that predisposed them to some social difficulty, was that they tended to be single males under thirty years old. Males outnumbered females nearly two to one before 1900. However, this imbalance had been eliminated gradually by 1940.

FARMS AND MINES

Finlanders

Sluggish industrialization and political oppression at home encouraged many Finlanders to pursue economic gain and freedom in America.[1] The Finns, however, were to discover that American wealth and freedom were not as easily accessible as they had envisioned from afar. Native hostility toward Finnish socialist organizations and residence in dirty mining towns became the ultimate reality for many. Finlanders had arrived too late for the prize farmland and lacked the skills to capitalize fully on industrial expansion. Rather, American primary industries benefited from Finnish muscle and cheap labor.

Actually the first Finns in America arrived with the Delaware Swedes in 1638 (Finland was then part of Sweden). Others came to America in the early years of the nineteenth century, either after having worked in the Russian–Alaskan fur trade (Finland was then a part of Russia) or after having jumped ship in California to join the gold and silver prospectors.

Nearly all of the approximately 275,000 Finnish immigrants, however, arrived after 1883. In fact, over half that number entered the country in the first decade of this century. By 1930 first- and second-generation Finns totaled 320,000. The largest number resided in the

---

[1] For scholarly works on Finnish Americans, see Walfrid J. Jokinen, "The Finns in the United States" (doctoral dissertation, Louisiana State University, 1955); and William A. Hoglund, *Finnish Immigrants in America: 1880–1920* (Madison, Wis.: University of Wisconsin Press, 1960).

agricultural and mining regions of Minnesota and Michigan; many later moved to Duluth and Detroit, respectively. Other urban areas favored by Finns were Worcester, Massachusetts, northeast Ohio, Puget Sound, and of course, New York City. As late as 1940, two-thirds of Minnesota and Michigan Finnish Americans were rural in residence.

Since Finnish industrialization started late, Finns were the least skilled of any Protestants to emigrate after 1880. More than two-thirds of the large 1899–1910 group were unskilled workers.[2] (The only European country with a higher percentage of unskilled immigrants for that period was Greece.) Many young Finns mined copper in upper Michigan, iron in northern Minnesota, and gold and silver in the mountain states. Others worked as lumberjacks, as they had in Finland. In Worcester and Fitchburg, Massachusetts, Finlanders labored in the textile industry. However, the largest group of Finnish workers were farmhands. The Finns, in short, entered the occupational structure almost entirely at the bottom, in the extractive industries, performing the most arduous physical tasks the economy had to offer.

"FINGLISH"

Finnish immigrants developed a comprehensive set of ethnic institutions in America. After studying an Ohio Finnish community, Kolehmainen wrote, "Flourishing immigrant institutions preserved and intensified Old World culture patterns and fostered the development of group solidarity."[3] He also noted, however, that Finnish cultural distinctiveness was waning in Ohio by the late 1920's.

Inasmuch as most Finns were literate but unable to read English, they were greatly dependent upon the foreign-language press. Scores of Finnish-language newspapers were printed in various Finnish locales, though most of them were short lived. Many first generation Finns spoke only what Jokinen has referred to as "Finglish," the now familiar mixture of the native tongue with that of the adopted land. Second-generation children enrolled in the public schools served as interpreters and transmitters of American culture for their Finnish-speaking parents.

The generation gap between foreign-born and native-born Finnish Americans was well marked, much more so than among Scandinavians. Perhaps the greater intergenerational differences among Finns were a

---

[2] Hoglund, *Finnish Immigrants in America*, pp. 60–62.

[3] John I. Kolehmainen, "A Study of Marriage in a Finnish Community," *American Journal of Sociology*, XLII (November, 1936), 372.

consequence of the stigma attached to Finnish ethnicity by the native American, an effective inducement to the second generation to dissociate themselves from the Finnish community. The lower degree of acceptance of Finns by native Americans is verified in early research on social distance: for example, only 16 per cent of natives would have approved of a close relative marrying a Finn, 27 per cent would have had a Finn as a close friend, and 36 per cent would have found them to be desirable neighbors.[4] By way of contrast, the degree of acceptance of Finns was only one-third of what it was for Swedes and about the same as for Italians—a remarkably low level for Protestants. Racial thinking of the time defined Finns as Asians. Small wonder, then, that the second generation was anxious over their ethnic visibility.

The anxiety of the American-born Finns regarding their national origin has been vividly documented in the following passages by a Finnish novelist in a scene where an immigrant mother and her daughter are preparing to go to town together:

> "Remember, mother, do not speak Finnish to me on the street."
> "Why not?" asked the mother in surprise.
> "Because I don't want anyone to think that I am an immigrant, let alone a Finlander."
> "But my good girl!" exclaimed the mother, "Is there anything wrong with that?"
> "There is. All those who have come from Europe are so uncivilized and stupid. They even got their first decent meal in this country. And our school books say that Finns are Mongolians. I don't want to be a slant-eyed Mongolian. Everyone in school began to laugh and looked at me when we read that . . . so don't speak to me in Finnish in town.[5]

Not all of the second generation turned away from the immigrant community.

> When I grew older I didn't even try to get into the English-language groups. . . . In our home we spoke often about Finland. . . . I learned the names of towns in Finland. . . . I learned to honor the long suffering Finnish nation. . . . I have never been ashamed that I am Finnish.[6]

Most of the second generation, however, lost interest in Finnish American life. As Jokinen has observed, "The institutions developed by the foreign-born Finns are in a rapid state of disintegration. The Ameri-

---

[4] Emory Bogardus, *Immigration and Race Attitudes* (Boston: D. C. Heath & Company, 1928), p. 25.
[5] Jokinen, "The Finns in the United States," p. 130.
[6] *Ibid.*

can-born generations of Finns have given little support to the socio-cultural aspirations of their parents." [7]

The efforts of the immigrants to salvage Finnish culture in the second generation were serious and systematic compared to, say, the efforts of the Swedes. During the early years of their lives, native-born Finns were compelled to participate in immigrant life and to further their knowledge of Finnish language and history. However reluctantly, the majority of the second generation completed the normal requirements of Finnish education and participation. Once independent, writes Kolehmainen, the teen-age Finn usually

> ... broke into rebellion against Finnish immigrant life. Resistance to Finnish customs and traditions crystallized into open opposition, participation in immigrant institutions ceased, and command of the language began to disappear rapidly. Conflicts with parents over choice of friends, dancing, habits, etc. were settled unilaterally in favor of the second generation. It became fashionable to disguise one's Finnish origin. . . . Finnish Christian names were changed to American equivalents (Toivo to Tom, Tyyne to Mary) and often surnames suffered the same fate (as from Koivumaki to Hill).[8]

Although segments of nearly every immigrant group struggled with the problem of heavy drinking, the Finns encountered more than the usual difficulties as young single males on the mining and lumber frontiers. The U.S. Immigration Commission singled out the Finnish in 15 iron mining towns of Minnesota as one of the two heaviest-drinking immigrant groups.[9] Saloon life, fighting, and gambling were frequent events among immigrant Finns in the mining towns and lumber centers of the Northland. As E. A. Ross once jibed, "Like the drunken Magyar and Lithuanian, the 'loaded' Finn is a terrible fellow." [10]

Outside the mining and lumber settlements, most Finlanders were teetotalers, even in time of festivals and celebrations. Indeed, the Finns played an active role in the temperance movement by forming their own anti-saloon leagues. Interestingly enough, Jokinen has argued that Finnish drinking patterns were not transplanted from the Old World, because drinking was not common in rural Finland during the period of heavy emigration. However, about the same time heavy drinking took root in America, it was beginning to be a problem in urban Finland among rural migrants.[11]

---

7 *Ibid.,* p. 201.

8 Kolehmainen, "Marriage in a Finnish Community," p. 377–78.

9 Hoglund, *Finnish Immigrants in America,* p. 103.

10 Edward A. Ross, *The Old World in the New* (New York: Appleton-Century, 1914).

11 Jokinen, "The Finns in the United States," p. 123.

ETHNIC COMMUNITY

There is no question concerning the strong communal tendencies among first generation Finns. As Hoglund has pointed out, "As soon as they came to America, Finnish immigrants sought each other's companionship. In their trials they found solace through informal contacts among themselves." [12] Or in Jokinen's words, "The foreign-born appear to be content to live out their lives within their own institutional framework." [13] Language and cultural barriers, of course, encouraged Finns to withdraw into their own groups for the satisfaction of their social needs.

The second generation had less reason and desire to restrict their social ties to the ethnic group. The object of frequent discussion in immigrant social circles was, How can we keep our children from associating with those of other nationalities and from marrying them? [14] No strategy proved successful. Just as most American-born Finns were eager to shed immigrant identity and customs, so did most tend to move outside the closed orbit of Finnish group life whenever possible.

Finlanders formed a variety of ethnic clubs and organizations. The most successful were the workingmen's societies organized during the 1890's. These groups later were replaced by or transformed into socialist clubs. The Finnish Socialist Federation was organized in 1906 at Hibbing, Minnesota around some fifty Finnish locals. By 1914, the federation counted some 16,000 members in over 160 different socialist locals.[15] After 1915, the federation gradually lost out to industrial unionism. During this period, however, Finns constituted a large minority of the American Socialist Party. To demonstrate their loyalty, other Finns concerned about their group's image organized *anti*-socialist leagues. Finnish socialist organizations were actually more social and athletic than political. Ethnic social life often centered in the halls built during the socialist movement.

The only type of immigrant organization that has survived and been supported by American-born Finns is the consumers' cooperative, a Finnish economic innovation, which also has had its social aspects. The cooperatives were instigated in 1917; by 1955, the Central Cooperative Wholesale of Minnesota, Wisconsin, and Michigan reported sales of $12 million. The American-born participants have tended to emphasize the economic benefits of the cooperative, the foreign-born the social benefits.

Finlanders as a group depended somewhat more than Scandinavians

12 Hoglund, *Finnish Immigrants in America*, p. 37.
13 Jokinen, "The Finns in the United States," p. xiii.
14 Kolehmainen, "Marriage in a Finnish Community," p. 375.
15 Hoglund, *Finnish Immigrants in America*, p. 44.

on secular ethnic institutions as against religious ones. The Finnish Evangelical Lutheran Church, however, played an important part in the Finnish community and continues to do so today. Suomi Junior College and Seminary, located in Hancock, Michigan, is the educational arm of the Finnish church.

The Finnish people had one of the highest rates of in-marriage of any European national origin group, and easily the highest among the northern Europeans. Though closest to the Swedes, Finlanders had no real close ethnic counterpart as did Scots in the English, Norwegians in Swedes, or the Dutch in Germans, which would contribute to a higher intermarriage rate. First- and many second-generation Finns veritably stood alone. Fully 92 per cent of first- and second-generation Finnish men married Finnish women in New York City.[16] In an ethnically mixed rural Minnesota area studied in 1942, 87 per cent of Finns were in-married.[17] As recently as 1956, three-fourths of Finns in another Minnesota area reported Finnish spouses.[18] In the Ohio community studied by Kolehmainen, more than half of all marriages involving a first- or second-generation Finn from 1895 to 1935 were endogamous.[19] However, the trend in Ohio was clearly away from in-marriage, since only about a fourth of all Finnish marriages toward the end of the period were endogamous. Whether in New York City or Minnesota country, intermarried Finns were nearly always wedded to Scandinavians or Germans. Taking intermarriage as a guide to assimilation, we thus see that the present generation of American Finns are becoming an accepted part of white Protestant society through the medium of the Scandinavian and German components.

SUMMARY

Finlanders have occupied the status of a definite "out-group" even though they are white Protestant. The timing of Finnish immigration and the cool reception of Finnish immigrants by native Protestants suggest that Finns belong more to the new immigration than the old, but as Protestants their descendants melted with those of the latter. Despite their high geographical concentration and the nearly complete social isolation of the first generation, Finns of native birth assiduously pursued accul-

16 Julius Drachsler, *Intermarriage in New York City* (New York: Columbia University Press, 1921), pp. 110–62.

17 Lowry Nelson, "Intermarriage among Nationality Groups in a Rural Area of Minnesota," *American Journal of Sociology*, XLVIII (March, 1943), 585–92.

18 Lowry Nelson, *The Minnesota Community* (Minneapolis: University of Minnesota Press, 1960), pp. 45–46.

19 Kolehmainen, "Marriage in a Finnish Community."

turation. With moderate difficulty, American-born Finns moved into the social and familial circles of Scandinavians and Germans. In possession of few industrial skills, Finnish laborers performed the most menial and strenuous tasks. However, the younger generations are competing quite favorably with a majority of other white Protestants for economic success.

To review German immigration and assimilation in America is a complete task in itself, both because of the enormous size and duration of the immigration and because of the diversity of the immigrants. Here we can hope to achieve only a brief outline.

Germany represents the only large immigrant country with a major Protestant-Catholic division. Whether common national origin served to override religious differences in social life or vice versa is a question of considerable interest concerning Germans. The Dutch, too, had the religious split, and Dutch Protestants and Catholics mutually preserved social distance. The impression one gets from the literature is that both German and Dutch Protestants moved more within their own respective social circles and that Catholics did the same.[1] However, not only does the literature often mix Protestant and Catholic Germans, but there is also a minor problem of distinguishing between the Germans and Dutch. In the colonial period, Germans were often referred to as "Dutch"; in the industrial era, Protestant Germans and Dutch often settled and mingled together, though in a number of places there were distinctively Dutch communities.

Deutsch and Dutch

GERMANS IN AMERICA

A handful of Germans were purportedly among the first settlers at Jamestown. In his monumental study of German Americans, Faust relates an anecdote concerning three "Dutch" carpenters who were employed by the colony's Captain Smith to construct a house for Chief Powhatan as part of a scheme to bring the chief under control of the English. The Germans, stigmatized and denigrated in the English colony, chose, as the story goes, to reveal the plot to the chief and remain with the Indians rather than return to Jamestown.[2] Germans were in New

[1] For a modern empirical analysis of the question of religion versus national origin in German social life, see Edward O. Laumann, "The Social Structure of Religious and Ethnoreligious Groups in a Metropolitan Community," *American Sociological Review*, XXXIV (April, 1969), 182–97.

[2] For a broad discussion of many aspects of German-American history, see Albert B. Faust, *The German Element in the United States* (New York: The Steuben Society of America, 1927).

Netherlands as well. Indeed, Peter Minuit, the man who paid the Indians 60 guilders for Manhattan Island, was born in Germany.

The "Mayflower" of German immigration, the *Concord,* sailed into Philadelphia in 1683 with a group of Mennonites attracted to Pennsylvania by the promise of religious freedom. These early sectarians were the vanguard of a German immigration which was to eventually exceed 6 million persons, the largest number to come to America from any other single European country. Tens of thousands of various German sectarians, Reformed, and Lutherans settled the valleys of Pennsylvania and neighboring areas throughout the eighteenth century. As early as 1750, a German population zone stretched from the Mohawk Valley in New York to Savannah, Georgia. German farmers moved with the frontier where land was the cheapest, often following after pioneering Scotch-Irish.

Some 200,000 Germans comprised 9 per cent of the population in 1790; fully half of these resided in Pennsylvania and comprised a third of its population.[3] New York, Maryland, Virginia, and Kentucky, and Tennessee also had relatively large German populations.[4] New England, on the other hand, contained very few Germans.

The magnitude of German immigration to industrial America was of epic proportions, surpassing that from England by 3.3 million and its nearest competitor Italy by 1.2 million. In all, 5.9 million German immigrants were officially enumerated during the 1820–1929 period. The massive influx of Germans began in the 1830's, a decade when Germans already ranked second to the Irish in total immigrants. A million and a half Germans arrived in the antebellum period alone. Yet, this figure was later matched in a single decade, the 1880's. In a single year, 1882, 250,000 Germans flooded American ports of entry. German stock (immigrants and their children) in America passed the 8 million mark as the country entered the twentieth century, rather dwarfing the 2.5 million first and second generation Englishmen who were their contemporaries.[5] Twentieth century America has witnessed still another million German immigrants. Thus, even as late as 1960, German stock numbered well over 4 million.

Industrial Germans were heavily concentrated along the Northeast seaboard from Maryland to Massachusetts, in the Great Lakes cities from Buffalo to Milwaukee, and across the Corn Belt from Indiana to

[3] Major works on the Pennsylvania Germans include Ralph Wood, ed., *The Pennsylvania Germans* (Princeton, N.J.: Princeton University Press); and Fredric Klees, *The Pennsylvania Dutch* (New York: The Macmillan Company, 1950).

[4] On the Maryland Germans, see Dieter Cunz, *The Maryland Germans* (Princeton, N.J.: Princeton University Press, 1948).

[5] E. P. Hutchinson, *Immigrants and Their Children* (New York: John Wiley & Sons, Inc., 1956), pp. 5, 10, 333.

Nebraska.[6] St. Louis and Kansas City, Missouri, southeast Texas, New Orleans, and the major cities of the West Coast have also been centers of German immigrant strength. The Mountain West received a proportionate share of Germans as well. That Germans were geographically dispersed, though not so much as the British, is suggested by the fact they have been the most numerous foreign-born group in more than half the states. German Missouri, Louisiana, and Texas settlements broke with the customary pattern of strictly northern occupancy of industrial immigrants. To be sure, Missouri and Texas ranked second and third behind Wisconsin in percentage of Germans in their foreign-born populations, though New York, Illinois, Wisconsin, Pennsylvania, and Ohio were easily the largest German-American states.

Most of the large cities of the North had substantial German-American sectors. For example, in 1900 three-fourths of Cincinnati's foreign-born population, two-thirds of Milwaukee's, and more than one-half of St. Louis's were German. Many rural areas were as predominantly German as any urban German-American sector. For example, 90 per cent of foreign-born persons in rural Franklin County, Missouri were German and 80 per cent of those in Jefferson County, Wisconsin.[7]

Class Location

Since the early colonial period, artisans and skilled workers have been fairly numerous among German immigrants. Skilled workmen were almost as plentiful as farmers among those who came to Pennsylvania in the eighteenth century.[8] Nineteenth-century Germans were, like other Protestants, most often employed in agriculture. Proportionately, Germans were only slightly less agricultural than Scandinavians and in absolute numbers far exceeded either Scandinavian or British in agricultural employment. The number of industrial workers did, however, gradually increase; by the end of the open immigration period, probably as many as half of all German immigrants were skilled or white-collar workers. Germans, nevertheless, have tended to lack the depth and scope of industrial experience of the British and possibly the Swedish. There were, to be sure, high-status German occupational groups that came to America in the nineteenth century, particularly middle-class political refugees.[9]

Persons of German parentage have gained the status of economic

6 T. Lynn Smith, *Population Analysis* (New York: McGraw-Hill Book Company, 1948), p. 56.

7 U.S. Bureau of the Census, *U.S. Census of Population*, 1900, Vol. I (Washington, D.C.: Government Printing Office, 1901), Table 34.

8 Klees, *The Pennsylvania Dutch*, p. 203.

9 For an account of one such group, the Turners, see Noel Iverson, *Germania, U.S.A.* (Minneapolis: University of Minnesota Press, 1966).

elite in numbers roughly proportionate to their representation in the general population, difficult as that may be considering British hegemony. For instance, both Keller [10] and Miller [11] reported that 12 per cent of their samples of business executives had German ancestry, and Sorokin found that about 10 per cent of American millionaires up to the time of his study were of German derivation.[12] Men of German background seem to have been overrepresented in the world of late nineteenth and early twentieth century American science.[13] Yet, only about 3 per cent of all Supreme Court justices have had German origins.[14] Mirroring the larger Protestant group, German Americans have been spread throughout the class structure. Few remained long near or at the bottom.

"SPRECHEN SIE DEUTSCH"

Germans preserved linguistic, cultural, and social ties rather well through several generations in both colonial and industrial America, especially in the colonial period. Pennsylvania Germans, or "Dutch" if you prefer,[15] were the only native group to emerge from the colonial period unassimilated. Colonial and industrial Germans shared less than one might expect. Colonial Germans remained as socially separate and culturally distinctive from the industrial Germans as each of them did from other national origin groups.

Spoken Pennsylvania German remained very much alive for over 200 years.[16] The dialect was used in the home, church, schools, and press right into the twentieth century and was often spoken in rural areas as late as 1941.[17] German was also the language of the day for most nineteenth-century immigrants living in German-American districts. As Cunz has noted, ". . . German-American sectors of Baltimore's population lived in their own world, cut off from their American surroundings by the

[10] Suzanne I. Keller, "The Social Origins and Career Lines of Three Generations of American Business Leaders" (doctoral dissertation, Columbia University, 1953).

[11] William Miller, "The Recruitment of the American Business Elite," *Quarterly Journal of Economics,* LXIV (1950).

[12] Pitirim Sorokin, "American Millionaires and Multi-Millionaires," *Social Forces,* III (May, 1925), 627–40.

[13] *Ibid.,* p. 633.

[14] John R. Schmidhauser, "The Justices of the Supreme Court: A Collective Portrait," *Midwest Journal of Political Science,* III (February, 1959), 1–57.

[15] The word "Dutch" is a corruption of the old German word *Deutsch,* which means "folk." Whether the people who settled Pennsylvania were more German or Dutch in culture is a moot point; they were, in fact, German by birth.

[16] Pennsylvania German is the eighteenth-century dialect of the Palatinate combined with a modicum of English words.

[17] Wood, *The Pennsylvania Germans,* p. 151.

language barrier." [18] Third-generation German-speaking Americans have been quite common, proportionately more common than third-generation Scandinavian-speaking persons.

German has been the language of more printed pages than any other foreign language in America. The first German newspaper was printed in 1739 in Germantown, Pennsylvania. Since then, literally hundreds of German newspapers and monthlies have been published. The German population of New York City could choose at once from among 12 local papers and Texas Germans from among 29.[19] Milwaukee's *Germania* claimed the largest circulation. The German-language press in 1910 had a total circulation of nearly 3.5 million for its 49 monthlies, 433 weeklies, and 70 dailies.[20] Even as recently as 1960, 40 German-language publications had a circulation of 300,000 and English-language publications for Germans had a total circulation of over 2 million—rivaled ethnically only by Jewish-directed English publications.

Immigrants to industrial America, however, were less successful than their colonial forebears in transmitting the distinctively German cultural legacy to subsequent American generations. German dramatic associations, literary groups, choral societies, gymnastic societies, lodges and fraternal orders, family beer gardens, and numerous other ethnic activities—usually stratified along social class lines—flourished among immigrants, but declined owing to apathy in American-born generations.[21] German-American cultural life was most vital in the last part of the nineteenth century, a period said to be characterized by the expression, "When three Germans meet they found a society." Informal group life was perforce strong in German-American districts; still, the following evaluation by an early German scholar of Texas Germans was probably typical of the larger German-American community: "... the Germans did not mingle much with the American population. The fact that the Germans were settled together and at some distance from the Americans, tended to separate the two groups. They made little acquaintance, observing one another, partly with unfeigned curiosity, often tempered with mutual contempt"; in later generations, however, "... relations are friendly, and in cities such as Galveston and Houston, the German has become merged with the American population." [22]

18 Cunz, *The Maryland Germans*, p. 393.

19 Gilbert G. Benjamin, *The Germans in Texas* (Philadelphia: Reprinted from *German-American Annals*, Vol. VII, 1909).

20 See Joshua A. Fishman, et al., *Language Loyalty in the United States* (The Hague: Mouton & Company, 1966), pp. 52–65.

21 For discussions of German-American cultural life, see John Frederick Nau, *The German People of New Orleans: 1850–1900* (Leiden: E. J. Brill, 1958); Cunz, *The Maryland Germans*, and Benjamin, *The Germans in Texas.*

22 Benjamin, *The Germans in Texas*, pp. 74–84.

Ethnoreligious Life

Colonial Germans were nearly all Protestants. The large majority were Lutherans or Reformed; others were members of various dissenting sects such as Mennonites, Amish, and Dunkards. Many Pennsylvania Germans were recruited to Methodism in the religious revivals of the early nineteenth century. Most Germans residing in homogeneous areas, however, remained loyal to colonial churches. The influx of German Catholics began shortly before the middle of the nineteenth century, but Protestants still continued to arrive in greater numbers. Most of the Texas Germans were Lutherans, as were a large majority of those who disembarked in New Orleans and migrated north into Missouri. St. Louis, in fact, became the headquarters of German Lutheranism in America. However, German Americans and especially their descendants have been Baptist and Methodist nearly as often as Lutheran.

Extensive systems of parochial schools were operated by both colonial and nineteenth-century Germans. Nearly every German church had at some time supported its own school. Numerous colleges have been founded by German Protestant churches, such as Muhlenberg (Allentown, Pennsylvania), Susquehanna (Selinsgrove, Pennsylvania), Valparaiso (Valparaiso, Indiana), and Concordia (Moorhead, Minnesota). Concordia Publishing House in St. Louis serves as the intellectual medium of German Lutheranism.

As among Scandinavians, the church often served as the chief institutional link between the individual and the German community. Pennsylvania Germans, writes Wood, ". . . usually lived in compact groups and formed close socioreligious . . . units." [23] German Americans of the industrial period also used the church as a center of communalism. Scandinavian Lutherans in the Midwest have been prone to view German Lutherans as clannish and aloof in social life. In part, this may be attributed to a tendency of the German Missouri Synod churches to remain outside interdenominational (including Lutheran) organizations and the absence of the Missouri Synod from the National Council of Churches.

The fact that Germans may be either Protestant or Catholic makes it somewhat difficult to ascertain how well Germans adhere to the multiple-melting-pot thesis. A German marriage to a Scandinavian may, for example, be a Catholic-Protestant marriage as well as a Protestant-Protestant one. Over-all in-marriage rates were fairly high in the first and second generations and in areas where Germans comprised a large portion of the population (Table 7–1). Although these figures attest to the

[23] Wood, *The Pennsylvania Germans*, p. 32.

TABLE 7–1

GERMAN IN-MARRIAGE RATES IN THE UNITED STATES, SELECTED STUDIES

Location	Time	Percentage Expected In-Marriages [a]	Percentage Observed In-Marriages [b]	Percentage Difference
New York City [c]	1908–1912	8	69	61
Nebraska [d]	1909–1913	48	81	33
	1921–1925	47	61	14
Wisconsin [d]	1908–1912	51	81	30
	1920–1924	40	61	21
New York State [d]	1908–1912	35	65	30
	1921–1925	32	56	24
New York State [e]	1939	29	40	11
Wright County, Minn. [f]	1942	46	80	34
Northeastern Minnesota [f]	1956	23	45	22
New Haven, Conn. [g]	1900	10	55	45
	1930	6	40	34
	1950	5	27	22
Protestant City [h]	1967	28	64	36
Catholic City [h]	1967	44	76	32

[a] The expected in-marriage rates were computed and represent the per cent of Germans (females if given) in the sample or community population.

[b] The observed in-marriage rates represent the percentage of German males married to German females of all German males in a given sample except in Protestant City and Catholic City, where the over-all male and female rates are given to maximize sample size.

[c] Julius Drachsler, *Intermarriage in New York City* (New York: Columbia University Press, 1921), first and second generations only.

[d] Edmund deS. Brunner, *Immigrant Farmers and Their Children* (Garden City, N.Y.: Doubleday & Company, Inc., 1929), first and second generations only.

[e] Lowry Nelson, "Intermarriage Among Nationality Groups in a Rural Area of Minnesota," *American Journal of Sociology*, XLVIII (March, 1943), 585–92, first and second generations only.

[f] Lowry Nelson, *The Minnesota Community* (Minneapolis: University of Minnesota Press, 1960).

[g] Ruby Jo Reeves Kennedy, "Single or Triple Melting-Pot? Intermarriage in New Haven 1870–1950," *American Journal of Sociology*, LVIII (July, 1952), 56–59.

[h] See Appendix B for source. A German with a mixed German-non-German spouse was considered an in-marriage.

continued importance of national origin in the German group, the extent of intermarriage between German Protestants and Catholics is not clear. Some evidence is available to suggest that German Protestants who intermarry tend to select British or Scandinavian spouses more often than they do German Catholics. In his study of a Minnesota area, Nelson grouped Germans living in communities with organized Catholic parishes (by implication Catholics) with French, Irish, and Polish respondents, and the remainder of Germans (by implication Protestant) with British and Scandinavian respondents; he discovered that 93 per cent of the latter and 90 per cent of the former married within the two ethnoreligious melting pots.[24] As a more direct piece of evidence, calculations based on Protestant and Catholic City data indicated that German Protestants preferred Scandinavian and British mates in intermarriage, while German Catholics more often chose Irish and Polish spouses.

Germanization

Germans have been the only national origin group to cause definite concern among natives over the possibility of a foreign-language group overwhelming Anglo-American institutions by dint of sheer numbers. Pennsylvania Germans, a large minority of Pennsylvania's eighteenth-century population, aroused nativist agitation against them. Benjamin Franklin once wrote to an English friend, asking

> ... why the Pennsylvanians should allow the Palatine Germans to swarm into our settlements, and be herding together to establish their language and Manners to the exclusion of ours? Why should Pennsylvania, founded by the English, become a colony of Aliens, who will shortly be so numerous as to Germanize us instead of our Anglifying them? [25]

Pennsylvania Germans developed their own biases against British groups. For example, as proud and assiduous farmers, they cast a critical eye at the "inferior" agricultural techniques of their neighbors, and poor fences became known as "(Scotch)-Irish fences" and poor plowing as "Yankee plowing." [26] New Englanders bore a particularly bad name among Germans as a result of the commercial activity of Yankee peddlers. "Yankee" became a handy synonym for "cheat." At the time of the Revolution, however, the large German population was instrumental in aligning

24 Lowry Nelson, "Intermarriage Among Nationality Groups in a Rural Area of Minnesota," *American Journal of Sociology*, LVIII (March, 1943), 585–92.

25 William Carlson Smith, *Americans in the Making* (New York: Appleton-Century, 1939), p. 394.

26 Wood, *The Pennsylvania Germans*, pp. 48–49.

Pennsylvania with the seven states voting for independence. Generals preferred Germans as their personal body guards.

In the nineteenth century, the seemingly countless millions of Germans evoked unprecedented nativist apprehensions. Especially threatening was the prospect of Germanization in Wisconsin, Missouri, and Texas. At the same time Americanization of German-American sectors in the large cities seemed to move much too slowly. Germans clashed with natives as the former vigorously pursued the support of their parochial school system. Nor did the Germans' anti-temperance stand appeal to the native Protestants. German socialists and political radicals also were feared and despised. Finally, World War I raised questions regarding the loyalties of the German-American community, a question apparently still unanswered at the time of World War II.

Politically, the early Germans tended to be at odds with the establishment; they were strong proponents of Jefferson and Jackson and generally supported Democrats as opposed to Federalists and Whigs. Later, most Germans were strongly opposed to the various Know-Nothing and American parties. Regional, religious, and changing economic interests led increasing numbers of Germans into the ranks of the Republican party. Indeed, one of the most famous Republicans of all, Herbert Hoover, came from Pennsylvania German stock. However, among the various Protestant national origin groups, Germans have no doubt made the largest contributions, relatively and absolutely, to the election of Democratic candidates in the North.

Although the threat of Germanization never materialized beyond a very limited sense, we might recall that Germans have made innumerable contributions to American life ranging from the kindergarten and university system to symphony orchestras (that of Philadelphia, for example) and the brewer's arts.

HOLLANDERS

Hollanders had a stake in America almost as early as the English and nearly 60 years before the Germans established settlements of their own. The Dutch were colonizers in the most rudimentary sense. Yet, Dutch claims were soon usurped by the English, and Dutch numbers far surpassed by the Germans. In Mulder's words, "Holland's failure to win a continent was basically a failure of emigration." [27] The freedoms and prosperity other peoples of the seventeenth and eighteenth centuries

27 For general works on Dutch life in America, see Arnold Mulder, *Americans from Holland* (New York: J. B. Lippincott Co., 1947); and Henry S. Lucas, *Netherlanders in America* (Ann Arbor: University of Michigan Press, 1955).

often went to America to find, the Dutch already enjoyed at home. Holland was herself absorbing labor from other countries and sheltering persecuted religious minorities. By the nineteenth century, however, Dutch commercial fortunes had waned, the population was plagued by food shortages, and religious freedoms were withdrawn. Still, emigration from Holland never attained the relative proportions of that from most other European nations.

The first Dutch interests in America were trading posts established in 1624 under the aegis of the West India Company on what is now Manhattan and Staten Islands and near Albany. The Manhattan settlement was known as New Amsterdam and the entire Hudson River Valley area as New Netherlands. As a tactic by which they hoped to colonize the whole Hudson River Valley, the Dutch developed the patroon system. The patroon system awarded a liberal grant of land, social and political rights and privileges, and the honorific title of "Patroon" to anyone who was able to persuade 50 adults to settle on the land within a four-year period. Except in a few cases, such as that of Kiliaen Van Rensselaer, who thereby acquired some 700,000 acres, the patroon system achieved little. After 40 years of Dutch rule, New Amsterdam and its 10,000 inhabitants became New York, and only half that number were actually Dutch. Dutch emigration was further reduced following the surrender of New Netherlands to the English. The total Dutch population in America at the end of the eighteenth century did not exceed 100,000 persons, more than half of whom resided in New York and more than a fourth in New Jersey, states where the Dutch comprised 18 per cent and 17 per cent of the population, respectively.[28]

The first nineteenth-century settlement of Hollanders in America was located in Michigan in 1846 by a group of some 50 religious dissenters who had left home to establish their own socioreligious community. Additional Dutch communities were soon founded in Wisconsin and Iowa. The large majority of Hollanders, however, emigrated as individuals or individual families rather than as religious collectivities. The Immigration Bureau reported nearly 250,000 Dutch newcomers as of the 1929 closing date. The Dutch patterns of immigration resembled the German, though obviously on a much smaller scale: beginning in the 1840's, cresting in the 1880's, but continuing at a relatively high rate through the early years of the twentieth century. In 1930 the census counted over 400,000 first and second generation Netherlanders.

Though the large part of the foreign-born Dutch population was scattered throughout the country in a pattern similar to German settle-

---

[28] *Annual Report of the American Historical Association,* Vol. I, 1931, (Washington, D.C.: Government Printing Office, 1932), pp. 124–25.

ment, certain areas developed unique Dutch characteristics or at least contained sizeable contingents of Dutchmen. Eastern Michigan, Chicago, northern New Jersey, New York City, and northwest and south central Iowa were the chief strongholds of Hollanders in America. In Michigan and Iowa, the Dutch were in several counties the most conspicuous national origin group. Towns such as Holland, Michigan, and Pella and Orange City, Iowa still preserve a Dutch identity and image. The larger body of Hollanders, however, resided near and eventually mingled with the Germans. In Passaic County, New York, for example, 7,000 foreign-born Dutchmen once neighbored with 9,000 Germans.

Dutch farmers and agricultural workers outnumbered any other occupational category throughout most of the immigration period, but a rather large minority of those who arrived in this century were clerical or skilled workers. The colonial Dutch were, by contrast, more often merchants and traders than farmers.

DUTCH TREAT, WASP PLEASURE

The Dutch image in America has been an unusually favorable one. To the nineteenth-century Hollanders living outside the tightly knit ethnic enclaves, assimilation posed no problems. The modern Dutch mingled first mainly with the German and then the larger Protestant community, except in the homogeneous communities of the Midwest where a degree of separateness continues even today. This is not to imply that Dutch and Germans did not at first recognize any differences between them. Much as foreign-born Norwegians and Swedes were often socially separated though culturally similar, first generation Dutch and Germans preserved ethnic lines despite the fact that they frequently settled in contiguous areas and shared behavioral ties.

An essay in early popular literature described the Dutch in America as "quiet, steady, and indefatigable persevering workers, a thrifty, frugal and prosperous people." [29] It further contended that "They [Hollanders] cluster in colonies in the rural districts, and do not concern themselves much with people of other nationalities. In the cities also they remain firmly in nuclei that are held together by their natural association in similar lines of occupation and in clubs founded and formed for natives of the Netherlands." [30] As Mulder has observed, Hollanders were often thought of as clannish by their neighbors and were accused of living within their own social shells.[31] Regarding the Protestant-Catholic divi-

[29] "Hollanders in America," *Literary Digest,* LXIII (December 6, 1919), 40.
[30] *Ibid.*
[31] Mulder, *Americans from Holland,* p. 199.

sion, Mulder argues, "There was an impassable gulf between the Protestant and Catholic [Dutch] communities." [32]

First generation Dutch living in ethnic communities dressed in a manner similar to that prevailing in the Netherlands. The immigrants spoke Dutch in the home as well as on the street and conducted regular church services in the native tongue. The first foreign-language newspaper, the *Sheboygan Nieuwsbode,* went to press in 1849 in Sheboygan, Wisconsin and was soon followed by *De Grondwet,* a Michigan publication that boasted an 80-year history. The longevity of Dutch customs and distinguishing life styles was easily equivalent to that of other Protestant immigrant customs, probably even more so in the homogeneous settlements of the Midwest.

The Dutch church was especially germane to ethnic life, understandably so in the religious communities of Michigan and Iowa, but also in more mixed areas. On the frontier, the church played a key role in the socialization of children, the administration of law and government, and the intellectual and artistic life of the community. The *koffee klatch,* a frequent focus of socializing among the women, also tended to be an informal extension of church life. In communities with a sizeable Dutch population, ecclesiastical divisions were also social divisions, even between two Dutch-based denominations.

The church's impact was plainly visible in the stringent moral code of the Dutch. Drinking, card playing, gambling, dancing, the theater, and much of the secular world of entertainment were strictly forbidden. Only the Norwegians, once the church was established, compared to the Dutch in rejection and denunciation of this-worldly pleasure. But quite understandably, the more rigorous the code of behavior, the greater the difficulty of its enforcement. And so like the Norwegians, the Dutch elders were often disappointed in the behavior of the younger generation. In an early volume on the Iowa Dutch, Van der Zee noted, "The young people tend more and more in their daily life to adopt the ways of the American public and to break with the orthodox views of their elders, and thus exert a softening influence on the hard tone of community life." The first generation, Van der Zee wrote, endeavored to instill in their children "the traditional hardihood, industry, frugality, thrift, morality, and religion for which the Hollanders are famous as a people." [33] Like those in Iowa, the Dutch in Michigan, according to Pieters, were confronted with surveillance problems in exacting conformity among the youth: "Many a father suffered heartache over the spiritual degeneracy of the sons, who all too soon learned to forsake the

[32] *Ibid.,* p. 174.
[33] Jacob Van der Zee, *The Hollanders of Iowa* (Iowa City, 1912).

straight and narrow way of the church for . . . worldly amusements." [34]

The religious organization that gave legitimacy to the austere behavior of the orthodox Dutchman was, of course, the Reformed church, whose official records date to 1639. Today the Reformed church counts nearly 250,000 members and the Christian Reformed church slightly more.

As for the ethnic life of the colonial Dutch, they maintained both a distinctive cultural style and social group boundaries for at least a century after yielding power to the English. As late as 1809, notes Mulder, the whole Hudson River Valley and parts of New Jersey and Delaware "were still strongly tinctured, some places even dominated, by Dutch mores." [35] The process of assimilation was underway earlier, however, as the intermarriages of Dutch families like the Roosevelts, Van Burens, Depews, Van Cortlandts, and Van Rensselaers with British stock suggests. Franklin D. Roosevelt, for example, descended from a family line that included Dutch, Swedish, English, and Scotch-Irish pre-Revolutionary antecedents.

Dutch tended to marry Dutch, of course, in the homogeneous settlements of the nineteenth century. Even more recently, however, a rather high percentage of Hollanders have continued to choose Dutch mates, but the large majority of such in-marriages involve persons still living in or near communities with strong Dutch churches. A study by Bouma of several Michigan congregations of the Christian Reformed church disclosed that 59 per cent of Christian Reformed marriages involved other members of the same denomination and fully 73 per cent of Christian Reformed marriages involved members of either the Christian Reformed or another Dutch Protestant denomination.[36] The record of Dutch intermarriage clearly indicates Dutch preference for Germans as partners in a mixed marriage. Because Dutch males were about a third again more numerous than females, men were considerably more often involved in a Dutch–non-Dutch marriage than were women.

Dutch Debts

Americans are indebted to the Dutch for the versatile name "Yankee." "Yankee" comes from the Dutch words *Jan* and *kaas,* which mean "John Cheese." *Jankaas* was an opprobrious appellation employed by New Netherlanders to refer to English settlers in the area. *Jankaas* became

---

[34] Aleida J. Pieters, *A Dutch Settlement in Michigan* (Grand Rapids, Mich.: The Reformed Press, 1923), pp. 103–4.

[35] Mulder, *Americans from Holland,* p. 68.

[36] Donald H. Bouma, "Religiously Mixed Marriages: Denominational Consequences in the Christian Reformed Church," *Marriage and Family Living,* XXV (November, 1963), 428–32.

"Yankee" and was eventually applied to New Englanders in general, who quaintly accepted it as descriptive of their own merit rather than as derogation. At the time of the American Revolution, the English adversaries applied the title Yankee to all Americans.

The colonial Dutch endeavored to recognize the freedoms of religion and speech in America—at a time when repression and intolerance characterized New England and the southern colonies. Among American Presidents of Dutch extraction who later swore to uphold these rights were Martin Van Buren, Theodore Roosevelt, and Franklin D. Roosevelt (Claes Martenszoon van't Rosevelt, the paternal ancestor of the Roosevelts, sailed for America from the Province of Zeeland in the Netherlands in 1650).

Other eminent Americans with Dutch background include film producer Cecil B. DeMille, biographer Carl Van Doren, and most of the so-called "Knickerbocker families," such as the Vanderbilts (Cornelius Vanderbilt was born to a poor Dutch family on Staten Island in 1794). American folklore has been enormously enriched through early Dutch presence in New York. Perhaps among the best known tales are Washington Irving's "Rip Van Winkle" and "The Legend of Sleepy Hollow." In education, Rutgers, the State University of New Jersey, was founded by the descendants of early Dutch settlers in 1766. And if the Germans were brewers, the Dutch were horticulturists. Annual tulip festivals in Holland, Michigan, and Pella, Iowa, attracted hundreds of thousands of persons during their efflorescence in the 1930's.

SUMMARY

Had Hollanders emigrated in greater strength to the New Netherlands, Dutch cultural patterns might have offered a significant challenge and alternative to Anglo-Saxon patterns in America. In Pennsylvania, Germans did in fact pose a viable cultural threat, and Germanization was again considered possible for some western areas in the nineteenth century. As it turned out, British numbers in the case of the Dutch and prior establishment of the British in the case of the Germans guaranteed that Anglo-Saxon patterns would prevail. The Teuton has been relatively assimilable in the second and third generations, aside from the Pennsylvania Germans and enclaves of Michigan and Iowa Dutch. The sheer size of the German immigration, combined with a foreign culture and language, stimulated an active ethnic life and permitted ethnic institutions to prosper for some time.

As the only two foreign contingents with a significant Protestant-Catholic division, the Germans and Dutch served to test the strength of common national origin against religion as community-making factors. Although national origin played an important role in the history of both Germans and Dutch in America, German and Dutch Protestants seemingly shared more with one another than either did with their respective Catholic counterparts.

Widely heralded as well-disciplined and persevering farmers and workers, the Germans and Dutch encountered few social obstacles to the intergenerational climb in the American class system.

WHITE PROTESTANTISM:
ITS PAST AND PRESENT STATUS
IN AMERICAN LIFE

Part Two

The substantive assimilation of the Protestant national origin groups into the white Protestant core society by the second quarter of the twentieth century shifted the focus of ethnic membership from national origin and national origin-based congregations to the Protestant religion as a whole. The reduction of national origin differences among Protestants and the consequent acceptance of these people into the status groups of the core society created a combined white Protestant component of the multiple melting pot.

In this part of the book we examine the specifically religious aspect of ethnicity and ethnic relations. Topics covered are similar to those in the first part, including Protestant-Catholic relations, religious identity and group life, location and mobility in the class structure, and political participation. Cultural patterns or life styles are not of direct concern here as they were in the part on national origin groups, because cultural traits of white Protestants, as has been frequently stated, are at least ideally coextensive with American culture—a topic clearly exceeding the limits of this book.

For much of American history, Protestantism has been formally or informally the nation's established religion. The time of greatest Protestant religious influence was the last half of the nineteenth century, though it would be difficult to say when Protestants as such have exerted the most influence; today's economic elite are largely Protestant but are not much concerned with spreading Protestant religious influences or Protestant power for its own sake. Since the nineteenth century, the balance of religious influence has been shifting, leaving white Protestants without the near total hegemony they had enjoyed. The rise of Protestantism into prominence; its defense through anti-Catholicism, Anglo-Saxonism, and immigration restriction; and its decline as a total influence shall be the topics of concern in the present chapter.

PROTESTANT AMERICA

Protestant America and American Protestants

Although 98 per cent of all colonial congregations were Protestant, a mere 5 per cent of the colonial population were church members.[1] As Lipset has pointed out, church membership in the colonial period was demanding and difficult.[2] In order to maintain church membership, a person was expected to attend several services each week, participate regularly in formal religious classes, live a life strictly consistent with the tenets of the faith, and dutifully perform frequent mission and benevolent work. The demands on a church member's time and financial resources simply excluded the majority of people from membership. Organized churches were, of course, unavailable to many people on the frontier. Nevertheless, the number of Protestant church attenders was probably several times the number of church members. Further, the number of self-identifying Protestants was probably two or three times the number of church attenders.

[1] Winthrop S. Hudson, *American Protestantism* (Chicago: University of Chicago Press, 1961), p. 4.
[2] Seymour M. Lipset, *The First New Nation* (New York: Basic Books, Inc., 1963), p. 147.

The actual number of self-identifying Protestants in colonial times is impossible to ascertain. Hudson has argued that "The vast majority of Americans even when not actual communicants, regarded themselves as 'adherents of one church or another.' " [3] Though the majority of colonial Americans may have identified themselves with a church, Littell has contended that the Protestant churches did not command the "loyalty or willing support" of the vast majority of the population. Early America, according to Littell, was "a heathen nation—one of the most needy mission fields in the world." [4]

Whatever might have been the extent of religious identity and participation, the people of colonial America were almost entirely Protestant in background. Suffice it to say that if any religion at all shaped the attitudes and behavior of early Americans and dominated early American institutions—consciously or unconsciously—it was Protestanism. As Alexis de Tocqueville observed in 1831, "There is no country in the world where the Christian religion retains a greater influence over the souls of men than in America." [5]

As de Tocqueville wrote, a large majority of the nation's 13 million persons in all likelihood identified themselves with some Protestant denomination. Religious feeling and identity at the time probably reflected to a large degree the influence of revivalism, which swept the country in the early nineteenth century. If colonial Americans were in fact more heathen than Protestant, mass evangelism provoked their descendants into a frenzy of religious activity that was to make the Protestant church singularly influential for generations to come. Evangelistic fervor, camp meetings, and nondenominational religious societies such as the American Bible Society, American Sunday School Union, American Tract Society, and American Home Missionary Society permeated the country and claimed various degrees of religious commitment from a large majority of the Protestant population. The religious successes of the time were partially solidified by the offering of church membership to the ordinary citizen, on a more voluntary basis; the organizing of frontier congregations; covering of the mission field with scores of (largely untrained) clergymen; and the establishment of dozens of church colleges and seminaries in which to train additional ministers. Mass organizational tactics such as these culminated in high growth rates for the Baptist and Methodist churches. Presbyterians also benefited, but to a lesser

[3] Hudson, *American Protestantism*, p. 110.
[4] Franklin H. Littell, *From State Church to Pluralism* (Garden City, N.Y.: Doubleday & Company, Inc., 1962), p. 29.
[5] *Democracy in America*, Vol. I (New York: Harper & Row, Publishers, 1954), p. 314.

degree. A more gradual growth characterized the reserved and traditional Congregational, Episcopalian, Lutheran, and Reformed churches.

Entering the last half of the nineteenth century, Protestants and their churches approached the high level of influence in American society that they were to maintain for over fifty years. A small, but rapidly growing, Catholic minority served only to heighten Protestant consciousness and activity.

ANTI-CATHOLIC NATIVISM

However, as early as the 1840's many Protestants were fully aware of impending Catholic strength. The response was various forms of nativism, that is, the belief that America is for "Americans" (native-born Anglo-Saxons and Protestants) and foreigners are subversive agents of other races, religions, and ways of life. As Higham has stressed, American nativism has not been a unidimensional phenomenon, but rather a complex of attitudes and behaviors with a number of possible outlets.[6] Three of the most prominent varieties of American nativism have been, in Higham's terminology, anti-radical, anti-Catholic, and Anglo-Saxon nativism. The latter two types have been closely related and obviously have special relevance to the study of white Protestants. Non-Protestants would not ordinarily be involved in anti-Catholic nativism or in a position to be proponents of Anglo-Saxon nativism. In combination, anti-Catholicism and Anglo-Saxonism were to be powerful forces behind the success of immigration restriction later on in the early twentieth century.

American Catholics have with varying degrees of intensity always encountered the open opposition of many white Protestants. Throughout much of American history, anti-Catholicism has not been particularly vicious; the anti-Catholic animus, however, has periodically erupted with great force. Between periods of relative calm and outbursts of enmity, white Protestants have typically viewed Catholics with palpable suspicion punctuated by fear. They have been suspicious of papal machinations against the democratic institutions of Protestant America and fearful of Catholic control in their cities, states, and nation. Catholics, though hardly deserving of Protestant allegations, have not in fact been a docile minority. Catholics have responded to Protestant threats and rejection with provocative recalcitrance. In Kane's words,

> Probably no other religious group in the United States has ever suffered such severe prejudice and discrimination as Catholics, at least not since

[6] For a thorough discussion of nativism in American history, see John Higham, *Strangers in the Land* (New York: Atheneum Books, 1965).

the colonial period. On the other hand, probably no other religious group in the United States, Protestants excepted, ever displayed such a militancy and belligerency.[7]

Anti-Catholicism in colonial times was manifest primarily in the area of civil and religious rights.[8] Only in Rhode Island could a colonial Catholic enjoy full civil and religious rights according to charter, decrees, and laws of the land. In Pennsylvania, where there were a number of Catholic churches, Catholics were permitted freedom of worship and enjoyed voting rights, but despite Quaker support were excluded from public office. In the other colonies, including Catholic Maryland, Catholics were categorically second-class citizens—variously disfranchised, barred from public office, repressed, banished, and even excluded (as in Georgia according to the charter of 1732). The Congregational and Anglican establishments oppressed Roman Catholics throughout most of the colonial period.

Hatred of Catholics by colonial Americans was not an indigenous growth. It had been transplanted from northern Europe where strong anti-Catholic sentiments had flourished since the Reformation. The handful of Catholics confronting colonial Americans were scarcely enough to create zealous religious animosities. (In the nineteenth century, however, American Protestants developed an anti-Catholic rationale of their own, although it was continually fed by Protestant immigration from northern Europe.)

Anti-Catholic feelings in America reached a low point in the post-Revolutionary period. As of 1807, a mere 100 Catholic churches dotted the nation's landscape.[9] Much more important than religious conflict was the imposing task of building a new nation: the Crown seemed a more immediate menace than the Pope. Yet, the new constitutions of many of the states contained discriminatory clauses against Catholics. By the 1820's, most of these antidemocratic statutes had been deleted, fortunately before Catholics entered the country by hundreds of thousands. Had such an inundation of Catholics been predicted, democratic impulses might not have been so successful in erasing discriminatory clauses such as those that excluded Catholics from public office. Not long after the repeal of that law, for example, frightened Protestant nativists were agitating for the reinstatement of similar discriminatory legislation.

[7] John J. Kane, *Catholic-Protestant Conflicts in America* (Chicago: Henry Regnery Co., 1955), p. 43.

[8] For summaries of anti-Catholicism in the colonial period, see Ray Allen Billington, *The Protestant Crusade 1800–1860* (Chicago: Quadrangle Books, Inc., 1964), pp. 1–31; and Littell, *From State Church to Pluralism*, Chap. 1.

[9] Edwin S. Gaustad, *Historical Atlas of Religion in America* (New York: Harper & Row, Publishers, 1962), p. 43.

The Nineteenth Century

As impoverished Irish Catholics started to accumulate in New England communities in the 1830's and 1840's, the native pulse began to sound a marked anti-Catholic beat. In Kane's words, "It was the immigration of poverty-stricken, ignorant and anti-Protestant Irishmen fleeing Ireland's greatest famine that revived and intensified religious prejudices." [10] To natives, Catholic immigrants appeared as pawns of the papacy involved in a plot to subvert American liberty, patriotism, education, democracy, morality, and above all, Protestantism. The Irish impressed all as despicably poor and dirty; class differences exacerbated religious dislike. Urban problems appeared to be directly proportionate to the number of Catholics in the population. The need for concerted Protestant action was "self-evident." Not only were there historic Protestant traditions to protect as in the colonial period, but more important, a new distinctly "American" way of life had to be preserved.

Playing major roles in the Protestant effort to contain Catholics and curb Catholic influence was a flotsam of secret societies (such as the Order of the Star Spangled Banner), which have been collectively designated in history as the Know-Nothing movement. Know-Nothingism, which culminated politically in the American or Know-Nothing Party, experienced brief but notable success in the 1850's.[11] Although Know-Nothings talked a great deal about American magnificence, the main adhesive for the national party was negative, namely, anti-Catholicism. As Billington has pointed out, "Only one force held members of the Know-Nothing party together, and that was their hatred for the Catholic Church." [12] As an indication of the party's anti-Catholic appeal, its greatest electoral successes were in the increasingly Catholic state of Massachusetts. Intimidation, violence, and death accompanied many Know-Nothing political campaigns. Nationally, Know-Nothing candidate Millard Fillmore polled 25 per cent of the vote in the 1856 Presidential election. The party disintegrated shortly thereafter as regional bitterness and war temporarily displaced religious conflict as a primary national problem.

Other antebellum organizations that were openly anti-Catholic and variously linked to Know-Nothingism were the Protestant Reformation Society (1836), the American Protestant Union (1841, headed by Samuel F. B. Morse), the American Protestant Association (1842), and

[10] Kane, "Catholic-Protestant Conflicts in America," p. 35.
[11] See Wallace D. Farnham, "The 'Religious Issue' in American Politics: An Historical Commentary," *Queens Quarterly*, LXVIII (Spring, 1961), 47–65, for a summary of Protestant-Catholic political tensions in American history.
[12] Billington, *The Protestant Crusade*, p. 387.

the American and Foreign Christian Union (1848).[13] Numerous local anti-Catholic groups, some linked to national organizations and some independent, contributed their support to the national Protestant effort. In addition, Protestant religious societies such as the American Home Missionary Society, American Tract Society, American Sunday School Union, and American Bible Society waged war against Catholics as well as against irreligion. Early workingmen's organizations, such as the Order of United Americans (1844), also had an anti-Catholic bent as well as patriotic, protective, and benevolent purposes.

Not long after the Civil War, anti-Catholic feelings were on the upswing once more. Anti-Catholic organizations formed anew. As noted previously, the Scotch-Irish were natural candidates for anti-Catholic movements. As Higham has remarked, "Few Americans hated the Catholic Irish more than did the Protestant Irish." [14] Thus, Scotch-Irish were solidly represented, along with other Britishers, in the American Protestant Association. The major Scotch-Irish organization, however, was the bellicose Loyal Orange Institution, which was transplanted from Great Britain about 1870.

The 1880's marked a sharp upsurge in the postbellum trend of anti-Catholic activity, and the decade hatched a host of nativist groups with titles confirming their patriotism—Red, White, and Blue; United Order of Native Americans; American Patriotic League; and Loyal Men of American Liberty, to name a few. The American Protective Association, founded in 1887 in Clinton, Iowa, had mainly political aims and centered its strength in the Midwest. By the mid-1890's the APA (not to be confused with the American Protestant Association) had mobilized a million members. Although the APA failed to match the Know-Nothings' achievements at the polls, it did control the balance of power in many local elections for a brief period of time. Much Scandinavian and German support in the Midwest defected as the APA assumed an increasingly antiforeign posture.

In addition to nativistic organizations, a plethora of anti-Catholic books, magazines, and pamphlets appeared and gained wide circulation. Some of these publications were organs of nativistic societies; others were independently written fulminations of hate, derision, and false allegation. The titles of anti-Catholic periodicals of the time confirm their focus on religion: *The Reformation Advocate, The Anti-Romanist,* and *The American Protestant Vindicator,* to note a few. Books such as *Master Key to Popery; Female Convents: Secrets of Nunneries Disclosed;* and *Jesuit Juggling: Forty Popish Frauds Detected and Disclosed* focused on

13 See *ibid.* for a discussion of many of these groups.
14 Higham, *Strangers in the Land,* p. 61.

Catholic "immorality." The most notorious of the "immorality" works was *Awful Disclosure of the Hôtel Dieu Nunnery of Montreal,* a book proven to be a total fabrication but considered credible by many persons at the time. The objectives of *Awful Disclosure* and other Protestant propaganda were to discredit Catholicism as a religion, reduce Catholic influence, and obstruct Catholic immigration. Anti-Catholic literature routinely raised the specter of a Roman "takeover."

Public school textbooks were sometimes blatantly anti-Catholic. A passage from a text used for 20 years in Philadelphia's primary schools read:

> To this day they [the Irish] consider Saint Patrick as in Heaven, watching over the interests of Ireland. They pray to him and to do him honor, set apart one day in the year for going to church, drinking whisky and breaking each other's heads with clubs.[15]

Beyond organizational strategies and malicious literature, violence was occasionally employed as a tactic of control. Anti-Catholic riots and arson broke out in Boston, New York, and Philadelphia. Violence was almost entirely directed toward Irish Catholics, whereas German Catholics were usually spared physical attack. Church and home burnings, beatings, and pitched battles between Protestants (mainly Orangemen) and Irish Catholics scar the history of religious relations in nineteenth-century America.

The Twentieth Century

Protestant-Catholic tensions subsided somewhat from the relatively high late nineteenth century level as the nation entered the twentieth century, world politics, and war. However, Protestant-Catholic hostilities, never close to being dead, flared to another high point in the early twenties as the country returned to peace and isolationism. As in the previous century, the concerns of the later anti-Catholics were grounded in nativistic assumptions regarding the subversive character of the Catholic church. The chief difference between nineteenth- and twentieth-century anti-Catholicism may be found in the fact that nineteenth-century anti-Catholics were more often urban dwellers, whereas those of the twentieth century were (and still are) more often rural folk.

One of the largest nativistic organizations of the twenties was the revived Ku Klux Klan. Organized in 1915, it counted approximately 3 million members by 1923. Most of its members resided in small towns across the Midwest and South. The Klan was weakest in the large cities,

15 John J. Kane, "Protestant-Catholic Tensions," *American Sociological Review,* LI (October, 1951), 664.

where, of course, the majority of Catholics lived. The exhortation of an Imperial Wizard of the Klan summed up the feelings of many white Protestants of his day:

> America was Protestant from birth. She must remain Protestant, if the Nordic stock is to finish its destiny. We of the old stock Americans could not work . . . if we become priest-ridden, if we had to submit our consciences and limit our activities and suppress our thoughts at the command of any man, much less a man sitting upon Seven Hills thousands of miles away. This we will not permit. Rome shall not rule us. Protestantism must be supreme. . . .[16]

To be sure, the Klan had vociferous opponents among the Protestant population itself. Klan activities were often assailed by angry anti-Klan mobs, which included Protestants and Catholics alike. Eventually, Klan anti-Catholic activity was largely discredited and disgraced. Although today's Klan has turned its main concerns toward black Americans, there remain Klan garments in the cedar chests of many Protestant homes as reminders of an earlier, cruder form of anti-Catholicism.

Early twentieth-century Americans, like those of the nineteenth century, had access to a wide selection of anti-Catholic journalistic diatribes. One of the most popular pieces of nativistic reading was *The Menace,* a periodical founded by W. F. Phelps of the Missouri Ozarks. In 1915, *The Menace* enjoyed a rather staggering circulation of 15 million.[17] Madison Grant's *The Passing of the Great Race* incited religious as well as racial bigotry. Sales of Grant's book were moderate after its 1916 publication date, but rose sharply during the nativistic revival of the early twenties.

With the country in dire economic peril in the thirties and at war in the forties, Protestants were too preoccupied to contemplate seriously the dangers of Catholicism. At mid-century, however, Protestant-Catholic altercations were again on the increase.[18] As an indication of this point, Kane has noted that the number of editorials, articles, and letters appearing in *The Christian Century* (a nondenominatinal Protestant weekly) critical of Catholicism rose from 15 in 1939 to 42 in 1949. Similarly, the number of pieces critical of Protestantism appearing in the Catholic magazine *America* (a Society of Jesus publication) also increased, though not nearly as sharply. Focal points of Protestant concern, according to Kane, have been rising Catholic influence in sociopolitical matters, as heralded by the election of Catholic officials, federal aid to education and the whole issue of the separation of church and state, censorship of the

[16] Peter H. Odegaard, ed., *Religion and Politics* (Englewood, N.J.: Oceana Publications, Inc., 1960), p. 45.

[17] Higham, *Strangers in the Land,* p. 184.

[18] Kane, "Protestant-Catholic Tensions," pp. 663–72.

media, and obstruction of social legislation opposed to Catholic dogma such as divorce, abortion, and birth control laws.

Anti-Catholicism has certainly not recovered its traditionally direct and overt style, but distrust, dislike, and abhorrence of Catholicism continues among substantial numbers of white Protestants, especially within the older generations. As Odegaard has evaluated prevailing sentiment, "The real indictment against the Roman Church is that it is fundamentally and irredeemably, in its leadership, in politics, in thought, and largely in membership, actually and actively alien, un-American and usually anti-American. The old stock Americans . . . see in the Roman Church today the chief leader of alienism, and the most dangerous alien power with a foothold inside our boundaries." [19] Many Protestants, from working people to intelligentsia, are more or less apprehensive over the "Catholic hierarchy of authority," "the monolithic structure of the Catholic Church," "Catholic authoritarianism," and "Catholic immorality." [20] Occasionally there is a trace of envy in the tone of Protestant complaints regarding the latter "problem" as illustrated by the remark of a New England Protestant: "Catholics have a comfortable, easy religion. All the Catholics have to do is to follow the forms, go to confessions, go to Mass, pay the priest, and all their sins are erased and they can start over. They can drink, gamble, run after women, cuss all they like." [21] As far as the "monolithic structure" problem is concerned, to the extent that such a structure has ever existed in America it is crumbling, but whether Protestants are fully aware of this decline of authority is another question. In all likelihood, a very substantial number of Protestants still consider Catholicism a "chief leader of alienism," probably more than consider Catholicism one of "three big sub-communities all equally American." [22]

Richard Means has raised the question regarding the extent of *anti-Protestant* sentiment in the American population.[23] As Means correctly observes, "In the voluminous studies of religious prejudice there is little sociological analysis of anti-Protestantism. . . ." The obvious explanation for the dearth of scholarly comment on anti-Protestant prejudice is the very absence of significant specifically Protestant prejudice.

---

[19] Odegaard, *Religion and Politics,* pp. 42–43.

[20] See Robert McAfee Brown, "Types of Anti-Catholicism," *Commonweal,* LXIII (November 25, 1955), 193–96.

[21] Kenneth Underwood, *Protestant and Catholic* (Boston: Beacon Press, 1957), p. 90.

[22] Will Herberg, *Protestant-Catholic-Jew* (Garden City, N.Y.: Doubleday & Company, Inc., 1960), p. 39.

[23] Richard L. Means, "Anti-Protestant Prejudice," *The Christian Century,* LXXVIII (August 16, 1961), 979–80.

Sociologists rarely conduct a study if they are fairly sure of insignificant results before they begin. As Herberg has pointed out, "The Anglo-Saxon Protestant type remains the ideal to the vast majority of Americans and the ideal self-image of even non-Protestants tends to be Anglo-American."[24] Few people are going to harbor strong prejudices against their own cultural ideal and against the source of their own ideal self-image. However, Means wisely cautions us against the tendency to equate all prejudice, discrimination, narrow-mindedness, and bigotry with the WASP. We might also remember that Protestantism has a history of progressive social action and reform to parallel a history of prejudice and discrimination.[25]

ANGLO-SAXONISM AND IMMIGRATION RESTRICTION

The step from anti-Catholic nativism to the notion of Anglo-Saxon supremacy (or vice versa) is logical and short. Contrary to some beliefs Anglo-Saxonism in America (or in Great Britain) did not originally include the notion of *racial* or genetic supremacy of British peoples.[26] Rather, the emphasis was on the unique moral and intellectual capacity of Anglo-Saxons for self-control and self-government (ethnocentrism), characteristics not then considered to be directly related to genetic and physical differences as they were to be later (racism).[27] Antebellum Anglo-Saxonism thus was not directed toward other ethnic groups, but simply exalted the superior institutions of Anglo-Saxon culture.

Because a person's culture (as opposed to his genetic inheritance) may be altered, early Anglo-Saxonists were confident in the assimilative potential of the core society. Many early champions of Anglo-Saxonism were ardent libertarians and democrats; they were often repulsed by the crude anti-Catholicism of the antebellum period. Anglo-Saxonists of the day believed these foreigners would soon be assimilated to American institutions and life styles.[28]

However, the optimism regarding the assimilative powers of Anglo-

---

[24] Herberg, *Protestant-Catholic-Jew,* p. 20.

[25] On black-white Protestant relations, see David M. Reimers, *White Protestantism and the Negro* (New York: Oxford University Press, Inc., 1965); and Joseph C. Hough, Jr., *Black Power and White Protestants* (New York: Oxford University Press, Inc., 1968).

[26] Higham, *Strangers in the Land,* esp. Chap. 6.

[27] For a discussion of the distinction between ethnocentrism and racism, see Pierre van den Berghe, *Race and Racism* (New York: John Wiley & Sons, Inc., 1967), pp. 9–25.

[28] See Barbara Miller Solomon, *Ancestors and Immigrants* (New York: John Wiley & Sons, Inc., 1965).

Saxon America began to fade in the latter part of the nineteenth century as it became increasingly evident that large numbers of immigrants and their descendants were not metamorphosing into paragons of Anglo-Saxonism. Those seeking an explanation began to postulate a link between genetics and the "un-American" behavior of the Irish Catholics and other foreign stock. The reason why non-Anglo-Saxons were not being satisfactorily assimilated became obvious: they were genetically incapable of adopting the Anglo-Saxon way of life. Thus, Anglo-Saxon ethnocentrism (belief in superior culture) was transformed into Anglo-Saxon racism (belief in superior culture *because of* superior genes). Non-Anglo-Saxons were now considered inherently inferior, incapable of self-determination and orderly social life, and unassimilable. Despite their belief in the Darwinian idea of the inevitability of the survival of the fittest, the exponents of Anglo-Saxon superiority decided shortly before the turn of the century that it would be prudent to guarantee the inevitable by halting the unrestricted flow of immigrants.

Anglo-Saxonists originally considered all non-British immigrants in similar terms. The increased proportions of southern and eastern Europeans among the more recent immigrants and the labeling of this group as "new" and northern Europeans as "old" generally did not occur until around the turn of the century. The status of Protestant Germans and Scandinavians vis-à-vis Anglo-Saxons had been somewhat problematic anyway, since most seemed similar in culture to Americans and capable of Americanization. Certain social scientists of the day helped to clarify the "old-new" distinction by demonstrating to their own and many others' satisfaction that the new immigrants (southern and eastern Europeans) were inferior mentally and physically, being predisposed to types of deviant behavior. For example, sociologist Kimball Young, after examining World War I army intelligence tests and discovering that British, German, Dutch, and Scandinavian foreign-born scored higher than the Irish, Russian, Italian, and Polish, maintained that "If the mentality of the South Europeans who are flooding this country is typified by the mentality of the groups studied by the writer and others, the problem of future standard of living, high grade of citizenship, and cultural progress is serious." [29] A popular journal of the period, appealing to "scientific" authorities, asserted that "It is clear... that the South Italians, Poles, and Russians... represent an extremely inferior racial contribution, measured by existing American standards." [30]

[29] Kimball Young, "Intelligence Tests of Certain Immigrant Groups," *Scientific Monthly*, XV (November, 1922), 430.

[30] "Measuring the Mentalities in our Melting Pot," *Literary Digest*, LXXVII (June, 1923), 27.

Germans and Scandinavians were generally accepted as members of the great Anglo-Saxon race. As an early physician once pointed out concerning all northern Europeans (Irish excluded):

> These northern peoples surpass all others in vigor, energy, and self-control; they are aristocratic in nature, domineering, oppressive to inferior races; but they are liberty loving, have an innate love for law and order, and are above all other races capable of self-government; and it is certainly not accidental that all the branches of this race are Protestants.[31]

For those who had any doubts, an article by an early essayist entitled "Are We Still Anglo-Saxon?" attempted to dispel them by declaring, "I'm glad to believe that an Anglo-Celtic-Germanic-Scandinavian stock will be as Anglo-Saxon as the oldest-minded of us old settlers can desire." [32] Catholic Celts, however, were excluded, as even the Immigration Restriction League—which began with an Irish Catholic on the executive committee—later formed alliances with anti-Catholic societies.

Voicing strong opposition to Anglo-Saxonist social scientists such as Edward A. Ross, John R. Commons, Franklin Giddings, and Richard Mayo Smith were a number of progressives, among them William James, Charles Beard, Charles Horton Cooley, John Dewey, and Thorsten Veblen. As Baltzell has noted, nearly all the progressives (Veblen of the above list excepted) were reared in old-stock Protestant families. [33] Nor did all of the upper class endorse the Anglo-Saxon theories of Henry Adams, Madison Grant, and their ilk; there were also liberal aristocrats such as Charles W. Eliot, Theodore Roosevelt, and Woodrow Wilson.

Nevertheless, the combined forces of urban Anglo-Saxons, rural anti-Catholics, and all of the anti-foreign and anti-radical persons in the interstices provided a sufficient base for passage of the 1924 Immigration Act that was to end open immigration by 1929. The prominent role played by Anglo-Saxonism in immigration restriction was clearly stated by Solomon when she wrote, "The intent was clear: to preserve the Teutonic composition of the American people in its present proportions so that the descendants of the foreign-born would never dominate the Yankees." [34] Hence, after 1929 total immigration was to be 150,000 with obvious discrimination against peoples from southern and eastern Europe. Restrictionist legislation, however, came too late. The heavy non-Protestant immigration of the late nineteenth and early twentieth centuries had assured a pluralistic society for America's future.

[31] Dr. Albert Allemann, "Immigration and the Future American Race," *The Popular Scientific Monthly*, LXXV (December, 1909), 588.
[32] *Literary Digest*, LXXIV (September 9, 1922), 32.
[33] Baltzell, *The Protestant Establishment*, pp. 143–53, 183–87.
[34] Solomon, *Ancestors and Immigrants*, p. 205.

AMERICAN PROTESTANTS

Thus, in response to the question, "What is your religion?" 57 per cent of those asked by the 1957 religious census were white Protestants.[35] Furthermore, as Petersen has pointed out, the census question, "What is your religion?" put considerable pressure on people to name some religion; in contrast, a Gallup survey posed the question on religious preference more neutrally by asking, "Have you a religion?" and found that only about half of white persons reported Protestantism.[36] Evidently, there are a number of persons whose religious identity is very weak, but when pressured a little, are willing to call themselves Protestants. That such is the case is confirmed by the fact that the census religious survey reported only 4 per cent of the population as having no religion or a fourth religion, whereas the "no pressure" Gallup survey found 16 per cent in this residual group.[37] White Protestant *church members* now constitute less than one-third of the nation's population and weekly Protestant church attenders about one-sixth.

White Protestants have long ceased to be a majority and no longer enjoy even a plurality in several of the nation's largest metropolitan areas. In the central cities, white Protestants may comprise only a small minority of the population. In many suburbs and elsewhere outside the East, however, white Protestants hold large numerical advantages. White Protestants possess two-thirds majorities over-all in the north central, southern, and western United States. The suburban and rural strengths of white Protestantism tend to be reflected in the social and political ideologies of these areas.

Owing to their entrenched social and economic position and disproportionate state and national political power made possible by a rural and small-town base, white Protestants have manged to perpetuate an image of supremacy and self-confidence until quite recently. Now, however, Protestants are being forced to consider relinquishing unilateral control over national political, economic, and status structures. And although Protestants still comprise the large majority of the upper middle class and exercise considerable control over its most central institutions,

[35] U.S. Bureau of the Census, "Religion Reported by the Civilian Population of the U.S.: March 1957," *Current Population Reports,* Series P-20, Number 79 (Washington, D.C.: U.S. Government Printing Office, February 2, 1958). The religious statistics in this section are all taken from this source unless otherwise indicated.

[36] William Petersen, "Religious Statistics in the United States," *Journal for the Scientific Study of Religion,* I (April, 1962), 165–78.

[37] Glenn M. Vernon has recently pointed out the need for research on individuals who have counted themselves out of any religious group. See his "The Religious 'Nones': A Neglected Category," *Journal for the Scientific Study of Religion,* VII (Fall, 1968), 219–29.

here, too, Protestants are facing increasing numbers of non-white, non-Protestant persons and interests.

Among the foremost problems facing white Protestants today, then, is that of coming to terms with new ethnic realities. Owing to the mental as well as physical isolation of many white Protestants, they often only vaguely sense the new national ethnoreligious balance. America is "post-Protestant" numerically, socially, politically, and economically, but this obviously does not mean that Protestants are no longer a very powerful and influential group, or that American ideas and culture are no longer preeminently Anglo-Saxon Protestant. However, the result of an altered ethnic balance within the mainstream of American life and an inadequate recognition of this alteration among white Protestants may well be increasing conflict among white Protestants and other groups, although regional and ethnic disputes are difficult to distinguish. "That men do not move over graciously," O'Dea has warned, "is one of the few undeniable generalizations from history." [38]

In addition to defending traditional areas of hegemony, white Protestants may respond to increased pluralism with a heightened sense of community and cooperation. At a time when American institutions served mainly white Protestants, self-conscious Protestant identity, cooperation, and community could hardly be expected. As more Protestants realize that local and national institutions can no longer be mere extensions of their own ethnic group, self-conscious Protestant community may become more marked. As Herberg has contended, "A growing number of Protestants . . . are coming to recognize the hard facts of the situation, and are proceeding, though haltingly, to build up their own Protestant communal institutions. . . ." [39] The question of white Protestant community will be our concern in the next two chapters.

SUMMARY

Although formal religion was practiced by only a small minority of early Americans, the Protestant churches exercised a major influence in the colonies, and nearly all the settlers came from Protestant countries. Evangelical religion in the nineteenth century stirred the masses to greater religious commitment and Protestant churches and religious organizations dominated much of the American social landscape.

[38] Thomas F. O'Dea, "The Missing Dialogue," in *Facing Protestant-Catholic Tensions*, ed. Wayne Cowan (New York: The Association Press, 1960), pp. 57–58.

[39] Will Herberg, "Religious Group Conflict in America," in *Religion and Social Conflict*, eds. Robert Lee and Martin E. Marty (New York: Oxford University Press, Inc., 1964), p. 151.

Increased Roman Catholic immigration gave rise to waves of anti-Catholic sentiment and activity in the 1840's, 1880's, and 1920's. Growing racial self-awareness among many Anglo-Saxons provided a strong impetus to immigration restriction in the 1920's but passage of such legislation came too late to prevent major ethnic realignments.

CHAPTER NINE

Throughout the nineteenth century and the first part of the twentieth century the various Protestant national origin groups maintained separate social communities based on common tradition and identity. These social networks were, in effect, bounded by religious belief as well as national origin. Indeed, the church was often the chief locus of social life in the national origin communities. The English, Scottish, and Scotch-Irish, and Welsh were the first foreign peoples to be absorbed socially into the Anglo-Saxon Protestant core society as it had been formed in the colonial period. In the second quarter of the twentieth century, large segments of the non-British Protestant groups—Swedes, Norwegians, Danes, Finns, Germans, and Dutch—merged with one another and with the Anglo-American group. The outcome of the assimilation of most members of Protestant national origin groups has been the development of an inclusive religious subsociety.

White Protestant Community: Cliques and Organizations

Of the several processes of assimilation, three have particular relevance for the evaluation of white Protestant community: group life, marriage patterns, and religious identification. If a white Protestant prefers coreligionists for close friends, supports religious and secular Protestant organizations, selects a Protestant spouse and opposes intermarriage, and holds a definite Protestant identification, then we should assume this person to be strongly oriented toward the religious community. Conversely, if a person participates in religiously mixed cliques, eschews the church and joins mixed organizations, intermarries and does not oppose intermarriage, and only weakly identifies with his religion, he should be considered outside the white Protestant community. As with any religious or ethnic group, the division among Protestants may be described as *community* versus *assimilation*. Many white Protestants are near the communal end; others participate in religiously mixed groups; the remainder are distributed at various points along an intervening continuum. Our main concern in this chapter and the next is to assess, on the basis of available evidence, the degree of communal participation among white Protestants subsequent to the decline of the national origin group.

A second question of related interest has to do with the *location* of white Protestant communal strength; that is, is religious community stronger in the middle class or the working class? Are older Protestants more communally directed than younger ones? Does communal strength center in particular denominations more than in others? Is communal strength greater in places where white Protestants are the majority or where they are the minority?

PRIMARY GROUP LIFE:
"BIRDS OF A FEATHER..."

A number of empirical inquiries into white Protestant community suggest that Protestants have been and continue to be strongly influenced by the religious factor in primary social interaction. Elin Anderson observed that Burlington, Vermont in the 1930's was separated into "two main camps of Catholicism and Protestantism, each with its own social stratification along economic lines." [1] A few years later, King learned that of 263 Protestant clique memberships in a Connecticut town, 61 per cent were in homogeneous Protestant cliques and another 16 per cent in cliques with a Protestant majority. [2] Of the 189 total clique memberships held by Catholics, 60 per cent were in homogeneous Catholic cliques and an additional 10 per cent in Catholic-majority cliques. Underwood's research in "Paper City" in the late 1940's again revealed sharp Protestant-Catholic social divisions. [3] Although many "Paper City" Protestants and Catholics occupied the same socioeconomic position, visiting and courtship behavior reflected a religious cleavage at each class level. The upper class consisted of a group of self-conscious Yankee families clustered in their own exclusive social institutions.

More recently, Lenski reported that nearly two-fifths of Detroit white Protestants counted all or nearly all their close friends from among members of their own religious group, and Catholics did the same. [4] Later Detroit area data (1966) analyzed by Laumann also indicated that a large percentage of white Protestants' three closest friends were members of their own denomination; the percentage exceeded what one would expect by chance by, for example, about 3 times for Lutherans and Methodists

[1] Elin Anderson, *We Americans* (Cambridge, Mass.: Harvard University Press, 1938).

[2] C. Wendell King, "Branford Center: A Community Study in Social Cleavage" (doctoral dissertation, Yale University, 1943), p. 171.

[3] Kenneth Underwood, *Protestant and Catholic* (Boston: Beacon Press, 1957), p. 191.

[4] Gerhard Lenski, *The Religious Factor* (Garden City, N.Y.: Doubleday & Company, Inc., 1963), p. 39.

and 33 times for Congregationalists.[5] In a similar vein, Wilensky and Ladinsky noted that a majority in largely Protestant samples of lawyers and engineers found all of three closest friends among other Protestants; in contrast, only a small minority of the lawyers and engineers counted three closest friends among persons of their own profession.[6] Two Midwestern communities studied by Schroeder and Obenhaus, one heavily Protestant and the other Catholic, were both scored by socioreligious divisions.[7]

Studies of Protestant friendship networks suggest that religious conservatives tend more often than religious liberals to limit their close friends to members of their own *congregations*. For example, Dynes discovered that Protestants with fundamentalistic orientations were much more likely to find friends within their own congregation than were liberal Protestants.[8] Similarly, Stark and Glock's research on a California sample disclosed that two-thirds of the sectarians and almost half the Baptists reported that at least three of their five best friends were members of their own congregation; about a quarter of the Methodists and Lutherans did so.[9] Over a third of the Catholics fell into this category. As a further refinement, differences in community orientation among white Protestants exist *within* given congregations. In a study of Lutherans, Demerath found that more manual workers than non-manual workers, more older persons than younger persons, and more females than males reported close friends within their own congregations.[10]

That religious conservatives, blue-collar workers, older persons, and females report more close friends within their own congregation than their status opposites should not be interpreted to mean that the former persons are necessarily more communally oriented than the status opposites when considered in the context of the larger Protestant group. Liberals, white-collar workers, younger people, and men are in most ways more mobile individuals and hence make more friends outside of their own church. These friends, of course, may also be Protestant. That

[5] Edward O. Laumann, "The Social Structure of Religious and Ethnoreligious Groups in a Metropolitan Community," *American Sociological Review*, XXXIV (April, 1969), 182–97.

[6] Harold L. Wilensky and Jack Ladinsky, "From Religious Community to Occupational Group: Structural Assimilation Among Professors, Lawyers, and Engineers," *American Sociological Review*, XXXII (August, 1967), 546–47.

[7] W. Widick Schroeder and Victor Obenhaus, *Religion in American Culture* (New York: The Free Press, 1964), pp. 86–87.

[8] Russell R. Dynes, "The Consequences of Sectarianism for Social Participation," *Social Forces*, XXXV (May, 1957), 331–34.

[9] Rodney Stark and Charles Y. Glock, *American Piety: The Nature of Religious Commitment* (Berkeley: University of California Press, 1968), p. 166.

[10] N. J. Demerath III, *Social Class in American Protestantism* (Chicago: Rand McNally & Co., 1965), pp. 88, 102.

this is indeed the case is suggested in data I gathered on "Protestant City" and "Catholic City" (See Appendix B for discussion of the samples, one of which is Mormon). These data indicate that if one considers the larger Protestant group as the unit of friendship community instead of

TABLE 9–1

NUMBER OF THREE CLOSEST FRIENDS OF OWN RELIGION
OF PROTESTANTS, CATHOLICS, AND MORMONS, BY SEX

Friends of Own Religion	Protestants in Protestant City		Protestants in Catholic City		Catholics in Protestant City		Catholics in Catholic City		Mormons in Mormon City	
	Respon-dents	Wives [a]	Respon-dents	Wives	Respon-dents	Wives	Respon-dents	Wives	Respon-dents	Wives
3 of 3	58%	63%	41%	40%	17%	16%	45%	57%	80%	81%
2 of 3	35	31	35	45	58	56	37	32	13	16
1 or 0 of 3	7	6	23	15	25	28	18	11	7	3
Total N's	(165)	(159)	(74)	(73)	(43)	(43)	(121)	(113)	(161)	(157)

[a] As reported by respondents.

TABLE 9–2

PERCENTAGE OF PROTESTANTS, CATHOLICS, AND MORMONS
REPORTING THREE OF THREE CLOSEST FRIENDS OF OWN RELIGION,
BY OCCUPATION

Group	White-Collar Workers	Blue-Collar Workers	Statistical Significance (d.f. = 1)
Protestants PC	58(N = 95)	56(N = 68)	No
Protestants CC	43(N = 61)	a	a
Catholics CC	44(N = 77)	45(N = 44)	No
Mormons MC	79(N = 101)	79(N = 52)	No

a Too few cases for analysis. Also too few cases for Protestant City Catholics.

TABLE 9–3

PERCENTAGE OF PROTESTANTS, CATHOLICS, AND MORMONS
REPORTING THREE OF THREE CLOSEST FRIENDS OF OWN RELIGION,
BY AGE

Group	39 and Under	Over 39	Statistical Significance (d.f. = 1)
Protestants PC	51(N = 72)	62(N = 93)	.01
Protestants CC	37(N = 35)	44(N = 39)	No
Catholics CC	47(N = 59)	42(N = 62)	No
Mormons MC	77(N = 69)	82(N = 92)	No

the congregation, white-collar people are as community oriented in primary-group life as blue-collar people, younger people as much as older people, and males as much as females (Tables 9–1, 9–2, 9–3). Denominational conservatives, however, were still more communally oriented than liberals (Table 9–4).[11] Mormons, who do not consider themselves Protestants, are significantly and consistently stronger in friendship community than either Protestants or Catholics.

Although Protestants of Protestant City more often reported three of three Protestant close friends than did those of Catholic City, the Protestants in the latter community actually counted three of three Protestant friends more often than those of the former considering the *relative opportunities and expected number* of Protestant friends (Table 9–5).[12] The fact that Catholics of Catholic City also had more Catholic friends

TABLE 9–4

PERCENTAGE OF PROTESTANTS REPORTING THREE OF THREE
CLOSEST FRIENDS OF OWN RELIGION, BY DENOMINATION

Group	Conservative Denominations [a]	Liberal Denominations	Statistical Significance (d.f. = 1)
Protestants PC	66(N = 92)	49(N = 55)	.01
Protestants CC	47(N = 43)	32(N = 28)	.10

a Lutherans, Baptists, and sectarians were considered conservatives and Methodists, Presbyterians, Congregationalists, and Episcopalians as liberals. For distribution of religious orthodoxy by denomination, see Rodney Stark and Charles Y. Glock, *American Piety* (Berkeley: University of California Press, 1968).

TABLE 9–5

PERCENTAGE OF PROTESTANTS, CATHOLICS, AND MORMONS
REPORTING THREE OF THREE CLOSEST FRIENDS OF OWN RELIGION,
EXPECTED AND OBSERVED FREQUENCIES

Group	Percentage Expected 3 of 3	Percentage Observed 3 of 3	Difference
Protestants, Protestant City	34	58	24
Protestants, Catholic City	5	41	36
Catholics, Protestant City	2	17	15
Catholics, Catholic City	25	45	20
Mormons, Mormon City	27	80	53

[11] See also Charles H. Anderson, "Denominational Differences in White Protestant Communality," *Review of Religious Research*, X (Fall, 1969).

[12] For further discussion, see Charles H. Anderson, "Religious Communality Among White Protestants, Catholics, and Mormons," *Social Forces, XLVI* (June, 1968), 501–8.

in terms of relative opportunities and expected numbers than did Catholics in Protestant City further suggests that majority or minority status is not the critical variable in either the Protestant or the Catholic religious community, but rather the number of Catholics in a given population. The more Catholics there are in a city the more often, it would seem, do Protestants and Catholics remain separate in primary group life.

Role of Kin

A question closely related to the problem of religious composition of cliques is that concerning the role of kin in primary-group life. White Protestants are often thought of as relying less on relatives for friends than other religious groups do. Is this assumption true?

Winch, Greer, and Blumberg in a study of an upper-middle-class suburb of Chicago found that Protestants had social contact with fewer households of kin than did Catholics or Jews.[13] Seventy-one per cent of the Jews, 33 per cent of the Catholics, and only 16 per cent of the Protestants reported interaction with more than four households of kin in the metropolitan area. However, the investigators also found that more Protestants had migrated into Chicago from other areas, and thus they had fewer kin in metropolitan Chicago with whom they *could* associate. At first glance, then, Protestants appeared to be less familistic simply because they were more migratory. However, holding migratory status constant, the investigators observed that Protestant nonmigrants (and migrants) still interacted with fewer households of kin than nonmigrant (and migrant) Catholics or Jews. Furthermore, fewer Protestants reported mutually supportive interaction with kin, that is, giving and receiving aid, services, loans, and so forth.

Winch and his associates demonstrated that Protestants had interaction with *fewer households* of kin than Catholics and Jews, but not that Protestants interact with kin *less often,* or that kin are not their most important category of friends. Indeed, Tomah found that 59 per cent of white Protestant respondents claimed social contact with kin "often," whereas 23 per cent reported contact "often" with co-workers, 40 per cent with neighbors, and 48 per cent with other friends.[14] Catholics relied on relatives only slightly more than did Protestants, in terms of frequency of contact (63 per cent "often" had contact). Earlier, Lenski reported that half the subjects in a sample of white Protestants visited kin every week, a figure only a few percentage points below that reported

[13] Robert F. Winch, Scott Greer, and Rae Lesser Blumberg, "Ethnicity and Extended Familism in an Upper-Middle-Class Suburb," *American Sociological Review,* XXXII (April, 1967), 265–72.

[14] Aida K. Tomah, "Informal Participation in a Metropolitan Community," *The Sociological Quarterly,* VIII (Winter, 1967), 98.

for Catholics for weekly visits.[15] These findings indicate that kin are, in fact, the most important category of social contacts for Protestants and only slightly less important in terms of frequency of visits than for Catholics (despite the fact that Catholics have significantly larger nuclear families and hence larger kinship networks).

ORGANIZATIONAL LIFE

Protestant formal groups or organizations may be categorized into at least four broad types. First, the churches themselves, along with their parish organizations such as Sunday schools, youth leagues, women's circles, and brotherhoods, are the largest and most important Protestant associations. Included as a subcategory here might be the interdenominational religious and quasi-religious groups such as the Bible and missionary societies, Salvation Army, and the Gideons (the various "Christian crusades" could conceivably be included as well). Second, secular nondenominational associations such as the Young Men's Christian Association and Young Women's Christian Association, which have been founded and largely funded and administered by white Protestants, are second only to the churches in importance and are often much more important than churches in the central city. Large numbers of Negroes and increasing numbers of Catholics are members of the YMCA and YWCA. Third, there are the fraternal orders and secret societies, such as the Odd Fellows and Masons (originally militantly Protestant), and the service clubs, such as Rotary and Lions, which usually have no formal Protestant ties but traditionally have been white Protestant strongholds and may incorporate some religious ritual. In this third category, but without the quasi-religious rites, we might also include Anglo-Saxon organizations like the Daughters of the American Revolution and exclusive metropolitan men's clubs. Finally, the extensive network of welfare and educational institutions founded and administered by churches and nondenominational Protestant organizations constitutes a significant aspect of Protestant organizational life.

Beyond these more specifically designated Protestant organizations there is little information as to the degree of community among white Protestants in the many special interest groups and clubs that proliferate in every town and city. Disparate bits of evidence suggest that religious affiliation is of some importance in these groups.[16]

15 Lenski, *The Religious Factor*, pp. 216–17.
16 For example, Mhyra Minnis, "Cleavage in Women's Organizations," *American Sociological Review*, XVIII (February, 1953), 47–53; for affiliation in country clubs, see E. Digby Baltzell, *The Protestant Establishment* (New York: Random House, Inc., 1964), p. 357.

There is substantial evidence, however, that Protestants are more frequent "joiners" than Catholics, regardless of social status. To illustrate, Schroeder and Obenhaus noted that in a predominantly Protestant community 59 per cent of white-collar Protestants but only 19 per cent of white-collar Catholics belonged to four or more organizations; and in another, predominantly Catholic, town the comparable figures were 58 per cent and 27 per cent.[17] This fact alone would expose Protestants to greater in-group than out-group contact. Whatever the extent of inter-religious contact that exists in social clubs and organizations, Protestant-Catholic contact is certainly much greater in this type of group than in primary-group life.

CHURCH PARTICIPATION

The Protestant church is, to point out the obvious, the "most Protestant" of any organization a Protestant might join. Participation in the church and commitment to the faith are very crucial to Protestants' communal strength. A person may, of course, be involved in the religious community without being active in an organized church, or even without being a believer. Nevertheless, formal religious participation and belief enormously enlarge the scope of communal life.

Over 60 million white Americans, representing about 30 per cent of the population, were members of various Protestant churches in 1966.[18] Between 55 and 60 per cent of all self-identifying white Protestants are church members, with perhaps another 10 to 15 per cent claiming church membership if asked. Thus, social surveys commonly record up to 75 per cent or even more of self-identifying white Protestants as claiming church membership. Up to a point, higher-status persons are more frequently church members than lower-status ones.[19] Church membership, without attendance, however, adds little or nothing to a person's religious communalism.

Attendance at church services is probably one of the most critical generating forces of white Protestant community. Involvement in the formal church structure vastly expands opportunities for involvement

[17] Schroeder and Obenhaus, *Religion in American Culture*, p. 51; see also Bernard Lazerwitz, "Membership in Voluntary Associations and Church Attendance," *Journal for the Scientific Study of Religion*, II (Fall, 1962), 74–84.

[18] *Yearbook of American Churches*, 1967 (New York: National Council of the Church of Christ in the U.S.A., 1967).

[19] For instance, see Louis Bultena, "Church Membership and Church Attendance in Madison, Wisconsin," *American Sociological Review*, XIV (June, 1949), 384–89; and Lee G. Burchinal, "Some Social Status Criteria of Church Membership and Church Attendance," *Journal of Social Psychology*, XLIX (February, 1959), 53–54.

in the informal dimension of religious group life. The informal social atmosphere often found in Protestant churches strongly encourages the formation of church-based friendships. Church attendance is moderately high among white Protestants. About four in ten attend church services weekly; three in ten at least monthly; two in ten at least yearly; and one in ten never (Table 9–6).[20] Protestants who are already church members

TABLE 9–6

FREQUENCY OF CHURCH ATTENDANCE BY PROTESTANTS, CATHOLICS, AND MORMONS, BY SEX

Frequency of Attendance	Protestants in Protestant City		Protestants in Catholic City		Catholics in Protestant City		Catholics in Catholic City		Mormons in Mormon City	
	Respon-dents	Wives [a]	Respon-dents	Wives	Respon-dents	Wives	Respon-dents	Wives	Respon-dents	Wives
At least once a week	44%	50%	41%	51%	93%	93%	93%	97%	62%	68%
At least once a month	34	29	41	26	2	0	5	3	15	18
At least once a year	16	7	15	10	0	3	1	0	17	8
Never	6	14	3	13	5	4	1	0	6	6

a As reported by respondents.

do much better in attendance than nonmembers; up to two-thirds of church members are weekly attenders.[21] Nor does church participation necessarily conclude with the Sunday morning service. Possibly as many as half the church members spend at least one evening a week in church, and a majority participate in at least one parish organization.[22]

Although the ubiquitous Sunday morning suit and tie sometimes obscure status differences among the faithful, casual observation confirms statistics indicating that, at least up to a point, the higher a person's social status is the more likely it is that he will go to church (Table 9–7).[23] For example, Burchinal found that 51 per cent of a sample of Iowa Protestant business and professional persons attended regularly, 40 per cent of clerical and skilled workers, and 22 per cent of unskilled

20 See Lazerwitz, "Membership in Voluntary Associations and Frequency of Church Attendance," p. 76; Schroeder and Obenhaus, *Religion in American Culture*, p. 39; and Stark and Glock, pp. 84–86.

21 Stark and Glock, *American Piety*, p. 84.

22 *Ibid.*, pp. 92, 94.

23 Lazerwitz, "Membership in Voluntary Associations and Frequency of Church Attendance"; Lenski, *The Religious Factor*, p. 48; and Schroeder and Obenhaus, *Religion in American Culture*, p. 41.

TABLE 9–7

PERCENTAGE OF PROTESTANTS AND MORMONS REPORTING
WEEKLY CHURCH ATTENDANCE, BY OCCUPATION

Group	White-Collar Workers	Blue-Collar Workers	Statistical Significance (d.f. = 1)
Protestants PC	46(N = 96)	41(N = 68)	No
Protestants CC	45(N = 62)	a	a
Mormons MC	71(N = 101)	43(N = 53)	.01

a Too few cases for analysis.

workers.[24] White-collar persons are also more active than blue-collar persons in extra-church activities within the parish. Further, higher-status Protestants are more active in church affairs than lower-status ones regardless of whether they belong to liberal, moderate, or fundamentalistic churches.[25]

Why are persons of higher social status more active in church than those of lower status? Do middle-class persons have greater interest in organized religious activities per se? Or is it because, as Lenski has suggested, higher-status persons participate more in all types of organizations than lower-status ones do, and hence the former would naturally be more active in church?[26]

Church attendance data analyzed by Glock and Stark disclosed that white-collar persons attended more frequently than blue-collar persons even when both belonged to the same number of nonchurch organizations; [27] however, the church attendance difference between the two occupational groups was then considerably reduced.[28] And as noted previously, higher-status persons are more apt to be church *members* in the first place than are those of lower-status; because church members attend more often than nonmembers, we would expect a comparison of higher- and lower-status church *members* with similar numbers of nonmembers to yield an even smaller difference in church attendance and activity by class position. Indeed, in exactly such a comparison, Goode discovered that blue-collar workers were *as* regular in church activities as white-collar persons.[29]

24 Burchinal, "Some Social Status Criteria."

25 Erich Goode, "Further Reflections on the Church-Sect Dimension," *Journal for the Scientific Study of Religion*, VI (Fall, 1967), 271.

26 Lenski, *The Religious Factor*, p. 49n.

27 Charles Y. Glock and Rodney Stark, *Religion and Society in Tension* (Chicago: Rand McNally & Co., 1965), p. 188.

28 See the reanalysis of the same data, and new data, by Erich Goode, "Social Class and Church Participation," *American Journal of Sociology*, LXXII (July, 1966), 105–10.

29 *Ibid.*

The evidence now available, then, would seem to at least partially confirm Lenski's view that higher-status persons are more active in church and church affairs as a consequence of their greater organizational activity in general. Why higher-status persons are more apt to be members of organizations in the first place is a question dealing with life styles and interests, and lies beyond the scope of the present study.

We have been careful to note that church membership and attendance increase with social status up to a point, for evidence is available to indicate that religious activities reach a peak at the upper-middle-class level but decline at higher levels. For example, Adams and Butler recently reported that 63 per cent of top professionals and managers in predominantly Protestant Greensboro, North Carolina attended church at least monthly compared to 78 per cent of the upper middle class, 68 per cent of the middle class, and 45 per cent of the working class.[30] Even using three of four occupational categories in the analysis of status differences in church participation, we may be certain that important individual occupational differences are being overlooked, especially at the white-collar level.

Looking over the pews of a Protestant church on Sunday morning, we may readily observe that age is also relevant to the question of church participation. Parishioners in their thirties, forties, and fifties are more common than those in their late teens and twenties (Table 9–8: Mormons

TABLE 9–8

PERCENTAGE OF PROTESTANTS AND MORMONS REPORTING
WEEKLY CHURCH ATTENDANCE, BY AGE

Group	39 and Under	Over 39	Statistical Significance (d.f. = 1)
Protestants PC	35(N = 72)	50(N = 94)	.01
Protestants CC	28(N = 36)	54(N = 39)	.01
Mormons MC	63(N = 70)	62(N = 94)	No

diverge from the Protestant pattern). Older teenagers, childless young adults (persons with children are more regular in church participation than childless ones [31]), and couples with very young children provide pastors with their greatest challenge. The above pattern strongly suggests that

[30] Bert N. Adams and James E. Butler, "Occupational Status and Husband-Wife Social Participation," *Social Forces*, XLV (June, 1967), 505.

[31] Bernard Lazerwitz, "Some Factors Associated with Variations in Church Attendance," *Social Forces*, XXXIX (May, 1961), 301–9; and Gerhard Lenski, "Social Correlates of Religious Interest," *American Sociological Review*, XVIII (October, 1953), 533–44.

changes in church participation by life cycle and family status account for most of the variation in age differences among the faithful rather than any general drift away from religion in the younger age brackets. Regular church attendance by parents, for example, serves as a standard of emulation for children and becomes almost obligatory for parents when children began to use church facilities and programs, which few parents—however irreligious themselves—are willing to deny to their children.[32] With a growing investment in the community and a growing family, young couples having weak church ties since their early teens often become loyal members of a congregation; and once started again, they tend to remain practicing members.

Though females are more faithful than males, church attendance differences by sex are slight and not nearly so great as age or occupational differences (Table 9–6).[33] Why are females somewhat more frequently involved in church activities? For one thing, women are usually responsible for seeing that children get to Sunday school and church. Further, men have access to people at work, whereas married women may rely more on the church for social contacts (not necessarily more for *close* friends). The notion that women are inherently more expressive than men and more attracted to the expressive aspect of religion is both far-fetched and unprovable.

Finally, as we might expect, the adherents of conservative Protestant churches tend to be more frequent church attenders than Protestants with liberal affiliations (Table 9–9).[34] Nearly all members of sects attend church at least once a week, as opposed to only a minority of Congrega-

TABLE 9–9

PERCENTAGE OF PROTESTANTS REPORTING WEEKLY
CHURCH ATTENDANCE, BY DENOMINATION

Group	Conservative Denominations [a]	Liberal Denominations	Statistical Significance (d.f. = 1)
Protestants PC	53(N = 93)	44(N = 55)	No
Protestants CC	51(N = 43)	27(N = 29)	.01

[a] See Table 9–4n for classification of denominations.

[32] See Dennison Nash and Peter Berger, "The Child, The Family, and the 'Religious Revival' in Suburbia," *Journal for the Scientific Study of Religion*, II (Fall, 1962), 85–93.

[33] Lenski, "Social Correlates of Religious Interest"; and Lazerwitz, "Membership in Voluntary Associations and Frequency of Church Attendance."

[34] Harry C. Dillingham, "Protestant Religion and Social Status," *American Journal of Sociology*, LXX (January, 1965), 416–22; Schroeder and Obenhaus, p. 41; Stark and Glock, *American Piety*, p. 84.

tionalists; Baptists and Lutherans, for example, fall in between these extremes. In the previous section we observed that adherents of conservative denominations exhibit greater Protestant friendship community than persons with liberal affiliations. This fact, together with the evidence just cited of greater church attendance within the same conservative denominations, suggests that we are correct in stressing the importance of church ties for the informal aspect of Protestant community. The data in Table 9–10 document this importance. The tie between church participation

TABLE 9–10

PERCENTAGE OF PROTESTANTS AND MORMONS REPORTING
THREE OF THREE CLOSEST FRIENDS OF OWN RELIGION,
BY FREQUENCY OF CHURCH ATTENDANCE

Group	Weekly Attendance	Less than Weekly Attendance	Statistical Significance (d.f. = 1)
Protestants PC	73(N = 73)	45(N = 92)	.01
Protestants CC	52(N = 31)	33(N = 43)	.05
Mormons	91(N = 102)	59(N = 59)	.01

and having Protestant friends is definitely not one-way, however; having churchgoing friends would in turn promote a person's own churchgoing tendencies.

Religiosity

A person's religious commitment may be measured in other ways than by church attendance.[35] As we have observed, Protestants tend to be quite reliable church attenders; but how *serious* do they tend to be regarding church attendance and their religion? Is church participation mainly a ritual one goes through for the sake of children and maybe to meet and see friends (not to devalue these as irreligious motives—I see little relevance in accusing the churches of being social clubs, as if socializing with fellow religionists is somehow a reprehensible activity)?

Recent data presented by Stark and Glock indicate that a substantial number of white Protestants are indeed serious about their church and their faith.[36] Half of a national sample of self-identifying Protestants

---

35 For discussions of the various dimensions of religiosity, see Yoshio Fukuyama, "The Major Dimensions of Church Membership," *Review of Religious Research,* 2 (1961), 154–61; and Glock and Stark, *Religion and Society in Tension,* Chapter 2.

36 Stark and Glock, *American Piety;* see also David O. Moberg, "Theological Self-Classification and Ascetic Moral Views of Students," *Review of Religious Research,* X (Winter, 1969), 100–107.

(which includes non-church Protestants) claimed their religion was "extremely important" to them and another quarter declared it to be "quite important." [37] Catholics followed suit. It is doubtful that job or family are held in such high regard in American society.

An important aspect of Protestant religiosity, which we might further take note of here, is belief in church doctrines. The overwhelming majority of white Protestants believe in a personal God, in the Divinity of Jesus, in life after death, and in the efficacy of prayer.[38] Indeed, two to three out of every five white Protestants are *absolutely* sure there is a devil. Larger proportions of sectarians, Baptists, and Lutherans are so categorical in their convictions, but even the liberal churches with their highly educated congregations are relatively firm in belief. The space age clergyman should be pleasantly surprised in the success of his vocation. What a Jonathan Edwards or a Dwight L. Moody might think of the extent and nature of modern-day Protestant religiosity, one can only guess. Although Stark and Glock themselves feel their data support the view that Protestantism and Christianity in America are withering on the vine, the rather large percentages of unwavering and occasionally wavering (is not an orthodox person in any situation, religious or otherwise, entitled to occasional doubts and questions?) respondents can to me only be an indication of religious viability—though no one can say for sure, since we have no previous empirical benchmarks as points of comparison.

Any given individual or group, of course, may be high in church participation and low in religious belief, or vice versa. For example, although higher-status Protestants are more frequent church attenders than those of lower status, evidence is available to indicate that persons of lower status *who are church members* are on the average more orthodox in belief than higher-status church members.[39] As Demerath has argued concerning low-status religiosity,

> If a lower-class individual is committed to religion at all, his internal involvement [belief and experience] is likely to be higher than that of his higher-status church-fellows. On the other hand, there is a large segment of the lower class that has no religious commitment whatsoever.[40]

[37] Stark and Glock, *American Piety*, p. 101.

[38] *Ibid.*, pp. 28–38; and Leonard Broom and Norval Glenn, "Religious Differences in Reported Attitudes and Behavior," *Sociological Analysis*, XXVII (Winter, 1966), 187–209.

[39] For instance, see Thomas R. Ford, "Status, Residence, and Fundamentalistic Religious Beliefs in the Southern Appalachians," *Social Forces*, XXXIX (October, 1960), 41–49; Demerath, *Social Class in American Protestantism*, pp. 20–25; and Fukuyama, "The Major Dimensions of Church Membership."

[40] Demerath, *Social Class in American Protestantism*, pp. 22–23.

SUMMARY

Like other ethnoreligious groups, white Protestants tend to form clique and organizational ties with persons of their own faith. Higher-status Protestants rely less on members of their own congregations for confidants than do lower-status ones, but no less on Protestants in general. Protestant friendship community is only slightly greater among older than younger persons and among females than males. However, Protestants affiliated with conservative churches are significantly more likely to prefer coreligionists as close associates than are liberal church members. Although kin are the most important category of associates for white Protestants, kin are slightly less important than they are for Catholics and much less than for Jews.

The organizational aspect of white Protestant community is moderately strong, in both secular and religious dimensions. The middle classes have been more active than working people in Protestant-dominated secular organizations as well as in the church. Lower-status persons, however, seem to be more orthodox in religious belief *if* they are already church members but are less often members in the first place than are higher-status persons. As in informal groups, older Protestants participate more frequently in organized religious activities than younger Protestants do; females participate more than males do; and denominational conservatives more than liberals, though only in the latter instance are the differences very important. On the other hand, in nonchurch organizations—many of which are very much white Protestant in composition and outlook—younger persons, males, and denominational liberals probably out-join their status opposites.

Although there are no figures from the past for comparison, white Protestant religiosity seems very strong within the large and most rapidly growing Baptist, Lutheran, and sectarian churches. Members of the Methodist, Congregational, Episcopal, and Presbyterian churches on the whole express more doubts about the traditional tenets of the faith and more often hold religious views that variously diverge from fundamentalism. Nevertheless, a large minority of persons in these more liberal churches hold to the most orthodox religious beliefs.

A GROWING
MINORITY CONSCIOUSNESS

"Protestantism in America today," writes Will Herberg, "presents the anomaly of a strong majority group with a growing minority consciousness." [1] Minority consciousness is not new to American white Protestants. Both as members of national origin groups and as members of ingrown denominations, many white Protestants have had the experience of being set off from the social mainstream. What is new is that a minority consciousness seems to be emerging among white Protestants qua white Protestants. A Protestant may, of course, identify with a church or denomination as well as with the larger Protestant collectivity. Whereas sectarians, Southern Baptists, Missouri Synod Lutherans, and a few other inward-looking churches may often exclusively stress denominational loyalty (often reinforced by class or regional differences), most Methodists, Baptists, Lutherans, and Presbyterians feel increasingly akin to one another as fellow Protestants and are less conscious of being members of separate denominations. Congregationalists, owing to their regional base, and Episcopalians, owing to their class base, may also feel set apart somewhat from these center churches. Nevertheless, as the original Anglo-Protestant churches in America they themselves constitute the historic center of Protestant identification.

White Protestant Community: Identification and Marriage

The notion of collective religious group identity among white Protestants was first given full sociological treatment in 1955 by Herberg in his *Protestant-Catholic-Jew*.[2] An amorphous and unarticulated sense of Protestant identity—refined, interpreted, and thus divided through the prisms of national origin and denomination—has been until recently almost synonymous with American identity. An increasing number of white Protestants, however, conform to Herberg's hypothesis of a growing collective minority consciousness.

[1] Will Herberg, *Protestant-Catholic-Jew* (Garden City, N.Y.: Doubleday & Company, Inc., 1960), p. 234.
[2] *Ibid.*

127

Minority consciousness as conceived here should not be confused with the "negative" type of group awareness Protestants often have had in regard to what they *are not*. As Littell explains the negative self-concept:

> "Protestants" who have never expressed any clear, disciplined, voluntary witness to the evangelical faith, who have never perceived any dichotomy between the Christian life and the norms of a heathen society, can still suddenly remember that they are children of the Reformation when "the Jewish threat" or "the Catholic threat" puts in an appearance.[3]

Rather, we are interested in what white Protestants feel they *are*, although a type of negation is part of any kind of group identity.

Unfortunately, empirical data on Protestant self-identity and collective consciousness are in short supply. Kuhn and McPartland asked a sample of Midwestern university students to respond with twenty statements to the question "Who am I?" in an attempt to decipher the most important components of self-concept.[4] Lutheran, Baptist, and sectarian respondents were highest in religious self-concept, as each made seven references to religious group ties. Next came Congregationalists (5.4), Presbyterians (4.5), and Methodists (3.2). Catholics (7.3) and Jews (6.9) were as high as the conservative Protestants. In view of the numerous potential dimensions of self-concept available to a university student and the relatively low religious interest in this age group, Kuhn and McPartland's findings attest to the importance of the religious component in self-concept. A second piece of evidence concerning religious self-concept comes from a study of professional persons by Wilensky and Ladinsky; 71 per cent of a predominantly white Protestant sample of engineers maintained strong *religious* identification compared to only 27 per cent reporting strong *occupational* identification.[5] Even among lawyers, more declared strong religious identification (66 per cent) than strong occupational identification (55 per cent). If occupational identification at the upper professional level fails to exceed religious identification, religious identification must surely be one of the most central—if not *the* most central—component of self-concept to much of the white Protestant population.

Responding to the question "How would you rate the strength of

3 Franklin H. Littell, *From State Church to Pluralism* (Garden City, N.Y.: Doubleday & Company, Inc., 1962), p. 147.

4 Manford H. Kuhn and Thomas S. McPartland, "An Empirical Investigation of Self-Attitudes," *American Sociological Review*, XIX (February, 1954), 68–76.

5 Harold L. Wilensky and Jack Ladinsky, "From Religious Community to Occupational Group: Structural Assimilation Among Professors, Lawyers, and Engineers," *American Sociological Review*, XXXII (August, 1967), 541–61.

TABLE 10–1

STRENGTH OF RELIGIOUS SELF-IDENTIFICATION OF PROTESTANTS,
CATHOLICS, AND MORMONS, IN PERCENTAGES, BY SEX

Religious Self-Identity	Protestants in Protestant City		Protestants in Catholic City		Catholics in Protestant City		Catholics in Catholic City		Mormons in Mormon City	
	Respon-dents	Wives [a]	Respon-dents	Wives	Respon-dents	Wives	Respon-dents	Wives	Respon-dents	Wives
Very Strong	25	28	18	30	19	33	21	30	47	48
Strong	30	32	37	32	53	49	51	56	24	30
Moderate	30	31	29	27	21	16	23	14	15	14
Weak or none	15	9	16	11	7	2	5	0	14	8

[a] As reported by respondents.

your identification with your religious group?" Protestant City and
Catholic City Protestants tended to confirm salience of their faith in self-
identity (Table 10–1). Interestingly enough, as many Protestants as
Catholics affirmed "very strong" religious self-identification. As typical of
sectarians, Mormons reported stronger religious group identification than
either Protestants or Catholics. White-collar Protestants were stronger in
religious self-identity than blue-collar Protestants, as were white-collar
Mormons and Catholics (Table 10–2). Younger Protestants in Protestant
City were more likely to acknowledge strong identity than were older
Protestants, whereas in Catholic City the reverse was strongly true (Table
10–3). Mormons and Catholics offered no further hints as to the role of
age in religious group identification, as the younger group was slightly
stronger among Mormons and the older group among Catholics. As we
might expect from statistics on religion of friends and church participation, members of the conservative denominations reported significantly

TABLE 10–2

PERCENTAGE OF PROTESTANTS, CATHOLICS, AND MORMONS
REPORTING STRONG RELIGIOUS IDENTIFICATION,
BY OCCUPATION

Group	White-Collar Workers	Blue-Collar Workers	Statistical Significance (d.f. = 1)
Protestants PC	60(N = 96)	50(N = 68)	No
Protestants CC	56(N = 62)	a	a
Catholics CC	75(N = 79)	71(N = 45)	No
Mormons MC	79(N = 101)	55(N = 53)	.01

a Too few cases for analysis.

stronger religious group identification than those with more liberal affiliations (Table 10–4). The interplay between church participation and religious group identity (Table 10–5) parallels that reported in the previous chapter between church participation and friendship community.

TABLE 10–3

PERCENTAGE OF PROTESTANTS, CATHOLICS, AND MORMONS
REPORTING STRONG RELIGIOUS IDENTIFICATION,
BY AGE

Group	39 and Under	Over 39	Statistical Significance (d.f. = 1)
Protestants PC	63(N = 72)	50(N = 94)	.05
Protestants CC	36(N = 36)	72(N = 39)	.01
Catholics CC	68(N = 60)	76(N = 66)	No
Mormons MC	51(N = 70)	44(N = 94)	No

TABLE 10–4

PERCENTAGE OF PROTESTANTS REPORTING STRONG
RELIGIOUS IDENTIFICATION, BY DENOMINATION

Group	Conservative Denominations [a]	Liberal Denominations [a]	Statistical Significance (d.f. = 1)
Protestants PC	69(N = 93)	47(N = 55)	.01
Protestants CC	65(N = 43)	45(N = 29)	.05

[a] See Table 9–4n for classification of denominations.

TABLE 10–5

PERCENTAGE OF PROTESTANTS AND MORMONS REPORTING WEEKLY
CHURCH ATTENDANCE, BY STRENGTH OF RELIGIOUS IDENTIFICATION

Group	Strong Identity	Moderate or Weak Identity	Statistical Significance (d.f. = 1)
Protestants PC	67(N = 92)	15(N = 74)	.01
Protestants CC	66(N = 41)	12(N = 33)	.01
Mormons	84(N = 116)	12(N = 48)	.01

MARRIAGE AND THE
RELIGIOUS COMMUNITY

An extremely important aspect of religious community is mate selection. Intermarriage strikes at the center of communal solidarity through possible loss of members and their offspring. New members gained through intermarriage and conversion may or may not weaken the socioreligious fabric of the receiving group. Though empirical evidence is as yet unavailable, my suspicion is that converts brought into a church through interfaith marriage are only slightly less religious and communal than those raised in the church.

Attitudes

Protestant attitudes toward intermarriage are less receptive than those of Catholics. A rather large minority of Protestants would strongly oppose a Protestant-Catholic marriage (Table 10–6). After having analyzed a set

TABLE 10–6

ATTITUDE TOWARD RELIGIOUS INTERMARRIAGE OF PROTESTANTS, CATHOLICS, AND MORMONS

Attitude Toward Intermarriage	Protestants in Protestant City	Protestants in Catholic City	Catholics in Protestant City	Catholics in Catholic City	Mormons in Mormon City
Strongly opposed	33%	36%	9%	19%	50%
Mildly opposed	39	40	40	41	35
No objection	28	24	51	40	15
Total N's	(166)	(75)	(43)	(126)	(164)

of national survey data, Broom and Glenn reported that 43 per cent of all Protestants would seriously object to a son or daughter marrying a Catholic; only 23 per cent of Catholics seriously opposed the marriage of a son or daughter to a Protestant.[6] Opposition among Protestants is higher among females, religious conservatives, and rural persons; there is a very slight tendency for higher-status and older persons to oppose mixed marriage more than lower-status and younger ones (Tables 10–7, 10–8, 10–9).[7]

Why should Protestants oppose intermarriage more than Catholics? It may be that Catholics have been confident that children of mixed marriages will be educated in the Catholic faith, whereas Protestants may have feared the intractability of the Catholic church's ante-nuptial agreement. However, as Croog and Teele have demonstrated with a large

---

[6] Leonard Broom and Norval Glenn, "Religious Differences in Reported Attitudes and Behavior," *Sociological Analysis*, XXVII (Winter, 1966), 187–209.

[7] See, for example, A. I. Gordon, *Intermarriage* (Boston: Beacon Press, 1964); Lee G. Burchinal, "Membership Groups and Attitudes Toward Cross-Religious Dating and Marriage," *Marriage and Family Living*, XXII (August, 1960), 248–53; and Victor A. Christopherson and James Walters, "Responses of Protestants, Catholics, and Jews concerning Marriage and Family Life," *Sociology and Social Research*, XLIII (October, 1958), 16–22.

TABLE 10–7

PERCENTAGE OF PROTESTANTS, CATHOLICS, AND MORMONS
REPORTING STRONG OPPOSITION TO RELIGIOUS INTERMARRIAGE,
BY OCCUPATION

Group	White-Collar Workers	Blue-Collar Workers	Statistical Significance (d.f. = 1)
Protestants PC	33(N = 96)	32(N = 68)	No
Protestants CC	34(N = 62)	a	a
Catholics CC	18(N = 79)	20(N = 45)	No
Mormons MC	58(N = 101)	23(N = 53)	.01

a Too few cases for analysis.

TABLE 10–8

PERCENTAGE OF PROTESTANTS, CATHOLICS, AND MORMONS
REPORTING STRONG OPPOSITION TO RELIGIOUS INTERMARRIAGE,
BY AGE

Group	39 and Under	Over 39	Statistical Significance (d.f. = 1)
Protestants PC	32(N = 72)	34(N = 94)	No
Protestants CC	14(N = 36)	56(N = 39)	.01
Catholics CC	17(N = 60)	21(N = 66)	No
Mormons MC	53(N = 70)	48(N = 94)	No

TABLE 10–9

PERCENTAGE OF PROTESTANTS REPORTING STRONG OPPOSITION
TO RELIGIOUS INTERMARRIAGE, BY DENOMINATION

Group	Conservative Denominations [a]	Liberal Denominations [a]	Statistical Significance (d.f. = 1)
Protestants PC	44(N = 93)	24(N = 55)	.01
Protestants CC	39(N = 43)	31(N = 29)	No

a See Table 9–4n for classification of denominations.

sample of army inductees who were children of Protestant-Catholic marriages, the popular stereotype of Catholics always "winning out" is far
from accurate; an over-all 35 per cent of these mixed-marriage children
identified themselves as Protestants.[8] Moreover, in the case of respond-

8 Sydney H. Croog and James E. Teele, "Religious Identity and Church Attendance of Sons of Religious Intermarriages," *American Sociological Review,* XXXII
(February, 1967), 93–103.

ents with Protestant mothers and Catholic fathers, 47 per cent claimed Protestant affiliation (note the relative power of the mother in religious concerns).

Marriage Behavior

More Protestants are receptive to the idea of religiously mixed marriage than have actually intermarried. This discrepancy is partly due to the fact that the random chance of a Protestant marrying a Catholic is much less than random chance for marrying a Protestant and partly due to the fact that verbal receptiveness is easier to express than behavioral receptiveness. Table 10–10 summarizes a number of empirical studies dealing with white Protestant and Catholic endogamy. Note that the percentages refer to the number of Protestants (or Catholics) who married someone *raised* as a Protestant (or Catholic). Owing to the religious conversion of one partner at the time of a mixed marriage or afterwards, a cross-sectional count of religious endogamy yields higher percentages than those studies dealing with the religious upbringing of marriage partners. For example, the religious census of 1957 reported that 91 per cent of marriages involving a Protestant were religiously endogamous at the time of the interview.

A perusal of Table 10–10 will reveal that in-marriage among Protestants may be higher than 90 per cent in the Midwest and 65 to 70 per cent in the East.[9] As many as or more than half of all white Protestants marry Protestant-reared persons beyond what one would expect on the basis of Protestant representation in a given population or, if you prefer, random mate selection.[10] Protestants who have higher than average out-marriage rates include teenagers, offspring of interfaith marriages, persons low in church participation, and persons of lower social status.[11] Probably the lowest Protestant intermarriage rate is found in the elite.[12]

The best estimation of *trends* in Protestant intermarriage must be inferred from data presented in the annual *Catholic Directory*. These

[9] We should always keep in mind that the percentage of mixed *marriages* is not the same as the percentage of *individuals* in any given group who intermarry. For example, if out of 100 marriages involving a Protestant 30 were religiously mixed, the intermarriage rate would be 30 per cent, but only 18 per cent of all Protestant individuals in the group would be religiously intermarried; that is, 30 Protestants who intermarried, out of 170 Protestants, equals 18 per cent.

[10] For a careful analysis of the religious census data regarding the ratio of actual to expected intermarriage, see J. Milton Yinger, "A Research Note on Interfaith Marriage Statistics," *Journal for the Scientific Study of Religion*, VII (Spring, 1968), 97–103.

[11] Lee G. Burchinal and Loren E. Chancellor, "Ages at Marriage, Occupation of Grooms and Interreligious Marriage Rates," *Social Forces*, XL (May, 1962), 348–54.

[12] Lawrence Rosen and Robert Bell, "Mate Selection in the Upper Class," *The Sociological Quarterly*, VII (Spring, 1966), 157–66.

TABLE 10–10

PROTESTANT AND CATHOLIC IN-MARRIAGE RATES IN THE UNITED STATES, SELECTED STUDIES

Location	Time	Percentage Protestant In-Marriages [a]	Percentage Catholic In-Marriages [b]
New Haven, Conn.[c]	1900	91	86
	1930	78	82
	1950	70(20)	73(70)
Branford Center, Conn.[d]	1942	63(41)	74(59)
Wright County, Minn.[e]	1943	93(83)	90(17)
New Haven, Conn.[f]	1948	74	94
Manhattan [g]	1950's	66	79
Iowa [h]	1957	91(83)	79(16)
Rural Pennsylvania [i]	1957	84(62)	60(18)
Detroit [j]	1958	73	70
Protestant City [k]	1967	92(68)	63(29)
Catholic City [k]	1967	77(35)	88(63)

[a] The in-marriage rates represent the percentage of Protestant males married to Protestant females of all Protestant males in a given sample. The expected rates, based on sample or city distribution of Protestants, if available, are given in parentheses.

[b] The in-marriage rates for Catholics, including the expected rates given in parentheses, have all been calculated in the same way as those for Protestants.

[c] Ruby Jo Reeves Kennedy, "Single or Triple Melting-Pot? Intermarriage in New Haven 1870–1950," *American Journal of Sociology,* LVIII (July, 1952), 56–59.

[d] C. Wendell King, "Branford Center: A Community Study in Social Cleavage" (doctoral dissertation, Yale University, 1943).

[e] Lowry Nelson, "Intermarriage Among Nationality Groups in a Rural Area of Minnesota," *American Journal of Sociology,* XLVIII (March, 1943), 585–92.

[f] August B. Hollingshead, "Cultural Factors in the Selection of Marriage Mates," *American Sociological Review,* XV (October, 1950), 619–27.

[g] Jerold S. Heiss, "Premarital Characteristics of the Religiously Intermarried in an Urban Area," *American Sociological Review,* XXV (February, 1960), 47–55.

[h] Loren E. Chancellor and Lee G. Burchinal, "Relations among Inter-Religious Marriages, Migratory Marriages and Civil Weddings in Iowa," *Eugenics Quarterly,* IX (1962), 75–83.

[i] F. K. Willits, et al., "Interreligious Marriage Among Pennsylvania Rural Youth," *Marriage and Family Living,* XXV (November, 1963), 433–38.

[j] Gerhard Lenski, *The Religious Factor* (Garden City, N.Y.: Doubleday & Company, Inc., 1963).

[k] See Appendix B for source.

data indicate that church sanctioned Catholic intermarriages have remained constant at about 28 per cent nationally since 1946.[13] However, Protestant-Catholic marriages may conceivably have increased within the category of nonsanctioned marriages and thus not have been included in the *Directory* figures. Also, the percentage of Protestant-Jewish intermarriages has in all likelihood slightly increased over the past generation.

One of the major arguments used against intermarriage, especially by Protestants, is that interfaith marriages are less successful than inmarriages and more often end in divorce.[14] There seems to be a factual basis to this claim: [15] Protestant-Catholic marriages break up about twice as often as Protestant-Protestant matches. However, as Vernon has pointed out, reporting the outcome of mixed marriage in terms of *success* rather than failure drastically alters the image of the comparative fragility of intermarriage.[16] An eight in ten chance of success looks nearly as good as a nine in ten chance (whereas the failure ratio is two to one).

RELIGIOUS COMMUNITY AND RELIGIOSITY

Our discussion of white Protestant religious community as manifested in primary groups, organizations, self-identification, and marriage attitudes and behavior has consistently pointed out the greater strength of religious conservatives on these variables as compared to religious liberals. Because the majority of church Protestants are members of the conservative denominations (Baptist, Lutheran, Christian, and sectarian), and because these churches have been and continue to be the fastest-growing ones, any over-all evaluation of the current status and future of white Protestant community should be very positive. The addition of the sizable minority of religious liberals with strong communal orientation further enlarges the scope of the operative white Protestant community. Nonchurch Protestants, on the other hand, add little or nothing to Protestant community.[17]

[13] See Paul J. Reiss, "The Trend in Interfaith Marriages," *Journal for the Scientific Study of Religion*, V (October, 1965), 64–67; Lenski similarly found no tendency for Protestant-Catholic marriages to increase by immigrant generation in America. See *The Religious Factor*, p. 55.

[14] Broom and Glenn, "Religious Differences in Reported Attitudes and Behavior."

[15] For example, see Loren E. Chancellor and Thomas P. Monohan, "Religious Preference and Interreligious Mixtures in Marriages and Divorces in Iowa," *American Journal of Sociology*, VI (November, 1955), 233–39; and Judson T. Landis, "Marriages of Mixed and Non-Mixed Religious Faith," *American Sociological Review*, XIV (June, 1949), 401–7.

[16] Glenn M. Vernon, "Interfaith Marriages," *Religious Education*, LV (July, 1960), 261–64.

[17] Charles H. Anderson, "Denominational Differences in White Protestant Communality," *Review of Religious Research*, X (Fall, 1969).

That a relationship exists between religious communalism and religious orthodoxy among white Protestants is quite evident. The question to be dealt with now concerns the direction of influence between the two phenomena. Are white Protestants highly communal because they are religious or are they religious because they are highly communal?

A white Protestant may not be religious and may nevertheless participate in the religious community; however, this type of person is clearly in the minority. Probably in an even smaller minority would be the religious person who is *not* involved in the religious community, since without the reinforcing influence of the group, religious commitment would seem exceedingly fragile. Although very probably communal orientation and religiosity reinforce each other, my contention is that the extent of a white Protestant's participation within the religious community (including church attendance if for the moment it may be considered an aspect of religious community rather than religiosity) conditions his specifically religious beliefs and feelings to a greater degree than his religious beliefs and feelings influence his communal ties and loyalties.

If the above argument is valid, *the viability of the Protestant faith depends to a large extent on the viability of Protestant communalism.*[18] *If it is also true that white Protestants are in the process of building a more self-conscious community, then the Protestant churches should be the beneficiary of continued or even heightened religiosity,* perhaps with a more this-worldly theological emphasis than in the past.

RELIGIOUS COMMUNITY AND THE WHITE PROTESTANT INTELLECTUAL

We have learned that a large portion of white Protestants sustain relatively strong inclinations toward the religious community; on the other hand, Milton Gordon has argued that a majority of intellectuals do not participate in *any* religious community. Instead, intellectuals of diverse religious and ethnic backgrounds, Gordon contends, "interact in primary group relations with considerable frequency and with relative comfort and ease." [19] By "intellectuals" Gordon means "people for whom ideas, concepts, literature, music, painting, the dance have intrinsic meaning—are a part of the social psychological atmosphere which one

[18] To argue the importance of religious community is not necessarily to argue from the Durkheimian position that religion is an epiphenomenon of group life. The psychology of religious belief and feeling may itself have an independent influence in generating socioreligious group life and identity.

[19] Milton M. Gordon, *Assimilation in American Life* (New York: Oxford University Press, Inc., 1964), p. 224.

breathes." [20] Gordon's hypothesis is that intellectuals of different ethnic backgrounds coalesce to form a type of ethnically neutral subsociety free of religious cleavages and based on a mutual and overriding interest in ideas. Religious origins are pushed into the background, as it were, making an occasional appearance as a topic of discussion without playing a role in group life or psychological identification.

Not all intellectuals, Gordon surmises, are part of this fluid and open subsociety. Some may prefer the familiarity and security of religious communities, and a small minority act as spokesmen and apologists for religious groups.

The Protestant intellectual may experience marginality to his religious group much as any minority-group intellectual faces the problem of social and psychological separation from his religious background community. He, too, may be a participant in a transethnic subsociety. As a member of this subsociety, the white Protestant intellectual would not be simply a member of an intellectual version of the white Protestant core society, which assimilated non-Protestants. He would be, like minority-group intellectuals, a participant in a non-ethnic group.

There is empirical evidence that intellectuals and academics, especially Protestants in the humanities and social sciences and Jews, are low in *religiosity*.[21] The preceding discussion regarding the probability that persons low in religiosity will be weak *communally* should be enough to make us skeptical over the prospects of Protestant intellectuals' contributions to the religious community. Nevertheless, direct information is needed concerning the extent of both their religious community and their involvement in ethnically mixed groups.

The evidence now available suggests that academic intellectuals, at least, do in fact exhibit extremely weak ties to the religious community; instead they tend to participate in and identify with groups consisting of persons from diverse ethnic backgrounds.[22] Academics with Protestant

20 *Ibid.*

21 Edward C. Lehman, Jr., and Donald W. Shriver, Jr., "Academic Discipline as Predictive of Faculty Religiosity," *Social Forces*, XLVII (December, 1968), 171–82; Fred Thalheimer, "Continuity and Change in Religiosity: A Study of Academicians," *The Pacific Sociological Review*, VIII (Fall, 1965), 101–8; and Rodney Stark, "On the Incompatibility of Religion and Science," *Journal for the Scientific Study of Religion*, III (Fall, 1963), 3–20.

22 Charles H. Anderson, "The Intellectual Subsociety Hypothesis: An Empirical Test," *The Sociological Quarterly*, IX (Spring, 1968), 210–27; also idem, "Marginality and the Academic," *Sociological Inquiry*, XXXIX (Winter, 1969), 77–83, and "Religious Communality Among Academics," *Journal for the Scientific Study of Religion*, VII (Spring, 1968), 87–96; John D. Murray, "The American Catholic Intellectuals: An Empirical Test of the Intellectual Subsociety Hypothesis," (doctoral dissertation, University of Massachusetts, 1969); and Allan Mazur, "Resocialized Ethnicity: A Study of Jewish Social Scientists" (doctoral dissertation, The Johns Hopkins University, 1969).

and Jewish origins tend to be weaker in religious community than those with Catholic backgrounds. However, the difference is almost entirely accounted for by Catholics teaching in Catholic schools.

As previously suggested, Gordon's explanation for greater religious assimilation among academics and intellectuals than the general population is their common overriding interest in ideas. We could also plausibly argue that some of the differences in assimilation between intellectuals and nonintellectuals are due to choice of intellectual professions by those persons originally weak in religious community orientation. Although such an explanation may account for some of the differences between intellectuals and nonintellectuals, in degree of ethnic assimilation, the available evidence indicates that it is mostly *after* participation in the academic and intellectual milieu that religious community declines and assimilation occurs.

Whatever the relative weights of intellectual milieu versus early religious socialization and self-selection might be in promoting more rapid and complete assimilation among academics and intellectuals, preliminary evidence strongly implies that Protestantism has incurred the loss of a large majority of its intellectuals, in terms of both religiosity and religious community.

SUMMARY

White Protestant group consciousness does not as yet seem to be as strong as Protestant friendship community or associational ties, though such identity seems to be heightening. A majority of white Protestants report strong identification with their religious group. A large minority of white Protestants are categorically opposed to religious intermarriage, and many more place a number of qualifications on it. Further, Protestant opposition to interfaith marriage is sharper than Catholic opposition. Actual white Protestant intermarriage rates are, however, lower than might be expected on the basis of attitudes and much lower than would be expected on the basis of random mating and are lower than Catholic rates. Empirical data are insufficient to support the notion that Protestant intermarriages have increased in the past generation. The locus of greatest opposition to interfaith marriage and the lowest intermarriage rate are in the expanding middle classes and the large church-affiliated population.

Over-all religious community orientation—including friends, organizational participation, religious group identification, and intermarriage—is somewhat greater among higher-status than among lower-status Protestants and greater among females than among males. Age does not seem to be consistently related to strength of religious community. By far the largest differences in Protestant communal orientation are between churchgoing and non-churchgoing Protestants. There is a lesser difference between church conservatives and liberals. Protestant intellectuals, the majority of whom belong to the non-churchgoing category, tend to be very peripheral participants in the white Protestant community. Thus, there seems to be a direct connection between communalism and religiosity; at one end of the scale is the highly communal and religiously orthodox Protestant, at the other the noncommunal and irreligious Protestant. Religious community ties, I have argued, are more basic to religiosity than vice versa, though mutual reinforcement occurs. Although Protestant intellectuals and unchurched Protestants in the larger society are similarly low in communal orientation, the unchurched in the larger society may be communally low owing to their irreligious views, whereas intellectuals may be so owing to their preoccupation with ideas.

White Protestants as a group have been members of no predominant or characteristic social class as have nonwhites, Jews, and until recently, white Catholics. The class distribution of white Protestants has been almost as diverse as the American class structure itself. (In view of the size of the group, this is understandable.) I say "almost as diverse" because white Protestants, particularly church-going Protestants, have historically been and continue to be overrepresented toward the top of the class structure. Indeed, the higher one goes in the class structure the more predominant are white Protestants, until at the very top we find nearly all white Protestants. Native white Protestants have historically been promoted into the middle classes by the influx of immigrants near the bottom of the occupational structure and, since the turn of the century, by a marked upgrading of the entire occupational structure. However, since the 1940's mobile non-Protestants have been in the process of moving middle-class white Protestants over and sometimes even down in the class structure. This accommodation of non-Protestants and nonwhites has been disconcerting to urban white Protestants, but especially to nonmobile rural white Protestants, and the trend is continuing. The latter share with nonwhites the very bottom of the socioeconomic ladder.

White Protestants in the Class Structure

The debate over the Protestant ethic and the relative worldly success of Protestants and Catholics, ignited by Max Weber [1] and fueled by several other scholars,[2] has been a topic of controversy in the sociology of religion and social class right through the 1960's.[3] The issues and research find-

[1] Max Weber, *The Protestant Ethic and the Spirit of Capitalism* (New York: Charles Scribner's Sons, 1958).

[2] R. H. Tawny, *Religion and the Rise of Capitalism* (New York: Mentor Books, 1961); Amintore Fanfani, *Catholicism, Protestantism, and Capitalism* (London: Sheed and Ward, 1951); and H. M. Robertson, *Aspects of the Rise of Economic Individualism* (Cambridge: Cambridge University Press, 1933).

[3] See, for example, Raymond W. Mack, et al., "The Protestant Ethic, Level of Aspiration, and Social Mobility," *American Sociological Review*, XXI (June, 1956), 295–300; Bernard C. Rosen, "Race, Ethnicity, and the Achievement Syndrome," *American Sociological Review*, XXVI (February, 1959), 47–60; Gerhard Lenski, *The Religious*

ings dealing directly with the question of Protestantism and social mobility will be considered later in the chapter. First we address ourselves to a cross-sectional view of Protestants' class location, looking initially at the upper strata mainly consisting of persons with national prestige and power.

THE UPPER CLASS

From earlier discussions of the class location of national origin groups, we would naturally anticipate a predominance of white Protestants at the upper levels of the class structure historically and even contemporarily, because large-scale alterations in the composition of social classes usually take a long time. The past ascendancy of native Protestants in New England and Midwestern towns has been described by several researchers as part of earlier community studies. An example is Underwood's research on a New England industrial town, where "... the mill-owning, mill-managing Yankee occupies a position of such great economic power and conspicuousness ... that the identification of most Protestants with the upper class is a prevalent stereotype." [4] In a similar vein, Hollingshead and Redlich have noted that "... old Yankee families controlled the city of New Haven and the suburban towns politically, financially, industrially, and professionally, as well as socially." [5] Baltzell has historically documented how Anglo-Protestants reigned supreme in Philadelphia's social and economic life.[6] Although white Protestants have continued to monopolize social prestige in most communities, non-Protestant minorities have made important gains in power and influence at the local levels of government, business, labor, and education. Then, too, suc-

---

Factor (Garden City, N.Y.: Doubleday & Company, Inc., 1963); Albert J. Mayer and Harry Sharp, *American Sociological Review,* XXVII (April, 1962), 218–27; Neil J. Weller, "Religion and Social Mobility in Industrial Society" (doctoral dissertation, University of Michigan, 1960); Harold N. Organic, "Religious Affiliation and Social Mobility in Contemporary American Society: A National Study" (doctoral dissertation, University of Michigan, 1963); Andrew M. Greeley, "The Protestant Ethic: Time for a Moratorium," *Sociological Analysis,* XXV (Spring, 1964), 20–33; and Norval D. Glenn and Ruth Hyland, "Religious Preference and Worldly Success: Some Evidence from National Surveys," *American Sociological Review,* XXXII (February, 1967), 73–85.

[4] Kenneth Underwood, *Protestant and Catholic* (Boston: Beacon Press, 1957), p. 194.

[5] August B. Hollingshead and Frederick C. Redlich, *Social Class and Mental Illness* (New York: John Wiley & Sons, Inc., 1958), p. 60. See also W. Lloyd Warner and Paul S. Lunt, *The Social Life of a Modern Community* (New Haven: Yale University Press, 1941), or any of a number of earlier community studies.

[6] S. Digby Baltzell, *Philadelphia Gentlemen: The Making of a National Upper Class* (New York: The Free Press, 1958), reprinted with an additional chapter as *An American Business Aristocracy* (New York: Crowell-Collier and Macmillan, Inc., 1962).

cessful minorities have constructed their own status and prestige hierarchies to parallel those of the white Protestant core society.[7]

As C. Wright Mills once pointed out, the sum of local upper classes and elites does not add up to the national upper class and elite. The national upper stratum of power and prestige derives almost entirely from the very largest metropolitan areas. Thus, in the case of Philadelphia cited above, Baltzell has dealt with both a local elite and a segment of the national upper stratum, understanding that there is considerable overlap between them. Our focus here is primarily national.

In his study of the power elite, Mills directed widespread attention to the Protestant religious base of the national upper class.[8] In Mills' words:

> Almost everywhere in America, the metropolitan upper classes have in common, more or less, race, religion, and nativity. There are, of course, exceptions, some of them important exceptions. But however important, these are still exceptions: the model of the upper *social* classes is still "pure" by race, by ethnic group, by national extraction. In each city, they tend to be Protestant; moreover Protestants of class-church denominations, Episcopalian mainly, or Unitarian, or Presbyterian.[9]

The most exhaustive treatment of the national upper class, its history, and its Protestant religious structure has been done by Baltzell.[10] Baltzell distinguishes between the *elite,* individuals who have achieved prominence in business, finance, the professions, science, and other functional hierarchies, and the *upper class,* a social stratum based in the largest cities and composed of the second or third or later generations descended from elite individuals. Toward the end of the nineteenth century, wealthy white Protestants developed a set of exclusive upper-class institutions, including churches, schools, resorts, clubs, and organizations, which preserved a member's social distance from the rest of the citizenry. Baltzell theorizes that in order to maintain respect and authority, an upper class must be socially open and representative of all groups in the population. If it is to be legitimate and authoritative, Baltzell argues, the upper class must assimilate the families of elite individuals regardless of race, religion, or national origin. Baltzell contends that the Protestant upper class in the twentieth century is in danger of degenerating into a closed caste owing to its failure to admit to membership the increasing non-Protestant elite and their descendants; thus it is in danger

---

[7] Baltzell, *An American Business Aristocracy,* Chap. 11.

[8] C. Wright Mills, *The Power Elite* (New York: Oxford University Press, Inc., 1956).

[9] *Ibid.,* p. 60.

[10] Baltzell, *An American Business Aristocracy,* and idem, *The Protestant Establishment* (New York: Random House, Inc., 1964).

of losing its representativeness, together with respect and authority. In Baltzell's words:

> A crisis in moral authority has developed in modern America largely because of the White-Anglo-Saxon-Protestant establishment's unwillingness, or inability, to share and improve its upper-class traditions by continuously absorbing talented and distinguished members of minority groups into its privileged ranks.[11]

Unless the upper class becomes truly representative of the aspirations of the population and especially of the functional elite, leaders must resort to manipulation, coercion, and dishonesty in lieu of respect and authority based on aristocratic traditions of responsible leadership. Whether or not one agrees with Baltzell's line or argument (and in light of the events of the late 1960's, it is difficult not to), he has etched in detail the white Protestant milieu of the national upper class.

A number of studies of top business and corporate executives document that Protestants have dominated these crucial areas of American and upper-class life. Keller's investigation of those in the topmost positions in the largest 200 corporations in 1950 revealed that 85 per cent who claimed a religion were Protestants.[12] In the areas of manufacturing, mining, and finance, 93 per cent were Protestant. Furthermore, the overall 1950 figure represented only a slight drop from the 89 per cent of top company men who were Protestant at the turn of the century. Indeed, during the 50-year interim, the proportion of Protestants in the key areas of manufacturing, mining, and finance actually *increased*. Only in entertainment, where they composed 63 per cent of the total, were Protestants found in numbers anywhere near proportionate to their representation in the population. The Jewish group were overrepresented in entertainment, and Catholics were underrepresented. Episcopalians (30 per cent) and Presbyterians (17 per cent) accounted for nearly half of all executives Keller studied. Conversely, Baptists and Lutherans were as badly underrepresented as Catholics. In a similar type of trend study, Newcomer reported nearly identical findings.[13] Analyses of *Who's Who in Commerce and Industry* have indicated that the very large majority of business executives included therein were Protestant.[14] A very recent survey

11 Baltzell, *The Protestant Establishment,* p. x.

12 Suzanne I. Keller, "The Social Origins and Career Lines of Three Generations of American Business Leaders" (doctoral dissertation, Columbia University, 1953).

13 Mabel Newcomer, *The Big Business Executive: The Factors That Made Him* (New York: Columbia University Press, 1955).

14 Kenneth Watson, "The Religious Affiliation, Motivation, and Opinions of Business and Labor Leaders in the United States" (doctoral dissertation, Southern California School of Theology, 1960); and Judson B. Pearson, "American Business Leaders: Social Characteristics and Occupational Ascent" (doctoral dissertation, University of Washington, 1953).

by a national magazine confirms that white Protestant control of the "command posts" of the corporate economy is nearly as secure today as it was in the late nineteenth century.[15] Of 790 directors in the 50 largest corporations, 88 per cent were "apparent" WASP's, as were most executives. The same report noted that of 241 directors in the nation's 10 largest commercial banks, 83 per cent were Protestants. Similar figures were reported for life insurance companies and foundations.

If top corporate personnel are mostly white Protestant, so are the very rich, for great (and small) American fortunes are anchored in the corporate economy.[16] Again to quote from Mills, "American-born, city-bred, eastern-originated, the very rich have been from families of higher class status, and . . . they have been Protestants. Moreover, about half have been Episcopalians, and a fourth, Presbyterians." [17]

Aside from the fact that the old Anglo-American churches have enjoyed accumulated advantages since colonial times, they have also inherited many non-British and sectarian persons through denominational switching undertaken to keep religious affiliation in line with status change. As Baltzell has pointed out with regard to the Philadelphia elite, many were originally Lutherans, Quakers, Baptists, and Presbyterians; but these eventually built more fashionable Episcopalian churches for themselves and their descendants.[18]

Other Elites

Not only in business have Protestants tended to occupy the top positions. Protestants have also been favored in science, education, government, and the military. An early investigation by Fry of the religious preferences of persons included in *Who's Who in America* (which includes many businessmen also) disclosed that of those who claimed church membership over 90 per cent were Protestant; over half of these were Episcopalians, Presbyterians, or Congregationalists.[19] A later analysis by Beverly Davis of *Who's Who in the East* similarly found Protestants of the Anglo-American churches vastly overrepresented.[20] A more recent questionnaire

---

[15] Fletcher Knebel, "The WASPS: 1968," *Look,* XXXII (July 23, 1968), 69–72. On the overlap between top corporate personnel and the upper social class, see G. William Domhoff, *Who Rules America?* (Englewood Cliffs, N.J.: Prentice-Hall, Inc., 1967), Chaps. 1 and 2.

[16] See Domhoff, *ibid.;* Mills, *The Power Elite;* Gabriel Kolko, *Wealth and Power in America* (New York: Frederick A. Praeger, Inc., 1962); and Arthur M. Louis, "America's Centimillionaires," *Fortune* (May, 1968), 152–57.

[17] Mills, *ibid.,* p. 106.

[18] Baltzell, *An American Business Aristocracy,* p. 24.

[19] C. Luther Fry, "The Religious Affiliation of American Leaders," *The Scientific Monthly* (February, 1933), 241–49.

[20] Beverly Davis, "Eminence and Level of Social Origin," *American Journal of Sociology,* LIX (July, 1953), 11–18.

study by Koch of high-ranking influentials in several institutional areas revealed that Protestants were overwhelmingly predominant in education, the military, and business, overrepresented in government, but slightly underrepresented in labor and religion.[21]

Persons of Protestant background have in the past almost totally dominated American science and tend to continue to do so.[22] In an early study by Lehman and Witty of the religious affiliation of over 1,000 persons listed in the 1927 edition of *American Men of Science,* Protestants as a whole were vastly overrepresented, though as in business, Methodists, Baptists, and Lutherans appeared in much smaller numbers than would be expected from their proportion in the population.[23] However, only a fourth of the 1927 scientists actually held church membership. Recent trends in this area are toward a higher percentage Protestant church members among scientists and a slightly better representation of Catholics and Jews. For example, an analysis by Vaughan, Smith, and Sjoberg of the religious orientations of 642 randomly selected persons in the 1955 edition of *American Men of Science* revealed that 63 per cent claimed Protestant church ties, 24 per cent were not members of any church (probably a majority being disaffected Protestants), 7 per cent were Catholic, and 6 per cent were Jewish.[24] Further, a recent review of ethnic backgrounds of the presidents of 775 of the nation's colleges and universities found that nearly all were white Protestants and 80 per cent of the trustees of the ten largest universities were white Protestants.[25]

The highest office in the land has to date been held by eight persons who did not claim Protestant church affiliation (four Unitarians, three with no religious preference—including Jefferson and Lincoln—and one Catholic), but only John F. Kennedy can be counted among all Presidents as clearly non-WASP in background. Once more, Episcopalians and Presbyterians accounted for over half the Protestant total. Of the major Protestant denominations, only the Lutherans have not had at least one President of the United States.

In Congress, particularly in the House of Representatives, where many voting constituencies have been ethnically mixed or non-Anglo, we might expect that white Protestants have not been so completely dominant. Nevertheless, as Killian has noted, "In spite of the growth of cities,

[21] Mary R. Koch, "The Family Background of Influentials" (doctoral dissertation, St. Louis University, 1963).

[22] For a discussion of the affinities between Protestantism and science in an historical sense, see Robert K. Merton, "Puritanism, Pietism, and Science," in *Social Theory and Social Structure* (New York: The Free Press, 1962).

[23] Harvey Lehman and Paul Witty, "Scientific Eminence and Church Membership," *The Scientific Monthly* (December, 1931), 544.

[24] Ted R. Vaughan, Douglas H. Smith and Gideon Sjoberg, "The Religious Orientations of American Natural Scientists," *Social Forces,* XLIV (June, 1966), 519–26.

[25] Knebel, "The Wasps, 1968," p. 72.

of industrial empires, of giant labor unions, and of ethnic political machines, the dominance of the white, Protestant, rural-minded representative in Congress has been evident throughout the nation's history. It has been even more evident in state legislatures." [26] Empirical data presented by Matthews on the 77th, 78th, and 81st Congresses indicate that the percentage of known Protestants increased in both the Senate and the House over the period of time covered.[27] At the time of the Ninetieth Congress (1967) 80 per cent of the Senators were Protestant *church members* (an additional 4 per cent were Mormon) plus 70 per cent of the Representatives; 78 per cent of all Governorships were held by Protestant church members.[28] Episcopalians, Presbyterians, and Methodists were vastly overrepresented in these offices, Baptists and Jews proportionately represented, Catholics underrepresented, and Disciples of Christ and Lutherans much underrepresented.

Finally, in the Supreme Court, statistics gathered by Schmidhauser indicated that of the 91 justices who served from 1789 to 1957 only six were Catholic and three Jewish.[29] Fifty-one were from two churches—Episcopalian and Presbyterian—but all the major Protestant denominations have had at least one representative on the Supreme Court.

Protestants are very concerned about what they feel to be the rising secular influence of Catholics in this country. Conversely, Catholics seem to be confident of their own power position while displaying very limited anxiety over a Protestant political threat. In view of Protestant hegemony in the upper class and various elites, these perceptions seem anomalous. However, Stark found that only 8 per cent of Catholics in his sample felt Protestants possessed "too much power" compared to 47 per cent of the Protestants who felt Catholics had "too much power." [30] Protestants are perhaps unaccustomed to sharing power privileges and are apprehensive about Catholic successes, whereas Catholics are accustomed to Protestant power but feel the tide of events to be on their side.

PROTESTANTS AND CATHOLICS

The over-all national trend in Protestant-Catholic socioeconomic differences (excluding the economic elite) has been one of a rather sub-

26 Lewis M. Killian, *The Impossible Revolution* (New York: Random House, Inc., 1968), p. 18.

27 Donald W. Matthews, *The Social Background of Political Decision Makers* (New York: Random House, Inc., 1954), pp. 26–27.

28 Edwin S. Gaustad, "America's Institutions of Faith," in Donald Cutler, ed., *The Religious Situation, 1968* (Boston: Beacon Press, 1968), pp. 851–54.

29 John R. Schmidhauser, "The Justices of the Supreme Court: A Collective Portrait," *Midwest Journal of Political Science,* III (February, 1959), 1–57.

30 Rodney Stark, "Through a Stained Glass Darkly; Reciprocal Protestant-Catholic Images in America," *Sociological Analysis,* XXV (Fall, 1964), 159–66.

stantial pre-World War II Protestant lead being narrowed in the post-war period and eliminated or surpassed in the 1960's. Empirical studies of Protestant-Catholic socioeconomic differences date back to Cantril's report on 1939 and 1940 national survey data.[31] At this time, a greater percentage of Protestants than Catholics were in the upper economic and college-educated categories. About 15 years later, national survey data analyzed by Bogue revealed that Catholics had pulled abreast with white Protestants in the percentage of white-collar jobs and incomes over $7,500, but continued to lag behind Protestants in education.[32]

National survey data gathered in 1964 and 1965 reported by Glenn and Hyland indicated that Catholics had by that time surpassed white Protestants in percentage of people with incomes over $7,500 and in non-manual occupations, but fewer Catholics than Protestants had some college education.[33] Above the $10,000 level and at the upper-white-collar level, differences between Protestants and Catholics were negligible.

National Protestant-Catholic comparisons, however, may be misleading. Although Protestants and Catholics may be viewed as national groups, individual Protestants and Catholics live in particular regions and communities, each with a different income distribution, occupational structure, and educational opportunities. White Protestants have been situated disproportionately in rural areas, small towns, and the South, whereas Catholics have much more often lived in cities, metropolises, and the Northeast. Clearly, broad educational and economic opportunities are inestimably greater in the city than in the country and in the Northeast than in the South. In national socioeconomic competition and comparisons, Protestants are thus at a disadvantage. For example, in the Glenn and Hyland study cited above, fully 40 per cent of white Protestant respondents lived on farms or in hamlets of fewer than 2,500 people, compared with only 15 per cent of the Catholics; over a third of the Protestants lived in the South, compared with only 8 per cent of the Catholics.

Taking residence differences into consideration, Glenn and Hyland further analyzed their data so as to include only those white Protestants and Catholics who lived in non-Southern metropolitan areas of 250,000 or more people. They then learned that more Protestants than Catholics earned $10,000 or more (24 per cent versus 18 per cent), were upper white-collar (38 per cent versus 24 per cent), and had some college education (35 per cent versus 24 per cent). Along similar lines of analysis, Organic

[31] Hadley Cantril, "Educational and Economic Composition of Religious Groups," *American Journal of Sociology*, XLVIII (March, 1943), 574–79.

[32] Donald Bogue, *The Population of the United States* (New York: The Free Press, 1959), 702–6.

[33] Glenn and Hyland, "Religious Preference and Worldly Success."

discovered that among non-farm sons of non-farm fathers in a large 1960 national sample, Protestants clearly exceeded Catholics in occupation, income, and education.[34]

Protestant-Catholic socioeconomic differences may vary greatly from community to community. For example, Protestant-Catholic differences in Detroit [35] have not been nearly so large as in New Haven [36] or Wichita.[37] Protestant-Catholic occupational distributions varied greatly in two neighboring towns studied by Schroeder and Obenhaus.[38] Similarly, twice as many Protestants as Catholics were in the upper-white-collar class and college graduates in Catholic City, whereas Protestant-Catholic socioeconomic disparaties were very small in Protestant City.

Local differences in the social status of Protestants and Catholics may be partially due to the national origin constituencies of the two groups. For instance, New Haven's Protestants were largely British, where Detroit's Protestants were much more diverse in national origin. The Catholics of Protestant City were largely Irish, whereas the Catholic City sample contained many Poles and Slavs. This, of course, points up what some people consider to be the explanation of religious group differences: Catholics as a group are more recent immigrants than Protestants.[39] However, the majority of respondents in the surveys and studies noted thus far have probably been at least of the third generation in both religious groups; many of the immigration handicaps should have been eliminated by the time of most of these investigations. The "catching up" that Catholics have done since the pre-World War II period has probably been due as much to the remarkable economic growth and prosperity in urban America (outside the largely black slums) as to the Americanization of the second and third generations.

RICH PROTESTANTS, POOR PROTESTANTS

Broad Protestant-Catholic status comparisons are misleading in a second way. Much as individual Protestants reside in particular places with distinctive economic opportunities, so do they belong to particular

[34] Organic, "Religious Affiliation and Social Mobility."

[35] Lenski, *The Religious Factor.*

[36] Hollingshead and Redlich, *Social Class and Mental Illness.*

[37] Donald O. Cowgill, "The Ecology of Religious Preference in Wichita," *The Sociological Quarterly,* I (April, 1960), 87–96.

[38] W. Widick Schroeder and Victor Obenhaus, *Religion in American Culture* (New York: The Free Press, 1964).

[39] For instance, S. M. Lipset and Reinhard Bendix, *Social Mobility in Industrial Society* (Berkeley: University of California Press, 1959), pp. 48–56.

denominations with characteristic socioeconomic status.[40] As Liston Pope's classic study of denominational stratification confirmed, Protestant churches have arranged themselves in an hierarchical order of social status (Catholics, too, are diversified socioeconomically by national origin).[41] Recent data indicate that stratification of the Protestant churches is as definite today as it was at the time of Pope's study (Table 11–1). Thus, broad

TABLE 11–1

SOCIOECONOMIC STATUS OF SELECTED AMERICAN RELIGIOUS GROUPS

Group	Median Family Income (1966) [a]	Median Years Education (1966) [a]	Percentage White-Collar (1957) [b]
Jewish	14,688	15.7	67
Episcopalian	13,000	13.0	63
Presbyterian	11,667	13.5	47
Methodist	10,703	12.1	32
Lutheran	10,375	12.0	31
No preference	10,357	12.1	30
Roman Catholic	9,999	12.0	29
Baptist	9,311	11.4	20

[a] Edward O. Laumann, "The Social Structure of Religious and Ethnoreligious Groups in a Metropolitan Community," *American Sociological Review*, XXXIV (April, 1969), 186.

[b] Bernard Lazerwitz, "A Comparison of Major United States Religious Groups," *Journal of the American Statistical Association*, LVI (September, 1961), 568–79.

Protestant-Catholic comparisons of socioeconomic status are misleading in the sense that Episcopalians, Presbyterians, and Congregationalists are much better represented than Catholics at the higher socioeconomic levels, Methodists and Lutherans only slightly better, and Baptists and sectarians worse. The postwar socioeconomic success of the Jews scarcely needs mention; as a group they have moved ahead of Episcopalians, the highest-ranking Protestant denomination. All Presbyterian and Congregational churches are not, of course upper-middle-class churches, nor all Methodist and Lutheran churches middle class, or Baptist and sectarian working class. The general trend in the social status of the over-all

[40] For the historical background of denominational stratification, see H. Richard Neibuhr, *The Social Sources of Denominationalism* (Cleveland: The World Publishing Company, 1962).

[41] Liston Pope, "Religion and the Class Structure," *The Annals of the American Academy of Political and Social Science*, CCLVI (March, 1948), 84–91.

membership of these churches is, however, in this direction.[42] There are few "prestige" Methodist, Lutheran, Christian, or Baptist congregations. There are also few déclassé Episcopalian, Congregational (outside of New England), or Presbyterian congregations.

A reason why Protestant churches may be class-typed, aside from the historical role of the churches of national origin groups and the frontier, is that their congregations are usually social communities as well as religious assemblies. A characteristic human practice is to participate in groups of people with whom one bears psychological affinities and holds common social and cultural interests. Marginal businessmen, white-collar workers, and skilled laborers may belong to Methodist and Baptist churches rather than Episcopalian or Congregational churches for the same reason that they participate in the Elks or American Legion rather than a country club or Town and Gown. Persons of all strata simply feel more comfortable among status equals. As a Jonesville resident put it:

> You see, the people in this church [Calvinist] are funny. Most of them are, well, they think they're so high and mighty just because they've got a little money. They're not my kind of folks. You see, they hold you at arm's length and kind of look down on you. You go over to the Baptist Church —they're my kind of folks. You'll notice the spirit there. There's the spirit of friendship. They all like one another and they're just common people.[43]

More than likely, what has been interpreted to be social snobbery was largely a lack of mutual interests and concerns upon which to make conversation and build friendships. Higher-level managers, businessmen, and professionals are more likely to run out of things to say to "nine-to-five" workers with a high school education than they are to each other, and vice versa. After church, when Protestants like to chat with one another, and at church socials, of which there are many, educational and occupational differences become crucial in social interaction among parishioners. Thus, Baptists and sectarians are not so much lower-status Protestants because they are Baptists and sectarians as because they are lower-status in general, and so on for members of other class-typed congregations. Obviously Protestants do a considerable amount of denominational and congregational switching in order to remain consistent with their status movements. Churches that still maintain national origin ties, such as the Lutheran and Reformed, are more or less an exception to de-

---

42 For evidence of the new middle-class status of Methodism and Lutheranism, see Samuel A. Mueller, "Changes in the Social Status of Lutheranism in Ninety Chicago Suburbs, 1950–1960," *Sociological Analysis*, XXVII (Fall, 1966), 138–45; and Frederick A. Shippey, "Social Class in Philadelphia Methodism," *Sociology and Social Research*, XLIII (September, 1958), 23–27.

43 W. Lloyd Warner, *Democracy in Jonesville* (New York: Harper & Row, Publishers, 1949), p. 167.

nominational switching for status reasons, although many members do engage in congregational switching to remain abreast with their status aspirations.

SOCIAL MOBILITY AND
THE PROTESTANT ETHIC

Max Weber argued that certain religious doctrines promulgated by Protestant reformers in the sixteenth and early seventeenth centuries had favorable unforeseen consequences for their adherents in the realm of economic life.[44] Weber contended that the Protestant emphases on work as a divine calling, rational and methodical conduct in worldly affairs, the doctrine of predestination and election, and ascetic and self-denying behavior produced the unintended results of economic growth and prosperity among Protestants, especially Calvinists. The purely religious supports of the work ethic and ascetic behavior did not, according to Weber, survive to the nineteenth century. But as Weber suggested, the sanctity of work and avoidance of personal dissipation in leisure need not be directly or consciously tied to religious beliefs in order to have an impact on worldly success. As Troeltsch has pointed out, "When all is said and done, Calvinism remains the real nursing-father of the civic, industrial capitalism of the middle-class." [45] Are contemporary Protestants, for these reasons or for other religiously related reasons, more successful in socioeconomic pursuits than Catholics? That is, are individual Protestants more socioeconomically mobile than individual Catholics?

As an indicator of the relative mobility of Protestants and Catholics, a comparison is usually made between fathers and their sons in order to ascertain whether Protestant sons have been more mobile than Catholic sons. However, in order to isolate religious influences per se on mobility, other related factors such as a person's race, residence, father's occupational and educational status, and national origin status must be held constant. If we are to believe that being Protestant is more conducive to worldly success than being Catholic, then we must be certain that any differences between the two groups are not merely an artifact of some third factor. (Though present in decreasing amounts, discrimination against Catholics would be nearly impossible to take into account in mobility studies; nevertheless we should be aware of its existence, however slight.)

Few studies of Protestant-Catholic mobility have imposed the neces-

44 Weber, *The Protestant Ethic.*
45 Ernst Troeltsch, *Protestantism and Progress* (Boston: Beacon Press, 1958), pp. 135–36.

sary controls on the data. There are, however, two studies of differential mobility of Protestants and Catholics that have matched the two groups on a number of important variables that might interfere with an evaluation of the influence of religion. The first was conducted by Weller, using Detroit area samples gathered from 1952 through 1958.[46] By excluding from his sample nonwhites, southern migrants, immigrants, and persons who grew up on farms, Weller automatically eliminated the influence of these factors on respondent's mobility. Then, with father's occupation held constant, Weller observed, for example, that Protestants who were raised in lower-blue-collar families achieved upper-white-collar status more often than Catholics from the same economic groups. The move from the working class or lower middle class into the upper middle class is of cardinal importance, and it is this step that Protestants take significantly more often than Catholics. The Protestants also earned higher incomes and had completed more years of education than Catholics of similar class origin. Moreover, within each level of educational achievement, Protestants were earning more than Catholics: in particular, among college graduates, three times as many Protestants reported high incomes as Catholics. Protestant socioeconomic advantages existed within both high-status and low-status national origin background groups (northwest and southeast European background). Finally, and most important, the Protestant-Catholic intergenerational achievement gap was significantly greater among respondents *under forty years of age* than in the older age category.

The second of the two studies alluded to above, this one conducted by Organic, had the added advantage of dealing with a national sample instead of one metropolitan area.[47] This analysis was also limited to sons of non-farm fathers, held class origins constant, and compared high- and low-status national origin groups. Organic's findings on the national level were very similar to those of Weller in Detroit. Protestants more often than Catholics made one- and two-step moves up from their father's occupational level, earned high annual incomes, and completed college. The educational gap *widened* in the younger age category.

How much of Protestant-Catholic mobility differences can be accounted for by the traditional Protestant ethic? Is there any evidence, for example, to indicate that Protestants hold more favorable attitudes toward work than do Catholics?[48] In response to a question asking if

---

[46] Weller, "Religion and Social Mobility."

[47] Organic, "Religious Affiliation and Social Mobility."

[48] The question being raised here does not pose a preference for work against a preference for paid idleness, but rather a preference for work against a preference for earned leisure. Nearly everyone, regardless of religion or status, prefers earned leisure over paid idleness. See Curt Tausky, "Meanings of Work Among Blue-Collar Men," *Pacific Sociological Review*, XII (Spring, 1969), 49–55.

hours on the job are enjoyed more than hours off the job, 48 per cent of Protestants in a 1955 national sample answered yes compared to 32 per cent of the Catholics.[49] However, in northern metropolitan areas, Protestants' attitudes toward work were closer to those of Catholics. Another question in the same survey asked respondents if they enjoyed work so much that it was hard to put aside: 52 per cent of Protestants compared to 42 per cent of Catholics answered positively. But again, northern metropolitan Protestants were similar to Catholics, at 42 per cent. The work ethic remains strongest in the rural Protestant population, and in rural areas it is more operative among older than among younger persons.[50] Like differences in mobility, Protestant-Catholic work attitudes diverge more in the upper middle class than in the middle mass.[51]

Do Protestants engage in more productive leisure time pursuits than Catholics and indulge themselves less? At least one piece of evidence would answer the former question in the affirmative. A sample of Protestant women were more likely than Catholic women to be involved in self-constructive leisure pursuits such as reading, taking educational courses, decorating, doing art work, doing social service work, and taking part-time jobs.[52] However, informal observation would suggest that, in general, devotion to mass culture and passive entertainment and the "camping-house-yard syndrome" characterizes Protestants and Catholics alike.

Differences between Protestants and Catholics in attitudes toward work and use of leisure, though perhaps relevant to a degree, would seem inadequate to account for more than a small part of mobility differences. If the metropolitan situation is indicative of a trend (as it usually is), Protestants are evidently changing their work-leisure values toward the Catholic norm, rather than vice versa. The notion of work as an end in itself is waning. Contemporary Catholics, we might note, are as materialistic and "ambitious" as Protestants, if not more so. Greeley's analysis of a national sample of 1961 college graduates disclosed that significantly more Catholics than Protestants held "making a lot of money" as an occupational value and a considerably larger proportion than Protestants were heading into the business world. In contrast, significantly larger percentages of Protestants than Catholics held service to others as an

[49] Leonard Broom and Norval D. Glenn, "Religious Differences in Reported Attitudes and Behavior," *Sociological Analysis*, XXVII (Winter, 1966), 187–209.

[50] Bernice Goldstein and Robert L. Eichorn, "The Changing Protestant Ethic: Rural Patterns in Health, Work, and Leisure," *American Sociological Review*, XXVI (August, 1961), 557–65.

[51] Lenski, *The Religious Factor*, pp. 89–98.

[52] *Ibid.*, pp. 227–28.

occupational value and expected to be employed in educational and welfare institutions.[53]

Regardless of whether modern Protestants emphasize educational values and achievement more than Catholics do (and this is very doubtful as we shall see in a moment), Protestants have continued to outdistance Catholics in educational mobility, and hence, occupational and income mobility. Why do Protestants more often complete college, professional, and graduate school?

THE FAMILY AND
SOCIOECONOMIC MOBILITY

Both popular and academic thinking has presumed that Protestants place greater emphasis on early independence training, intellectual autonomy, and achievement orientation in child rearing than Catholics and less on strict obedience and discipline. Despite some evidence that would tend to confirm this image of relative Protestant-Catholic value emphasis in socialization, especially in regard to the upper middle class,[54] it is not clear that differences in mobility are a related phenomenon. Discipline and obedience, for example, would seem just as essential to educational and economic mobility in American schools and business as independence and autonomy, if not more so.

Lenski has suggested that Protestants are more successful than Catholics because Protestants are not so strongly attached to the kin group as Catholics, and thus are more able to make the break with home and family that is often required of socially mobile persons.[55] However, attachment to the kin group has advantages in mutual aid and support, which probably offset any disadvantages. Indeed, persons in the more successful socioeconomic groups tend to exchange aid and services with family members more frequently than do persons in the less successful ones.[56] Moreover, as previously discussed, kin *are* the most important category of social ties for Protestants. *And the reason why Protestants move geographically more often than Catholics do is not so much that*

53 Andrew M. Greeley, *Religion and Career* (New York: Sheed and Ward, 1963).

54 Rosen, "Race, Ethnicity, and the Achievement Syndrome"; D. C. McClelland, et al., "Religious and Other Sources of Parental Attitudes Towards Independence Training," in *Studies in Motivation,* ed. D. C. McClelland (New York: Appleton-Century-Crofts, 1955); Richard E. Carney and Wilbert J. McKeachie, "Religion, Sex, Social Class, Probability of Success, and Student Personality," *Journal for the Scientific Study of Religion,* II (Fall, 1963), 32–42; Lenski, *The Religious Factor,* pp. 222–23; and Broom and Glenn, "Religious Attitudes in Reported Attitudes and Behavior."

55 Lenski, *The Religious Factor,* p. 345.

56 Marvin B. Sussman, "The Isolated Nuclear Family: Fact or Fiction," *Social Problems,* VI (1959), 333–40.

Protestants have weaker kinship ties as it is that the rural Protestant population has been caught up in the process of metropolitanization. Large numbers of Protestants *must* leave their homes and families if they desire better socioeconomic opportunities; Catholics and especially Jews have always been more strategically located residentially.

If there are any other factors that today seem to be sufficiently important to generate and sustain differences in the socioeconomic mobility of Protestants and Catholics, especially into the upper middle class (where, in fact, differences are the greatest), they are family size and child spacing.[57] The more children a couple has and the more rapid the succession, the less capital is available to be invested in each child's upbringing and education.[58] The tie between family size and higher education is evident to a parent who has underwritten four years of college for a son or daughter. Few couples with three or four children, or even two, if they are born in rapid succession, have either ample time or financial resources to assure each child a four-year college education, not to mention placement in the more prestigious colleges, graduate and professional schools—the real gateways to the upper middle class.[59]

Do Protestants have smaller families than Catholics? The evidence is unequivocal.[60] Protestants desire and actually have fewer children than Catholics. Important differences in fertility between Protestants and Catholics have persisted under the most rigorous methodological controls. An authoritative source noted that Protestant-Catholic family-size differences "have persisted . . . and now appear to be widening. Moreover, there is no indication that they are reduced by the upward socioeconomic mobility of Catholics. In fact, the largest Catholic-Protestant differentials in family-size expectations are usually found in the higher social and economic groups. . . ." [61] (This is the level at which Protestant-Catholic

---

[57] For evidence concerning the relationship between family size and personal and intergenerational mobility, see Jerzy Berent, "Fertility and Social Mobility," *Population Studies*, V (March, 1952), 244–60.

[58] For a discussion concerning the relationship between the small-family norm, capital formation, and differential Protestant-Catholic mobility, see Lenski, *The Religious Factor*, p. 352.

[59] Children from larger families also tend to score lower on intelligence tests and may later compete less successfully on entrance examinations to prestige schools and for grants and scholarships.

[60] For example, see Pascal Whelpton, Arthur A. Campbell, and John E. Patterson, *Fertility and Family Planning in the United States* (Princeton, N.J.: Princeton University Press, 1966); Charles F. Westoff and Raymond H. Potvin, *College Women and Fertility Values* (Princeton, N.J.: Princeton University Press, 1967); and Ronald Freedman, Pascal Whelpton, and John Smit, "Socio-Economic Factors in Religious Differentials in Fertility," *American Sociological Review*, XXVI (August, 1961), 608–14.

[61] Whelpton, Campbell, and Patterson, *Fertility and Family Planning in the United States*, p. 77.

socioeconomic mobility differentials are the greatest.) Catholics are several times more likely than Protestants to expect and have families of four children or more. Furthermore, as is untrue among Protestants, the more a Catholic is involved in religious activities, the larger is the family he desires.[62] Interestingly enough, a *larger fertility difference* between younger Protestants and Catholics than among older ones is matched by the *wider mobility gap* (as noted above) among the younger than among older age groups.

Of probably even greater importance than family size and its attendant impact upon life chances and social mobility is the correlative phenomenon of child spacing. Children born only a year or so apart will be ready to enter college, for example, at about the same time, bringing heavy financial pressure to bear on reserves and credit. Conversely, a three- or four-year interim between births alleviates the financial burdens of education temporarily and improves the educational chances of second or third children, especially if they happen to be girls, who usually fall heir to any educational deficit if born close in age to a boy. Data presented by Whelpton revealed that Protestants definitely space their children at longer intervals than do Catholics.[63] Jews, in turn, space births more widely than Protestants, although the two groups' family sizes are very similar.

Thus, on the individual average, each Jewish child would enjoy a greater investment of time and capital than each Protestant child, and Protestant children more than Catholic. In view of the relationship between family size, child spacing and socioeconomic mobility among Jews, Protestants, and Catholics, there are grounds for arguing that the higher mobility rates of Protestants than of Catholics (and among Jews than among Protestants) are due in part if not largely to differences in fertility behavior.

But why do Protestants *want* and *have* fewer children, further apart, than Catholics? Briefly stated, Protestants tend to hold a two-child norm more than Catholics do, a norm which at least for American Catholics does not appear to harmonize very well with religious values or socioreligious participation. Catholics have been socialized in and participate in a religious and socioreligious value system which, if it does not enhance fertility, at least is antithetical to the two-child norm. Even for Catholics who would prefer the small family model, Church doctrines that militate against family planning and birth control discourage its realization.

A final piece of my own evidence might be cited, which brings

---

62 Westoff and Potvin, *College Women and Fertility Values,* p. 153.

63 Pascal Whelpton, "Trends and Differentials in the Spacing of Births," *Demography,* I (1964), 83–93.

TABLE 11–2

PERCENTAGE OF PROTESTANT AND CATHOLIC RESPONDENTS
WITH GIVEN NUMBERS OF CHILDREN IN TWO CITIES

Number of Children	Protestant City		Catholic City	
	Protestants (N = 161)	Catholics (N = 42)	Protestants (N = 68)	Catholics (N = 122)
0	11%	7%	14%	3%
1	14	24	22	7
2	34	17	25	15
3	19	12	26	25
4	12	12	4	17
5 or more	10	28	9	34

together in an admittedly suggestive and indirect way the proposed relationship between fertility and socioeconomic mobility. In Protestant City, where Protestant-Catholic fertility differences were relatively small (Table 11–2), Protestants were only slightly more likely to have climbed into the college-educated ranks from working-class backgrounds than were Catholics. In Catholic City, where Protestant-Catholic fertility differences were large, Protestants were much more likely than Catholics to have left their working-class backgrounds for a college education and an upper-white-collar job. For example, fully 45 per cent of the Protestant respondents whose fathers had a high school education or less (N = 70) themselves completed college, compared to only 18 per cent of the Catholics with similarly educated fathers (N = 92). These data confirm, albeit indirectly,[64] the suggested relationship between fertility behavior and social mobility.

SUMMARY

Owing to the size and diversity of the group, white Protestants are distributed in sizeable numbers throughout every level of the class structure. At both local and national levels, Protestants have traditionally dominated the apexes of occupational hierarchies and upper-class social institutions. Locally, other minority groups have recently moved into leading positions in government and business, but have developed their own parallel upper-class social institutions. In areas of national promi-

[64] The confirmation is indirect in the sense that size of respondent's family of procreation is being considered and not family of orientation, a comparison that would be necessary for more direct substantiation of the relationship between fertility and intergenerational mobility. A degree of intergenerational continuity in fertility behavior is here being assumed. Since it can only be assumed in this case, an actual cross-tabulation of intergenerational mobility with family size would not be warranted.

nence, Protestants have been more successful in preserving control of top leadership positions. Yet, here too, white Protestants no longer rest entirely secure. New technology, new wealth, and new and scarce expertise sometimes outweigh ethnic purity, although we have considerable distance to travel before a meritocratic system is achieved. The prestige and status institutions of the upper class have remained largely impermeable to minority persons, despite the fashionability of a certain amount of ethnic liberalism.

Nationwide Protestant-Catholic socioeconomic differences have been largely eliminated. However, in the cities, white Protestants have perpetuated socioeconomic advantages, especially in education and at the upper-middle-class level. White Protestants also enjoy higher socioeconomic mobility rates than do Catholics. Explanations of Protestant-Catholic socioeconomic differences that point to factors such as the Protestant ethic, personal autonomy, or restricted kinship ties are either invalid or weak. The fact that white Protestants have fewer children further apart than Catholics, thus giving the children greater educational opportunities and access to the upper middle class, outweighs other explanations in importance.

White Protestants have seldom acted in concert on a public issue. On questions of public morality, the role of government in economy and society, civil rights and civil liberties, and electoral offices, white Protestants may be found at all points on the attitudinal and behavioral spectrum. Diversity among Protestants in civic affairs has reflected differences according to region, denomination and belief, social class, and national origin.

On certain points of public concern, however, a dominant perspective has been characteristic of at least the majority of white Protestants, particularly if there has appeared to be a definable Catholic position (such as controversies over the direct or indirect use of public monies or facilities for religious purposes). Protestant opinion has not, of course, always been a mere inversion of a real or imagined Catholic interest. Among noteworthy Protestant civic triumphs have been immigration restriction, Prohibition, and bans against the teaching of evolution. The latter issue has continued to crop up in various Protestant strongholds even in the past decade.

White Protestants in the Civic Arena

Though most liberal and progressive movements have relied heavily on white Protestant leadership and support, the consistent and pervasive thrust of white Protestantism has been and continues to be rural and conservative. As Grimes has pointed out,

> Traditionally, American politics has reflected in its principles the composition of its constituents. For much of our history, the country has been predominantly Protestant and has reflected in its politics a Protestant prejudice....[T]he country has been predominantly rural and has reflected in its politics this rural hegemony.[1]

Later, in connection with a discussion of voting behavior, we shall observe that the more a white Protestant is involved in his religious community, the more likely he is to vote conservative.

[1] Alan P. Grimes, *Equality in America* (New York: Oxford University Press, Inc., 1964), p. 125.

CIVIC ISSUES

White Protestants have evinced the least internal division of opinion and the greatest degree of consensus on questions of public and ascetic morality. That there has been consensus among white Protestants on these kinds of questions has been documented by Stark; he found slight difference in outlook among the various Protestant denominations concerning drinking, gambling, divorce, and birth control.[2] A majority of Protestants agreed with the statements: "Catholics are very lax about drinking and gambling as compared to Protestants" (Catholics disagreed); "Compared to Catholics, Protestants do not oppose divorce as often as they should" (Catholics agreed); and "Catholics interfere with the rights of others to practice birth control if they wish" (Catholics disagreed). A majority of Protestants personally disapproved of gambling, whereas only 23 per cent of the Catholics did so; a large majority of Protestants approved of artificial birth control, compared to 28 per cent of Catholics. National poll data have indicated that a third of Protestants favored nationwide prohibition of alcoholic beverages as opposed to 8 per cent of Catholics, and about half abstained from drinking alcoholic beverages compared to a quarter of the Catholics.[3]

Protestant opinion on questions like those above crosses class lines as well as denominational ones. Middle- and working-class Detroit Protestants were about equally opposed to gambling, drinking, and conducting business on Sunday, and equally in favor of allowing birth control and divorce. On each of these issues except Sunday business, Catholics tended to assume an opposite stance.

Another point on which Protestants largely agree among themselves and conflict with Catholics concerns federal aid to parochial schools. Most Protestants abhor the prospect of tax support to Catholic education and the issue sparks the most volatile feelings surrounding any Protestant-Catholic civic difference.

In other matters of government and economy, class interests directly compete with religious influences. Working-class Protestants, whose class interests tend to be liberal and align them with the Democratic party, in particular find class interests conflicting with the conservative influences of their religious group. Protestantism has traditionally been more allied with "individualism" than with "collectivism," historically the ideology of the working class. For instance, only about one-fourth of the

---

2 Rodney Stark, "Through a Stained Glass Darkly: Reciprocal Protestant-Catholic Images in America," *Sociological Analysis*, XXV (Fall, 1964), 159–66.

3 Leonard Broom and Norval D. Glenn, "Religious Differences in Reported Attitudes and Behavior," *Sociological Analysis*, XXVII (Winter, 1966), 187–209.

Protestants residing in a Midwestern town favored a program of federal health insurance, compared to over half the Catholics.[4] A national poll conducted a generation ago found approximately one-third of the Protestants favoring guaranteed economic security as opposed to well over half the Catholics.[5]

The pull of class interests against religious influences in political and economic matters may be observed in the same national poll data on guaranteed economic security. Twice as many Baptists (who are typically working-class people) as Congregationalists (who are typically middle-class people) were in favor of the government's instituting a program of basic economic security. Moreover, within each denomination blue-collar workers were much more receptive toward this idea than were white-collar persons.

As a broader indicator of the pull of political and economic liberalism among working-class Protestants, Lenski found that on a battery of questions dealing with governmental powers in unemployment, education, social security, medical care, and housing, the mean percentage of blue-collar Protestants giving answers consistent with a welfare state philosophy was 65, compared to 39 per cent for white-collar Protestants.[6] Indeed, blue-collar Protestants were nearly as supportive of governmental action in these areas as blue-collar Catholics and more so than *white-collar* Catholics. White-collar Protestants, however, were far less supportive of the welfare program than were white-collar Catholics. We shall return to the question of religion and politics later in the chapter.

Social Tolerance

On matters concerning civil rights, civil liberties, and tolerance, white Protestants are again scattered across the liberal-conservative continuum. On attitudes toward minority groups such as Jews and Negroes, white Protestants as a group are slightly less liberal than Catholics, though conflicting evidence does exist.[7] Considerably more Catholics than Protestants, for example, would vote for a qualified Negro or Jewish candidate for President, though a majority of Protestants would vote for the latter.

[4] W. Widick Schroeder and Victor Obenhaus, *Religion in American Culture* (New York: The Free Press, 1964), p. 169.

[5] Wesley Allinsmith and Beverly Allinsmith, "Religious Affiliation and Political-Economic Attitude," *Public Opinion Quarterly,* XII (Fall, 1948), 377–89.

[6] Gerhard Lenski, *The Religious Factor* (Garden City, N.Y.: Doubleday & Company, Inc., 1963), p. 155.

[7] For example, see Paul Sheetsly, "White Attitudes Toward the Negro," *Daedalus,* XCV (Winter, 1966), 217–38; and Broom and Glenn, "Religious Differences in Reported Attitudes and Behavior"; for conflicting evidence, see Harold J. Abramson and C. Edward Noll, "Religion, Ethnicity, and Social Change," *Review of Religious Research,* VIII (Fall, 1966), 11–26.

By contrast, Protestants tend to be more liberal than Catholics in the area of civil liberties.[8] The more a Protestant is involved in his religious community, the greater is his support for such rights as criticism of the President and attacks upon religion; conversely, the more a Catholic is involved in his religious community, the less is his support for these freedoms.

Class or educational differences, however, are much more important than religious differences in determining social tolerance among Protestants and Catholics. Liberal and conservative tendencies by class in social tolerance are the reverse, however, of what they are in economic and political matters. Higher-status Protestants tend to exhibit more openness than lower-status Protestants toward free speech, free press, racial desegregation, the United Nations, and minority groups. Higher-status Catholics are, in fact, more liberal socially than lower-status Protestants. Middle-class Protestants are not, of course, all enlightened social liberals and working-class Protestants all intolerant bigots. Social tolerance *tends* to be related to social status, especially to education (educated people, however, may only feel it less acceptable to *express* prejudice). Poorly educated and lower-status people often display a remarkable openness to and tolerance of other groups and points of view. Many more simply don't care one way or the other, whereas higher-status persons more often have definite opinions.

The belief that religious persons are more prejudiced and intolerant than nonreligious persons has the weight of very prestigious names and research behind it.[9] The evidence is not, however, unequivocal. Rosenblum, for instance, discovered that regular church attenders evinced *less* ethnic prejudice and *greater* democratic tendencies than irregular church attenders.[10] A study by Keedy of southern college students turned up a low correlation between religious orthodoxy and ethnocentrism and none at all between religious orthodoxy and authoritarianism.[11] Lenski found that Protestants with records of faithful church attendance more often took a liberal stand on freedom of speech and racial integration than the less faithful. Finally, an investigation of college students by Maranell re-

---

[8] Abramson and Noll, "Religion, Ethnicity, and Social Change," p. 17; and Lenski, *The Religious Factor*, pp. 190–92.

[9] T. W. Adorno, et al., *The Authoritarian Personality* (New York: Harper & Row, Publishers, 1950); Gordon Allport, *The Nature of Prejudice* (Reading, Mass.: Addison-Wesley, 1954); Samuel A. Stouffer, *Communism, Conformity, and Civil Liberties* (Garden City, N.Y.: Doubleday & Company, Inc., 1955); and Milton Rokeach, *The Open and Closed Mind* (New York: Basic Books, Inc., 1960).

[10] Abraham L. Rosenblum, "Ethnic Prejudice as Related to Social Class and Religiosity," *Sociology and Social Research*, XLIV (March-April, 1959), 272–75.

[11] T. C. Keedy, Jr., "Anomie and Religious Orthodoxy," *Sociology and Social Research*, XLIII (September-October, 1958), 34–37.

vealed that religiosity was unrelated to bigoted attitudes toward Negroes and Jews.[12]

These data suggest that to link orthodox Protestantism directly to social intolerance is unwarranted. Religiosity is complex and many-faceted, as is the whole notion of social tolerance. Methodological problems are especially imposing in this area. We should have to take into account a host of other intervening factors, especially the nature and type of religiosity (for example, whether it is this-worldly or other-worldly), before making a responsible statement regarding the influence of religion on social tolerance and democratic thinking. A similar caution should be exercised in relating strength of religious community orientation to social tolerance. As the case of the Jews suggests, there is nothing inherently antithetical in strong religious community and social liberalism.

VOTING BEHAVIOR

The outcome of some of the civic issues discussed in the preceding section are often decided by ballot. White Protestants have customarily constituted the very large majority of conservative party members in American history. But again, class interests have worked against Protestantism's conservative influence on voting, as have many liberal churches and clergymen.

Before the onset of heavy immigration, Protestants as such had had no particular party identification. However, in the first decades of party politics, the different Protestant denominations tended to have links with specific political parties. Denominational beliefs concerning the relationship of church and state and the social class and geographical location of the denominations were early factors that allied the denominations to specific parties.

The first party manifestation of conservatism was the Federalist party, support for which came largely from among the higher-status and established Congregationalists and Anglicans.[13] The Federalists also drew support from Quakers, Lutherans, and Reformed. The liberals of the period, the Democratic-Republicans, found their most ardent supporters in the ranks of lower-status and rural Presbyterians, Methodists, and Baptists. With the decline of the Federalists, conservative Protestants shifted loyalty to the Whigs, and workers and farmers provided the backbone of the Jefferson-Jackson Democrats.

---

[12] Gary Maranell, "An Examination of Some Religious and Political Attitude Correlations of Bigotry," *Social Forces*, XLV (March, 1967), 356–74.

[13] See Seymour M. Lipset, "Religion and Politics in the American Past and Present," in *Religion and Social Conflict*, eds. Robert Lee and Martin E. Marty (New York: Oxford University Press, Inc., 1964).

As the modern Republican and Democrat parties emerged around the middle of the nineteenth century, Congregationalists and Episcopalians remained within the conservative tradition, that is, in the Republican party. Northern Methodists, Baptists, and Presbyterians, then the three largest denominations, began making a transition from left to right. As Lipset has pointed out, the transition for many Protestants was mediated by association with the American and Know-Nothing parties of the late 1840's and 1850's. Thus, by the time the Republican and Democratic parties as we know them had crystallized, the majority of northern Protestants had affiliated with the Republicans.

What encouraged the shift to the Republican party by the largest Protestant denominations? For one thing, many of the children of lower-status Presbyterians, Methodists, and Baptists had developed middle-class interests. Second, the Democratic party had been identified as the political vehicle of Catholics, immigrants, and city people, all anathema to the native rural-oriented Protestant. Protestant immigrants, especially German and Scandinavian, were faced with choosing between an anti-Know-Nothing, pro-immigrant, but Catholic and urban-oriented Democratic party, and a frequently nativist, anti-immigrant, but abolitionist and rural-oriented Republican party. More often than not, their Protestantism prevailed over their foreignism.

The Republican party thus became the repository of conservative Protestantism in the North in the latter half of the nineteenth and first part of the twentieth centuries, whereas the Democratic party took on a working-class and Catholic character. A majority of white Protestants voted Republican, and the Republican party was proportionately more Protestant than the Democratic party. The large bloc of Protestant votes delivered to Hoover in the 1928 Presidential election against the Catholic Democrat Smith bore witness to the strength of the religious issue in American politics of the period.

What can be said concerning the influence of religious affiliation on voting behavior since the 1930's? Have Protestants continued to deliver a disproportionate number of votes to Republican candidates and points of view? In many small towns outside the South to be a Protestant has been to be a Republican and to be a Catholic has been to be a Democrat. Although the relationship between religion and voting is by no means that simple, the tendency in Presidential elections since 1936 has been for a much larger proportion of non-southern white Protestants than of Catholics to vote Republican.[14] Class position, of course, has also

14 See, for example, Lipset, *ibid.*; Robert Alford, *Party and Society* (Chicago: Rand McNally & Co., 1963); Bernard Berelsen, Paul F. Lazarsfeld, and William N. McPhee, *Voting* (Chicago: University of Chicago Press, 1954); and Oscar Glantz, "Protestant and Catholic Voting Behavior in a Metropolitan Area," *Public Opinion Quarterly*, XXIII (Spring, 1959), 73–82.

been an important influence in Protestant voting behavior. Almost twice as many working-class as middle-class white Protestants vote Democratic. For example, in the 1956 Presidential election, 44 per cent of non-southern white Protestant manual workers voted Democratic, compared to 21 per cent of Protestants who were not manual workers. Indeed, blue-collar Protestants tend to vote Democratic almost as often as white-collar Catholics do.

Of religion and class, which has been the most important determinant in voting behavior? From 1936 to 1956, the percentage difference between Protestants and Catholics voting Democratic has been on the average slightly larger than the percentage differences between manual and nonmanual workers voting Democratic within the two religious groups, indicating that religion has been a degree more important than class influences. However, in 1960, with a Protestant running against a Catholic for President, the differences between religious groups were much larger than the differences between classes within religious groups. In the East, three-fourths of the Protestants voted for Richard M. Nixon and three-fourths of the Catholics voted for John F. Kennedy.[15]

In the Democratic Presidential landslide victory of 1964, the unusually light Protestant Democratic vote of 1960 was reversed; one of the largest percentages of Protestants voted Democratic since the inception of the current two-party system. Religious voting in the 1968 Presidential election was more typical of pre-1960 elections, as a majority of northern white Protestants returned to the Republican candidate while a majority of Catholics chose the Democrat.[16] George Wallace received proportionately twice as many votes from Protestants as Catholics, but the balance of the Protestant vote for former Governor Wallace was polled in southern states.

Voting information gathered on Protestant City and Catholic City residents for the 1960 and 1964 Presidential elections disclosed the customary relationship between religious and political preference (Table 12–1). The countering influences of class on religion were especially visible among Protestants. The majority of blue-collar Protestants were, in fact, Democratic voters, more than the national average. Mormons, like Protestants, were as a group Republican only because of the small Democratic vote among white-collar persons.

Before turning to the next topic, we might caution that white Protestantism is far from being incontrovertibly conservative in outlook, especially in the large cities. Fully 47 per cent of northern metropolitan white Protestants in the optimistic years of the early 1960's stated a

---

[15] Leo Rosten, ed., *Religions in America* (New York: Simon and Shuster, Inc., 1963), pp. 286–91.

[16] *New York Times*, December 8, 1968, p. 84.

TABLE 12–1

PERCENTAGE OF PROTESTANTS AND CATHOLICS IN TWO CITIES
WHO VOTED FOR OR PREFERRED THE DEMOCRATIC CANDIDATE
IN THE 1960 AND 1964 PRESIDENTIAL ELECTIONS,
BY OCCUPATIONAL GROUPS

City, Occupation, and Election	Protestants	Catholics	Statistical Significance (d.f. = 1)
Protestant City			
Total			
1960	48(N = 161)	84(N = 43)	.01
1964	43(N = 160)	74(N = 43)	.01
White-Collar Workers			
1960	38(N = 96)	85(N = 27)	.01
1964	29(N = 96)	74(N = 27)	.01
Blue-Collar Workers			
1960	67(N = 63)	81(N = 16)	No
1964	66(N = 62)	75(N = 16)	No
Catholic City			
Total			
1960	36(N = 70)	80(N = 122)	.01
1964	44(N = 72)	64(N = 121)	.01
White-Collar Workers			
1960	31(N = 58)	75(N = 77)	.01
1964	42(N = 60)	60(N = 78)	.01
Blue-Collar Workers			
1960	80(N = 10)	88(N = 43)	No
1964	60(N = 10)	70(N = 43)	No

preference for the liberal party "if there were only two parties in the U.S.—one for liberals and one for conservatives." [17] Because white Protestants have historically formed the backbone of the Republican party, one may easily overlook Protestant liberalism in both parties among politicians, clergymen, and laymen alike. The National Council of Churches, for example, has taken a consistently progressive stand on contemporary social problems.

THEOLOGY AND PARTY PREFERENCE

A question of considerable interest concerns the extent to which liberal or conservative religious affiliation and belief of white Protestants coincides with liberal or conservative political position (a different issue,

[17] Broom and Glenn, "Religious Differences in Reported Attitudes and Behavior."

we might note, from that of the relationship between religious belief and social tolerance discussed earlier in the chapter). We know that as a group Catholics and black Protestants tend to be religious conservatives and political-economic liberals. What, if any, relationship exists between these two phenomena among white Protestants?

The work of Benton Johnson has given us some insight into this question. Johnson's study of the political preferences of Methodist and Baptist ministers in Eugene, Oregon revealed that among the theological conservatives 80 per cent preferred the Republican party compared to 43 per cent of the theological liberals (all of the theological liberals were Methodists).[18] Theological liberals were six times as likely to be Democrats as the theological conservatives. Elsewhere, Johnson reported that the religiously liberal ministers were more often in favor of federal aid to education, the income tax, the United Nations, and foreign aid than were the religious conservatives.[19] Thus, among clergymen at least, liberal religious belief evidently finds harmony in liberal politics. Can the same thing be said of their parishioners?

One might first ask if liberal Protestant ministers exert a liberal political influence on their congregations, and vice versa for conservatives. Two separate studies, again by Johnson, suggest that they do. In the first, Johnson found that members of Eugene, Oregon churches with liberal pastors (which included Methodist, Congregationalist, and Presbyterian churches) who attended church services frequently were more likely to vote Democratic than those who seldom went to church. Similarly, persons belonging to churches with conservative pastors (Baptist, Disciples of Christ, and Reformed churches) who frequently attended church services more often voted Republican than those who seldom attended.[20] Significantly, both white- and blue-collar respondents fit the pattern of greater Democratic voting in liberal churches and greater Republican voting in conservative churches if they attended frequently. The findings above were reproduced in a second study.[21]

On the basis of this evidence, Johnson has argued that Protestantism has served to dilute class interests, according to which higher-status persons would affiliate with conservatism and lower-status persons with liberalism. The liberal clergy encourage a liberal vote in middle-class

[18] Benton Johnson, "Theology and Party Preference Among Protestant Clergymen," *American Sociological Review,* XXXI (April, 1966), 200–207.

[19] Benton Johnson, "Theology and the Position of Pastors on Public Issues," *American Sociological Review,* XXXII (June, 1967), 433–42.

[20] Benton Johnson, "Ascetic Protestantism and Political Preference," *Public Opinion Quarterly,* XXIV (Spring, 1962), 35–46.

[21] Benton Johnson, "Ascetic Protestantism and Political Preference in the Deep South," *American Journal of Sociology,* LXIX (January, 1964), 359–66.

Republican congregations, whereas conservative clergy stimulate a conservative vote in working-class Democratic congregations. The impact of liberal clergymen on their congregations is still open to some question, however, because members may choose congregations and regularity of attendance according to the compatibility of the pastor's political beliefs with their own.

Liberal clergymen may be political liberals and conservative clergymen political conservatives, and both may influence active members of their congregations. However, we still have no answer to the question concerning the relationship between religious and political position among the Protestant laity as such. Unfortunately, there is little in the empirical literature that is addressed directly to this question. However, by assuming that members of religiously more liberal denominations (Methodist, Congregationalist, Episcopalian, and Presbyterian) are religious liberals and members of conservative denominations (Baptist, Lutheran, and sectarian) are religious conservatives, we may get some idea from the Protestant City data concerning the tie between religious belief and political preference among Protestants. In this case, respondents affiliated with liberal denominations were as likely to vote Republican as those belonging to conservative denominations in 1960, and more than likely to vote Republican in 1964 (Table 12–2). In both conservative and liberal denominations, the more frequent church attenders more often voted Republican than the less regular church attenders. Evidently, if John-

TABLE 12–2

PERCENTAGE OF PROTESTANTS IN TWO CITIES WHO VOTED FOR
OR PREFERRED THE REPUBLICAN CANDIDATE IN THE 1960 AND 1964
PRESIDENTIAL ELECTIONS, BY FREQUENCY OF CHURCH ATTENDANCE,
AND MEMBERSHIP IN CONSERVATIVE AND LIBERAL DENOMINATIONS [a]

Frequency of Church Attendance	Conservative Denominations [b]		Liberal Denominations [b]
		1960	
At least weekly	63(N = 68)		66(N = 32)
Less than weekly	47(N = 62)		48(N = 50)
		1964	
At least weekly	69(N = 65)		77(N = 30)
Less than weekly	56(N = 61)		73(N = 49)

[a] Occupational status has been automatically held constant, because both religious classifications contain nearly the same proportion of white-collar and blue-collar persons.

[b] See Table 9–4n for classification of denominations.

son's hypothesis concerning the influence of the clergy is correct, there were few political liberals among Protestant City clergymen in the liberal denominations.

Conceivably, religious liberalism has no relationship to political liberalism among the laity as it does in the clergy.[22] A Protestant businessman with liberal religious leanings who is a member of the Methodist church, for example, may be no more inclined to vote Democratic than a fundamentalist Baptist worker is likely to vote Republican. Indeed, the opposite happens to be true much more often.

Why are liberal preachers more often political liberals than religiously liberal laymen? First, the *kind* of religious liberalism held by clergy may be a more "educated" liberalism, perhaps more secular, than mere skepticism regarding religious doctrines sometimes common among their parishioners. A more authentic religious liberalism could be more easily translatable into political liberalism. Second, a clergyman's religious liberalism would seem to harmonize better with his class interests than, say, a businessman's class interest would harmonize with his religious liberalism.

RELIGIOUS COMMUNITY AND PARTY PREFERENCE

As noted at the outset of the chapter, a series of historical developments involving residence, social class, and immigration set the stage for the affinity of white Protestantism with the Republican party. Once established, the alignment of religious groups with political parties may be to a large extent transmitted through the socialization process from one generation to the next. Protestant fathers who have been reared as Republicans tend to remain so and in turn rear their own children in the same political framework. Catholic Democratic fathers do much the same, and for that matter, so do Protestant Democrats and Catholic Republicans. A perusal of Table 12–3 will reveal that political inheritance is a powerful factor in the perpetuation of religious voting.

However, the socialization mechanism is not entirely efficient. Fathers affiliated with the minority political party in Protestantism (Democrat), Catholicism (Republican), and Mormonism (Democrat) were noticeably less successful in eliciting conformity in their children than those fathers who had the added support of their religious group's cen-

[22] The finding that a theological liberal is a political liberal in the case of clergymen but not laity was corroborated for Catholics by Norbert Wiley. See his "Religious and Political Liberalism Among Catholics," *Sociological Analysis,* XXVIII (Fall, 1967), 142–48.

tral political tendency. The fact of being Protestant, for example, appeared to draw many sons out of Democratic families into the Republican party. As Table 12–4 indicates, the higher the involvement of Protes-

TABLE 12–3

AGREEMENT OF PROTESTANT, CATHOLIC, AND MORMAN RESPONDENTS' PARTY PREFERENCE (1964) WITH FATHER'S PARTY PREFERENCE: PERCENTAGE

| | Protestant City | | Catholic City | | Mormon City | |
| | Protestant Fathers | | Catholic Fathers | | Mormon Fathers | |
Respondents' Preference	Republican (N = 96)	Democrat (N = 42)	Republican (N = 35)	Democrat (N = 55)	Republican (N = 66)	Democrat (N = 52)
Republican	73	36	66	19	72	47
Democrat	27	64	34	81	28	53
	P = .01		P = .01		P = .01	

TABLE 12–4

CORRESPONDENCE OF PROTESTANT AND MORMON RESPONDENTS' POLITICAL PREFERENCE (1964) WITH FATHERS' PARTY PREFERENCE AND RESPONDENTS' STRENGTH OF RELIGIOUS COMMUNITY: PERCENTAGE

Protestant Fathers' Preference
Protestant City

	Republican		Democrat	
		Respondent		Respondent
	Respondent	Medium	Respondent	Medium
	High	and Low	High	and Low
Respondents' Preference	Community (N = 41)	Community (N = 55)	Community (N = 14)	Community (N = 28)
Republican	88	64	72	22
Democrat	12	36	28	78
	P = .01		P = .01	

Mormon Fathers' Preference

	Republican		Democrat	
		Respondent		Respondent
	Respondent	Medium	Respondent	Medium
	High	and Low	High	and Low
	Community (N = 43)	Community (N = 21)	Community (N = 30)	Community (N = 22)
Republican	77	67	60	28
Democrat	23	33	40	72
	N.S.		P = .01	

TABLE 12–5

PERCENTAGE OF PROTESTANTS IN TWO CITIES WHO
VOTED FOR OR PREFERRED THE REPUBLICAN CANDIDATE IN
THE 1960 AND 1964 PRESIDENTIAL ELECTIONS, BY STRENGTH
OF RELIGIOUS COMMUNITY AND OCCUPATIONAL GROUPS

City, Occupation, and Election	High Community	Medium and Low Community	Statistical Significance (d.f. = 1)
Protestant City			
Total			
1960	65(N = 60)	43(N = 100)	.01
1964	73(N = 60)	46(N = 99)	.01
White-Collar Workers			
1960	69(N = 39)	57(N = 56)	.01
1964	85(N = 39)	61(N = 56)	.01
Blue-Collar Workers			
1960	57(N = 21)	21(N = 42)	.01
1964	52(N = 21)	24(N = 42)	.01
Catholic City [a]			
Total			
1960	81(N = 27)	51(N = 41)	.01
1964	65(N = 26)	50(N = 46)	.10

[a] Too few cases for occupational separation.

tants (and Mormons) in the religious community and its prevailing rural and conservative normative system, the greater the chance that he will be influenced to vote Republican.[23] Note, for example, the poor success of Democratic fathers in transmitting Democratic voting among sons highly involved in the Protestant religious community and the good success among sons weakly involved therein.

The pull of class interests, like the influence of family political background, is very palpably moderated by participation in the religious community (Table 12–5). As one would expect, the effect of participation in the religious community on class interests is most easily observed among blue-collar workers. More than twice as many Protestant blue-collar workers who were strong in religious community orientation voted Republican in the 1960 and 1964 Presidential elections as blue-collar workers with weaker communal orientations. Precisely the same pattern existed among Mormons (Table 12–6). Hence, one of the social engineering strategies Republican leaders might consider would be the en-

23 For a discussion of the construction of the religious community index, which includes religion of friends, strength of religious identification, attitude toward intermarriage, and frequency of church attendance, see Charles H. Anderson, "Religious Communality and Party Preference," *Sociological Analysis*, XXX (Spring, 1969), 32–41.

TABLE 12–6

PERCENTAGE OF MORMONS WHO VOTED FOR OR PREFERRED
THE REPUBLICAN CANDIDATE IN THE 1960 AND 1964
PRESIDENTIAL ELECTIONS, BY STRENGTH OF RELIGIOUS
COMMUNITY AND OCCUPATIONAL GROUPS

Occupation and Election	High Community	Medium and Low Community	Statistical Significance (d.f. = 1)
Total			
1960	68(N = 88)	40(N = 69)	.01
1964	71(N = 88)	47(N = 69)	.01
White-Collar Workers			
1960	74(N = 64)	52(N = 35)	.01
1964	77(N = 64)	62(N = 34)	.05
Blue-Collar Workers			
1960	43(N = 16)	22(N = 28)	.01
1964	57(N = 16)	28(N = 29)	.01

couragement of Protestant religious community. Perhaps the visits of the
Reverend Billy Graham to the White House during President Richard
M. Nixon's term of office is an indication that such an awareness already
exists!

SUMMARY

In civic life, white Protestants have been both self-conscious allies
and enemies. However, white Protestant leanings have generally been
toward an overt or covert conservatism supported by rural imagery and
presuppositions. The tendency toward conservatism has been evident in
white Protestant attitudes toward public morality, political economy, and
electoral office. The more a white Protestant is involved in his religious
community the greater is his conservatism. If a white Protestant is highly
involved in his religious community, he is likely to vote Republican even
if he was raised in a Democratic family or is a blue-collar worker. There
does not seem to be, however, any direct link between how religious a
Protestant is and how tolerant or democratic he is; if anything, Protestant
religiosity encourages tolerance, especially if it is this-worldly in orientation. Protestant clergymen with liberal theological views tend to convert
religious liberalism into political liberalism and to have a politically
liberalizing influence on active parishioners. On the other hand, the
brand of religious liberalism found among many Protestant laymen does
not seem to encourage political and economic liberalism.

CHAPTER THIRTEEN

The sociologist is inescapably a generalizer, and generalization always involves risks. Generalizing about white Protestants, however, is an especially precarious activity. In some ways, white Protestants seem so variegated as to defy categorization beyond the most perfunctory limits. As colonist and immigrant, Englishman and Swede, Episcopalian and Baptist, cosmopolite and hillbilly, executive and laborer, liberal and conservative, northerner and southerner, the "white Protestant" is so various that the label appears meaningless.

But "white Protestant" is not a meaningless label. Diversity is often more apparent than real, distracting us from underlying similarities. A common faith, high-status national origin, "Old American" identity, a pioneering and individualistic ethos, ruralism, voluntarism, and local church organization, to name a few underlying similarities, have each contributed to the utility and meaningfulness of the label "white Protestant."

Into
the Future

PAST DIFFERENCES,
PRESENT CONVERGENCES

In the past, differences and conflict among white Protestants have perhaps been more salient than similarities and cooperation. Protestant national origin groups were at times mutually antagonistic. Old Americans pressed their privileges at the expense of immigrants. Denominations feuded bitterly with one another as well as internally. Owners and workers engaged in rancorous labor confrontation. Agricultural interests fought industrial interests militarily and politically. To an important extent, conflict in earlier American history was between separate white Protestant groups rather than between Protestants and non-Protestants —though there was no dearth of the latter. Internecine Protestant conflict prevailed because powerful and contentious interests tended to be Protestant ones.

Many of these past differences have been toned down or erased. Protestants of various national origins largely accept one another. With a few exceptions, denominational divisiveness has moderated and interchurch cooperation is progressing; denominational switching and interdenominational marriages help expand narrow church loyalties. As the farm population dwindles and agriculture becomes concentrated into large, company-owned farms, the rural-urban cleavage among white Protestants diminishes. The rural-urban conflict, serious as it is, today is more ideological than residential as white Protestants import rural values into towns and cities. Labor battles that often polarized white Protestants have to a considerable extent been routinized. Passionate Protestant regional loyalties subside in the face of pervasive geographical mobility and industrialization.

As white Protestants cultivate common ground, the nation itself gropes toward a more perfect pluralism. Catholic, Jewish, Spanish, Negro, and Indian subgroups have demanded and variously received recognition. The combination of diminishing internal cleavages within white Protestantism and the relative external gains of non-WASP groups has contributed to a heightened sense of white Protestant community. A more self-defined group life depends upon the recognition of underlying commonalities that white Protestants have historically shared.

New Community Orientations

Of all American ethnic groups, white Protestants are the least equipped for and the least able in the task of ethnic community building. As members of national origin groups, previous generations of white Protestants demonstrated constructive abilities in ethnic life. Their descendants, however, have too often relied on the identification of the general community with Protestantism. It is in the general community where white Protestants have acquired valuable experience in organization and group development.[1] These talents, I presume, will be increasingly made use of within more self-conscious boundaries of the ethnic group.

The focus of white Protestant community will continue to be found in church participants, though not necessarily in the church. The national origin and neighborhood congregations will decline in both number and importance. The new Protestant churches, in their tendency toward larger size and bureaucratization, seem better suited to serve as a framework and reference point of white Protestant community rather than as its main context. Nonchurch groups and organizations, some built within the framework of the church and others outside it, promise to assume more important positions in Protestant religious community. Church schools and colleges, local units of the Boy Scouts and Girl Scouts, YMCAs and YWCAs, athletic clubs, leisure and service organizations, summer camps, and even rest homes are among the kinds of groups and institutions that may accommodate the communal interests of white Protestants. Cliques and families will, of course, continue to be the most immediate and intimate ethnic subgroups. Church organization itself may respond in original ways to meet parishioners' interests in group life. Indeed, the fulfillment of organized religion's ostensible main interest,

[1] See Scott T. Miyakawa, *Protestants and Pioneers: Individualism and Conformity on the America Frontier* (Chicago: University of Chicago Press, 1964).

religiosity among laymen, may ultimately depend on the church's ability to encourage and accommodate the communal orientations of its members inasmuch as it is in the social context of interpersonal relationships that religious belief and practice are sustained.

At the core of white Protestant community stands the regular churchgoer. The most important fracture within the white Protestant group portends to be not regional, denominational, doctrinal, or even socioeconomic, but rather affiliational: those who regularly and dutifully participate in the church may foreseeably come to view one another as brothers and allies, as minority-group partners in the enterprise of conserving and promoting white Protestantism in America. The distinction between the active and inactive, church and nonchurch, committed and uncommitted will at least increase in importance if it does not become decisive.

STILL THE POWER STRUCTURE

A prospective rise in white Protestant consciousness and self-defined group life is paralleled by a relative decline in social, economic, and political privilege. The two processes are interactive. External threats animate group feeling and solidarity. Insofar as the Protestant middle classes have more fully experienced the social and economic competition of other ethnic groups, the white-collar worker and small businessmen mirror the interaction of religious community and socioeconomic prerogative more than do top executives and professionals. The upper echelons of prestige and privilege may even welcome the addition of a black, a Mexican, a Jew, or an Italian into their organizations and social circles. To do so is fashionable and good public relations, up to a point. These incentives will decline as increasing numbers of non-WASP's become eligible for elite and upper-class status, much as large numbers are now eligible for and many participating in middle- and upper-middle levels of prestige and reward.

The Protestant upper strata of economic and social privilege have considerably more to defend and to lose than do middle-class white Protestants. As previously noted, the white Protestant elite of power and privilege has monopolized the highest positions in government and business, the military and the university. It has to a large extent exercised its own prerogatives in the definition of national security, foreign policy, the law, and the economy. Members of the elite have had the most of what the system has to offer in the way of prestige, money, material goods, and personal freedom.

Although large urban areas have long ceased to be the sole political domain of the white Protestant, the control of the political apparatus of a big city is hardly a privilege. It is rather an onerous task and seemingly insoluble problem. White Protestants fare well, however, at the state level (Republicans controlled about 30 state governments at the beginning of the Nixon Administration) and the national level. And control of the latter level, in contrast to control of the big city, has far-reaching implications for social and economic continuity or change.

As graduate and professional schools turn out non-Anglo-Saxon scientific, technical, economic, diplomatic, social, and planning experts in greater quantities, the Anglo-Saxon Protestant elite would appear to have little choice, as these experts appear, but to accommodate, share with, and increasingly defer to them. If it is to succeed, a socially and technologically complex society cannot afford the luxury of evaluating and rewarding individuals in terms of their ethnic group membership.

The Responsibility of White Protestants

In a number of ways, this study has been a documentation of the advantages of being white and Protestant in American society. Along with the privileges of being white Protestant have gone most of the responsibilities of leadership and power. Although responsibility may be considered undesirable by some, positions of responsibility are usually pursued because of associated prestige, power, and material gain.

As the privileged ethnic group in American society, white Protestants have at times acted both responsibly and irresponsibly toward other ethnic peoples and the lower strata of white Protestants themselves. Too often, many contend, the Anglo-Saxon Protestant has pursued only his own self-aggrandizement. Regardless of the conception of their own ethnicity, white Protestants with disproportionate wealth, power, and responsibility will be judged by others as members of an ethnic group, and their actions will serve to credit or discredit that ethnic group both in this land and others.

White Protestants have in the past been less willing to accept minority religious and racial groups than these groups have been willing to accept white Protestants. Yet, as the largest and dominant ethnic group, a major part of the responsibility of promoting inter-ethnic cooperation, tolerance, and equality resides unalterably with white Protestants. What white Protestants do or fail to do will weigh heavily in, indeed determine, the outcome of social pluralism in American society. Important segments of white Protestant society have commendably worked toward the realization of these responsibilities, in particular many of the churches. The need in the future is for a larger commitment by white Protestants, especially among the various elites, to a more equitable distribution of political, economic, and social resources in American society. A commitment to fundamental change in values and social organization will be required. In the event that this occurs, white Protestants can expect little thanks for their efforts; if it does not, they can expect mounting hostility toward them and the system that has served the majority of them so well in the past. To grasp and accept these facts requires yeoman understanding and gentlemanly grace.

Appendix A

SOURCES OF UNITED STATES IMMIGRATION FROM 1820 TO 1929

Decade	Total Immigrants N	%	Northern and Western Europe [a]	Canada	Southern and Eastern Europe	Unspec- ified and Other
1820–1830	151,824	100	68.0	1.6	2.2	28.2
1831–1840	599,125	100	81.8	2.2	1.0	15.0
1841–1850	1,713,251	100	93.0	2.4	0.3	4.3
1851–1860	2,598,214	100	93.6	2.3	0.8	3.3
1861–1870	2,314,824	100	87.8	6.6	1.4	4.2
1871–1880	2,812,191	100	73.6	13.6	7.2	5.6
1881–1890	5,246,613	100	72.0	7.5	18.3	2.2
1891–1900	3,687,564	100	44.6	0.1	51.9	3.4
1901–1910	8,795,386	100	21.7	2.0	70.8	5.5
1911–1920	5,735,811	100	17.4	12.9	58.9	10.8
1920–1929	3,865,509	100	30.7	22.2	19.6	17.5
Total	37,520,312	100	48.6	7.6	37.0	6.8

Source: Annual Report of the Commissioner General of Immigration (Washington, D.C.: Government Printing Office, 1929), Table 82, p. 184.

[a] Northern and western Europe includes Belgium, Denmark, France, Germany, the Netherlands, Norway, Sweden, Switzerland, England, Ireland, Scotland, Northern Ireland, and Wales. Southern and eastern Europe includes all other European countries.

PERCENTAGE OF "OLD" AND "NEW" EUROPEAN IMMIGRANTS ARRIVING BEFORE AND AFTER 1880

Date of Arrival	Northern and Western Europe [a] N	%	Southern and Eastern Europe N	%
1820–1880	8,718,271	47.8	271,618	2.0
1881–1929	9,516,503	52.2	13,622,516	98.0
Total	18,234,774	100.0	13,894,134	100.0

Source: Annual Report of the Commissioner General of Immigration (Washington, D.C.: Government Printing Office, 1929), Table 82, p. 184.

[a] Northern and western Europe includes Belgium, Denmark, France, Germany, the Netherlands, Norway, Sweden, Switzerland, England, Ireland, Scotland, Northern Ireland, and Wales. Southern and eastern Europe includes all other European countries.

RELIGIOUS BACKGROUND OF IMMIGRANTS FROM NORTHERN AND WESTERN EUROPE
AND CANADA BY NATIONAL ORIGIN, 1820–1929

	Great Britain and English Canada [a]		Ireland [b]		Scandinavia [c]		Netherlands		Belgium	
	%	N	%	N	%	N	%	N	%	N
Protestant	93	6,723,683	10	364,440	98	2,562,862	80	195,097	–	–
Catholic	6	433,787	90	3,279,956	2	52,323	20	48,774	100	152,479
Jewish	1	72,297	–	–	–	–	–	–	–	–
Total	100	7,229,767	100	3,644,396	100	2,615,165	100	243,871	100	152,479

	Switzerland		France and French Canada [d]		Germany		Total	
	%	N	%	N	%	N	%	N
Protestant	66	190,396	5	64,332	62	3,646,419	64	13,747,229
Catholic	34	98,083	95	1,222,317	36	2,117,275	34	7,404,974
Jewish	–	–	–	–	–	–	–	–
Total	100	288,479	100	1,286,649	100	5,881,320	100	21,342,126

Sources: The religious background percentages were obtained from Gilbert Kelly Robinson, "Nationality Origin and Religious Background," *American Journal of Sociology,* XLIV (March, 1939), 716. The total number of immigrants for each national origin was obtained from the *Annual Report of the Commissioner General of Immigration* (Washington, D.C.: Government Printing Office, 1929), Table 83, p. 186. The number of Protestants, Catholics, and Jews was then derived from Robinson's percentages.

[a] Includes England, Wales, Scotland, Northern Ireland, and English Canada. Because Ireland and Northern Ireland were not held separate in census and immigration records prior to 1930, immigration totals for these two countries were estimated by extrapolating from figures for the 1930 foreign-born population from these two countries. The Scotch-Irish comprised about 20 per cent of the total Scotch-Irish and Irish foreign-born population in 1930; hence, 20 per cent of the 4,455,496 total immigrants from all of Ireland were assigned to Northern Ireland and the Great Britain total. A similar step had to be taken to obtain the English Canadian figure: 75 per cent of the 1930 foreign-born Canadians were from English Canada—hence, 75 per cent of the total Canadian immigration to 1929 of 2,831,947 was assigned to English Canada and the Great Britain total.

[b] The Ireland total was obtained in the same manner as the Scotch-Irish total, described above: 80 per cent of immigration from Ireland and Northern Ireland was assigned to the Irish Free State.

[c] Includes Finland (1871–1930) as well as Sweden, Norway, and Denmark.

[d] The total immigration from French Canada to 1929 was obtained in the same manner as the English Canadian total described above: 25 per cent of immigration from all of Canada was assigned to French Canada.

Appendix B

The data gathered on "Protestant City," Catholic City," and "Mormon City," were compiled from questionnaires sent to random samples of male heads of households. The three communities were selected on the basis of prior information regarding their religious composition. Each contained a different religious majority. As footnoted where appropriate, some of these findings have been published elsewhere. The information on Catholics and Mormons (Latter-Day Saints) has been included here for comparative purposes, although the latter group is very similar to the fundamentalist Protestant denominations in ascetic morality and religious orthodoxy. Thus, the Mormon sample is useful here not only in an independent comparative sense, but as a reasonable facsimile of white Protestant sectarianism.[1]

Out of 500 questionnaires sent to Protestant City, a North Central urban center of over 70,000 people, 212 were returned completed—166 (78 per cent) from Protestants and 43 (20 per cent, though church officials placed the percentage for Catholics in the city at 29 per cent) from Catholics. A second set of 500 was sent to Catholic City, another North Central urban place with a population of nearly 40,000, of which 207 were returned—126 (61 per cent) from Catholics and 75 (36 per cent) from Protestants. Finally, of 500 sent to Mormon City (an Intermountain central city of about 200,000), 225 were returned—164 (73 per cent, though the city is purportedly 65 per cent Mormon) from Mormons and the remainder mostly from Protestants and Catholics, but too few to analyze here.

All respondents were white males above the age of twenty-one, but nearly all were over twenty-five. More than half of each sample were over forty years old. These figures compare closely to those in the respective universes as enumerated in the 1960 census. Over-all, about two-thirds of respondents were white collar and about half had some college, larger proportions of these categories than in the universes according to the

[1] For a social history of the Latter-Day Saints, see Thomas F. O'Dea, *The Mormons* (Chicago: University of Chicago Press, 1957).

1960 census. Denominationally, Lutherans were the most prevalent group in both North Central samples, with Methodists being the second most numerous group. The large majority of all respondents reporting a religious preference claimed church membership. In regard to national origin, Germans, Scandinavians, Irish, and British, in that order of importance, largely made up the Protestant City sample. In Catholic City, Germans, Slavs, and Scandinavians were the major national groups.

Index

Abramson, Harold J., 161*n*, 162*n*
Adams, Bert N., 122*n*
Adams, Henry, 108
Adorno, T. W., 162*n*
Alford, Robert, 164*n*
Alleman, Albert, 108*n*
Allinsmith, Wesley, 161*n*
Allport, Gordon, 162*n*
American Protective Association (APA), 102
Amory, Cleveland, 21
Anderson, Charles H., 116, 135*n*, 137*n*, 171*n*
Anderson, Elin, 18*n*, 22, 24, 27, 113
Anglo-Americans (*see* British-Americans)
Anglo-Saxons (*see also* specific nationalities):
  genetic composition of, 13–14
  supremacy, doctrine of, 106–8
Assimilation:
  fusion distinguished from, 22*n*
  process of, 6–7

Babcock, Kendric C., 46*n*, 48*n*, 62*n*, 70*n*
Baltzell, E. Digby, 108, 118*n*, 141*n*, 142–44
Beard, Charles, 108
Bell, Alexander Graham, 41
Benjamin, Gilbert G., 83*n*
Benson, Adolph B., 47*n*
Berelson, Bernard, 164*n*
Berent, Jerzy, 155*n*
Bergmann, Leola Nelson, 59*n*, 62*n*, 63*n*
Berthoff, Rowland T., 15, 17*n*, 18*n*, 21, 22, 24*n*, 27, 29, 35*n*, 37*n*, 38*n*, 40*n*
Billington, Ray Allen, 100*n*, 101
Bjork, Kenneth O., 61*n*, 66*n*
Blair, Peter H., 33*n*
Blegen, Theodore, 21*n*, 59*n*, 63*n*, 65*n*
Bogardus, Emory, 27*n*, 41, 74*n*
Bogue, Donald, 147
Bouma, Donald H., 91

British-Americans (*see also* specific nationalities):
  communal tendencies of, 21–25
  ethnic identity, sense of, 25–28
  in-marriage, 24–25 (*table,* 26)
Broom, Leonard, 131, 135*n*, 153, 154*n*, 160*n*, 161*n*, 166*n*
Brown, Robert McAfee, 105*n*
Bultena, Louis, 119*n*
Burchinal, Lee G., 119*n*, 120, 121*n*, 131*n*, 133*n*

Caledonian clubs, 38
Calvinism, 151
Canadians, English, 31–32
Cantril, Hadley, 147
Carnegie, Andrew, 41
Carney, Richard E., 154*n*
Catholics:
  intermarriage, attitude toward, 131–33, (*tables,* 131, 132)
  kin, role of, 117
  marriage behavior, 133–35 (*table,* 134)
  organizational life, 118–19
  primary group life, 113–18 (*tables,* 115, 116)
  religious identification of, 127–30 (*tables,* 129, 130)
Catholics and Protestants (*see also* Political participation, Catholics and Protestants):
  child spacing, 155, 156
  conflict between, 99–108
  education, 154–55, 157
  family, mobility and, 154–57 (*table,* 157)
  leisure, attitude toward, 153
  materialism, 153–54
  mobility, 151–57
  socioeconomic status, 146–48, 154–57 (*table,* 157)
  work, attitude toward, 151, 153